Literary Criticism

JOSEPH NORTH

Literary Criticism
A Concise Political History

▌▌▌ Harvard University Press
CAMBRIDGE, MASSACHUSETTS, AND LONDON, ENGLAND   2017

First printing

Library of Congress Cataloging-in-Publication Data
Names: North, Joseph, 1980– author.
Title: Literary criticism : a concise political history / Joseph North.
Description: Cambridge, Massachusetts : Harvard University Press, 2017. | Includes bibli-
    ographical references and index.
Identifiers: LCCN 2016046677 | ISBN 9780674967731
Subjects: LCSH: Criticism—History—20th century. | Criticism—History—21st century. |
    Criticism—Political aspects. | Neoliberalism.
Classification: LCC PN94 .N67 2017 | DDC 801/.950904—dc23
LC record available at https://lccn.loc.gov/2016046677

Contents

Preface

IN THIS BOOK, I offer a rapid, synoptic overview of the basic paradigms that have governed the academic criticism of literature in much of the English-speaking world for the last century or so. If this is not the most pressing matter of our time, it is not the least pressing one, either. The study of literature is a test case—just one test case, but an important one—for a larger question that many people, I take it, acknowledge as central: the question of how and to what extent the societies in which we live allow us to cultivate deeper modes of life.

People write histories of many different kinds, and for many different reasons. It may therefore help readers to frame and evaluate the book if I begin by saying a few words about the kind of history it is intended to be. Clearly, it is not an exhaustive history. No attempt has been made to cover all—or even most—of the major figures and movements in the history of literary criticism. Some important figures and movements do appear, of course—in fact, the book is largely structured around a very short list of individual figures—but many that were obviously central to the history of literary studies appear only in the notes, if indeed they appear at all. Nor, I am afraid, is it a particularly illustrative history: it has little interest in painting a rich and detailed picture of the periods it describes, nor in bringing the reader into close imaginative contact with the minds of historical actors. Lastly, it is not an evaluative history of the kind sometimes written by professors of literature: readers will find that I have made few attempts to come to any broader assessment of the lasting value or significance of the figures concerned, beyond making the (often somewhat ruthless) judgments necessary for the task at hand. Certainly I would be disappointed if anyone understood the book as a belated attempt to assemble some kind of "canon" of criticism, in which role it would serve very badly. In this regard, it is worth stating from the outset that I have made no programmatic attempt to recover the work of thinkers who have been ignored or marginalized because of their subject position. That would have been an entirely different book; I leave it to readers to decide whether or not it would have been a better one.

If the book is none of these things, what is it? It is perhaps better thought of as an attempt to write a strategic history: a working analysis of existing tendencies in the present situation, as indicated by past trajectories. History of this kind is explicitly motivated by present concerns: one has something like a goal and something like a plan for reaching it, and so one turns to the past not "for its own sake," as is sometimes said, but in order both to clarify the goal and to identify tendencies in the present that seem likely either to help or hinder one's attempts to reach it. One therefore reflects on the past less for the sake of seeing the "full picture" and more for the sake of discovering its main lines of force; and not even for the sake of discovering all the forces that were relevant at the time, but instead limiting oneself to those lines of force that still seem to condition what occurs today. In this sense, the objects of the analysis here are not really the various historical periods through which the discipline has passed, but the present lines of force themselves. In such an analysis, a lean account has certain advantages over a thick one. In observing this, I am not attempting to exempt the work from critique, merely asking that the necessary critique is made with a sense of the author's aims in mind. It is of course right to note that more flesh could be put on the skeleton, but to see this as a crippling flaw is to assess the history by another standard than that which it is trying to meet. The more serious critiques will be those that draw attention to the flaws in my model of the skeleton itself. For at this level, one must do more than simply point to additional local complexities—one must bind those local complexities into a convincing general account. It is against the existing general account, which lurks unacknowledged within the work of so many who claim the privilege of speaking only about local cases, that my argument is principally ranged.

Accordingly, my basic method has been to step back from individual figures and movements in order to bring into focus the basic paradigms that have determined the development of Anglo-American literary studies throughout its history, and that therefore seem likely at least to condition its possible lines of development in the future. Thus, the particular thinkers assembled here have been selected not because I recommend them, nor in all cases because of their actual influence, fortunate or unfortunate, on the subsequent history of literary study, but for the quite different reason that they provide convenient emblems for the larger paradigms that are my real objects of analysis. Considered together, they offer a means by which to sketch a historical plan of the basic structures of assumption underlying some of the central work in the discipline throughout the century of its development. Pursuing an end of this kind naturally involves making claims at a high level of generality, and has thus risked putting me at odds with those within the discipline who still pride themselves on their commitment to particularity per se. I have felt this to be a risk worth taking.

While writing, I have had the sense of addressing two audiences rather different in nature. On the one hand, at many moments I have attempted to find a tone appropriate to addressing readers within and around academic literary studies: those who already have an obvious stake in the history and future of the discipline, can be expected to be familiar with many of the figures to which I refer, are versed in at least some of the methodological debates that have surrounded "close reading," the "aesthetic," and so on. On the other hand, there are also many moments at which I have attempted to find a tone appropriate to addressing readers on the radical left, which I understand as indicating the collective, or incipient collective, of those who have found themselves in the difficult and vexed position of trying to articulate and even to live a critique, not merely of the excesses of capitalism in its current form, but of capitalism itself. Thirty years of quite public debate about the "politicization" of the discipline notwithstanding, the area of overlap between these audiences is in truth rather slight. This has meant that the choice of a dual mode of address has carried with it certain risks, and has indeed led to certain failures. Readers within the discipline who are not on the left in the sense I indicate here may find themselves somewhat at odds with the political sensibility, and associated ranges of tone, at work in certain parts of the book; readers on the left who are not within the discipline may need more convincing that there is really something at stake, for the larger movement, in an extended discussion of matters literary, aesthetic, and methodological.

My reason for nevertheless persisting in trying to address both audiences is that I am seeking to expand the area of overlap between them. Indeed, from a certain angle, one might see this as the burden of the book as a whole: one of my larger claims is that many of the deeper interests of these two audiences would be the same, if only we could come to recognize them as such, in that the incipiently materialist account of the aesthetic that lies at the root of the discipline, and continues to mark its central practice of "close reading," is properly understood as part of a longer history of resistance to the economic, political, and cultural systems that prevent us from cultivating deeper modes of life. It is therefore a matter of some intellectual and political importance to try to find a tone that will speak to both audiences, in the hope that each will come to recognize at least some part of its own image in the whole formation. I cannot say I have succeeded, but readers should at least know what I understand myself to be attempting. I hope not to try their patience too much, wherever on this particular spectrum of views they happen to sit.

This question of audience brings me to another charge that I probably ought to meet head-on: the charge of writing an interested, rather than disinterested, history. In this respect, I should put on record from the outset my sense that a history of this kind need make no general claim to methodological objectivity or neutrality, and would indeed be compromised were it to do so. It is a nice historiographical question to consider what a truly disinterested historical inquiry would look like, since we have yet to see one: what we keep getting instead are inquiries in which the claim to disinterestedness masks the real interests at stake. Rejecting the old historian's principle of neutrality in this way does not amount, as is still sometimes said, to the claim that one can make anything one likes of the past; nor I think is there anything inherently dishonest or intellectually spurious about a history motivated by real interests. The idea that having interests—paradigmatically, political interests—makes one less willing to acknowledge the force of truth is a trick of the dominant liberalism about which I shall have more to say in the pages that follow. It seems better to ask where one's will to acknowledge the force of truth comes from, since it can then be seen that one's interests— even one's political interests—are what motivate and give meaning to the search for truth. For in fact the demand to identify the true contours of a situation is most pressing when one is in active pursuit of some desired objective. The task of writing a committed history thus holds the historian to as high a standard as does the attempt to write a purportedly objective history, though in a different way.

I hope that readers will forgive me if I close this preface by confessing some of my personal hopes for the book, such as they are. First, I hope that interested general readers may find here a useful overview of some of the central ways in which the dominant parts of the English-speaking world have managed to conduct serious collective thinking about literature in recent times. Second, I hope that readers with a more directly institutional interest in the literary—chiefly, students and professors of literature—may find here a new account of the discipline's present situation, and one that is troubling enough to convince them, if they need further convincing, that we need to work out how to do things differently in future. If it does nothing else, I hope that the book will at least help graduate students in the literary disciplines to understand what may be at stake when their supervisors encourage them, under the sign of either "scholarship" or "politics," to produce yet another historicist/contextualist paper, article, dissertation. If they resist doing this, and are then somewhat confused by the speed with which the rhetoric of the market ("job market") arrives to enforce the norm, then perhaps at least they will be better equipped to understand why.

But the final word really ought to be addressed to my friends on the left, who cross all these categories. I hope that those of you who read this book will find within it a history of literary criticism that is properly attentive to political concerns. I hope also to convince you that, for all the problems of the history of the discipline throughout the twentieth and now the twenty-first centuries—chiefly, its continual default to the mainstream of liberalism—there is much at stake here for the left. For the struggle is being fought, must be fought, on the terrain of sensibility. Not on the terrain of sensibility alone, of course—a mistake that keeps being made—but never entirely outside it. If we continue to surrender our ability to fight on that ground, we cannot win.

Literary Criticism

Introduction

I

To many who observe it, the field of literary studies appears quite heterogeneous—perhaps even fractious. I think this is wrong, and that in fact, for many decades now, Anglo-American literary studies has been proceeding on the basis of a fairly firm consensus: a consensus broad enough, and also generally unremarked enough, to constitute something like a Kuhnian paradigm. We might call this the "historicist/contextualist" paradigm, by which I simply mean that almost all of the most influential movements in literary studies since the 1980s have proceeded on the assumption that, for academic purposes, works of literature are chiefly of interest as diagnostic instruments for determining the state of the cultures in which they were written or read. If one is prepared to take this formulation in a fairly broad sense, then it describes the vast majority of work in the field at present.

It was not always thus. Among those who write the history of the discipline, there is a tolerably general agreement that for the first three-quarters of the twentieth century—which is to say, up until the crisis decade of the 1970s—literary studies was not unified under a single paradigm, but rather split between two rather different paradigms sometimes thought to be competing with one another and at other times thought to be complementary. The field's central axis of dispute was between literary "scholars" and literary "critics," the key distinction being between those who treated the study of literature as a means by which to analyze culture and those who treated the study of literature as an opportunity intervene in culture.[1] From this central opposition, a whole range of further oppositions followed, any of which could be taken as defining the central axis of the dispute at a given moment: specialists and generalists; professionals and amateurs; objectivity and subjectivity; understanding and appreciation; facts and values; the sciences and the humanities; producing knowledge and cultivating taste; *wissenschaft* and *bildung*—and so on. A dispute so broad and mobile naturally involved much confusion, yet for the most part, those involved were still able to identify it as a coherent dispute between two clearly opposed paradigms—a dispute significant enough to be considered characteristic of the structure of the discipline as a whole.

Yet once we arrive at the last three or four decades, this dispute seems to fade out—replaced either by debates over "theory," or else by the claim that, in the words of John Guillory, "for us it's not scholars versus critics. . . . [For us] scholars and critics . . . inhabit the same body."[2] I think we are now in a position to see that neither of these answers is really correct. On the contrary, the central fact of the discipline's development over the last generation—a fact so central it keeps being overlooked—is that at some point in the late 1970s or early 1980s, the literary "scholars" effectively won the dispute. This makes our own period—the period since the early 1980s— rather an exceptional one, since for the first time in the history of the discipline, one of the two paradigms has managed to dominate the field. Indeed, in the longer view, one of the defining features of our period has been the relative absence of "criticism" in anything quite like the sense used by earlier thinkers. There has been what I will call a "scholarly turn," by which "scholarly" approaches, which have tended to treat literary texts chiefly as opportunities for cultural and historical analysis, have replaced "critical" approaches, which, in their day, had tended to treat literary texts as means of cultivating readers' aesthetic sensibilities, "aesthetic" here of course being understood in a range of rather different senses. If most of those who study literature now primarily see themselves as professionals in the field of cultural and historical analysis, this is because for the first time in the history of literary studies, almost all of them are "scholars." For better or worse, one half of the discipline is all but gone. It is in the context of this "scholarly turn," and the associated demise of "criticism," that we must see the rise of our current historicist/contextualist paradigm.

A number of questions then impose themselves. Given that the "scholarly" and "critical" tendencies had existed side by side for the first three-quarters of the century, what particular arrangement of forces led to the eventual victory of the former in the late '70s and early '80s? What was the political character of those forces? What is then at stake in the discipline's continuing commitment to the historicist/contextualist paradigm? Or else, on the other side of the coin, might there now be some reason to call for a movement toward another paradigm, one quite different in nature? Even if one has set aside any residual temptation to be nostalgic about a lost "heroic age" of criticism in the mid-century—a "heroic age" we are right to be glad to have seen the end of—might there nevertheless be reasons to feel a renewed commitment to something like the project of criticism today?[3] Criticism, that is, viewed as a programmatic commitment to using works of literature for the cultivation of aesthetic sensibility, with the goal of more general cultural and political change.

I think there are such reasons, and it is largely in an attempt to give some substance to them that I have written the book that follows. *Literary Criticism: A Concise Political History* is an introduction to the lost "critical" paradigm in literary studies, as well as an overview of the historicist/contextualist "scholar" paradigm that has replaced it. The aims of the history are three: to account for the rise to dominance of the present consensus, to offer a preliminary assessment of the political character of that consensus, and to suggest that those of us who are in search of alternatives might begin by reconsidering our inherited views of the political character of older critical modes. The book is therefore not without its political elements. Perhaps the simplest way to summarize these is to observe that, though the turn to the historicist/contextualist paradigm has generally been understood as a local victory for the left over the elitisms of mid-century criticism, this has been largely an error. In fact, it is better to say that the opposite is true: in its most salient aspects, the turn to the current paradigm in the late 1970s and early 1980s was symptomatic of the wider retreat of the left in the neoliberal period and was thus a small part of the more general victory of the right. Seeing the matter in this light has the benefit, not only of accuracy, but of re-opening the question of how the left should organize its thinking about literature—a question that has lain dormant for too long.

Over the last three decades, the discipline has tended to assume that any attack on the historicist/contextualist paradigm must originate in cultural conservatism, particularly if the offending party makes use of such terms as "criticism," "aesthetic," "sensibility," and similar. This assumption has allowed much to pass for progressivism, even for radicalism, that under other circumstances would have been seen more clearly for what it was. But the political failings of the mid-century critics are now self-evident, the discipline having repeated its arguments against them, in ever-less-nuanced form, for the last three decades. What needs now to be emphasized is the critical paradigm's potential as a source of alternatives to the presently dominant mode. As neoliberalism enters into crisis, literary study, among other things, will once again be re-oriented, and alternatives will have to be found if the left is to have a hand in determining what that orientation might be. My hope is that this book, with its exploration not only of the historicist/contextualist paradigm but of the rather different critical paradigm that it replaced, may be of assistance to those trying to rethink what useful contributions literary studies might be able to make to the struggle for a better society in this new period, beyond the "scholarly turn."

II

But what is "literary criticism"? The phrase has many meanings, and it is perhaps worth taking a moment to specify which of them I intend to rely on here. Outside the academy, the phrase usually refers to literary journalism of an evaluative kind—book reviewing in particular. I will not be using the phrase in quite that sense, though the history of literary journalism is bound up in important ways with the history of "literary criticism" traced here. Nor will I be using the phrase in the way it is usually used within the academy today, as indicating the whole research activity of disciplinary literary studies. If one is trying to understand how the current paradigm in literary studies relates to the longer history that preceded it, then this rather sweeping use of the phrase creates some confusion, since most of what literature professors now do would best be described as "literary scholarship" if using the older terms. The "literary criticism" that will be the central concern of this book was of course never entirely separable from the various discourses that surrounded it, but nonetheless it had a real claim to be considered its own distinctive thing.

What, then, is "literary criticism" when one speaks of it in this sense? One way to begin to grasp what "literary criticism" once represented is to think of it as a significant intellectual discourse that, from about the 1920s through to about the early 1970s, provided a crucial bridge between literary journalism on the one hand and literary scholarship on the other—though of course it connected to many other discourses, too. The primary institutional site of "literary criticism," taken in this sense, was the academy, where it justified itself by reference to the distinctiveness of its research program and classroom methods, both of which were grounded in its founding innovations: "close reading" and "practical criticism." Yet if "criticism" was an academic discourse in the first instance, it was nevertheless one defined precisely by the strength and directness of its connection to the world outside the academy. Here the old caricatures can come to assist us: where the archetypal "scholar" was a highly specialized professional researcher—and thus susceptible to caricature as dry, anxious, dusty, myopic, and fixated on small details of language or etymology to the exclusion of broader, more worthwhile concerns—which is all to say, profoundly out of touch with the nonspecialist life of the general public—the archetypal "critic" was a generalist, sometimes even a "public intellectual," and was thus susceptible to caricature not only as an amateur and dilettante, but also as a mere journalist, popularizer, or "educator." That last charge is perhaps worth reflecting on, as a way to measure the difference between the older discourse of criticism and anything that goes on within the upper reaches of the literary disciplines today: for better or worse, the discourse of criticism was once the site of the discipline's strongest and most explicit ties, both intellectual and institutional, to education at the primary and secondary levels—ties that no longer exist in any significant form.

The history that follows does not attempt to track the development of all these elements of the discourse—I am afraid that readers looking for a history of disciplinary criticism's classroom methods, or its changing institutional sites, or its ties with journalism, or its role in primary and secondary schooling, will not find it here. Instead, this book is concerned specifically with the intellectual paradigm that once defined and justified "literary criticism" in the eyes of its practitioners. The modern university being what it is, this has meant focusing on its research program above all. To modern eyes, perhaps the most striking element of that research program is its strong commitment to evaluating the aesthetic merits of specific literary works, typically via "close reading" or "practical criticism." But criticism, in its day, was also more than this—like any long-standing disciplinary paradigm, it pursued a research program that was necessarily quite diverse. Thus in the hands of its various practitioners, "criticism" also involved the development of new hermeneutic and interpretative methods; sociological research into the present state of the culture; advanced pedagogical theory; extended enquiries into the nature of educational institutions; philosophical enquiry into the nature of the "literary," the "aesthetic," "language," "culture" itself, and so on. It was this complex array of interlocking projects that constituted the paradigm for "literary criticism" in the academy. What held all these diverse elements together? In a sense, the answer to that question occupies much of this book, but one can frame a rapid, provisional answer by observing simply that "literary criticism" was an institutional program of aesthetic education—an attempt to enrich the culture directly by cultivating new ranges of sensibility, new modes of subjectivity, new capacities for experience—using works of literature as a means. Of course, all these terms cry out for elaboration; for now, I offer them simply as signposts pointing away from the project of scholarly cultural analysis that occupies so much of the discipline today.

III

Very few people, it seems to me, start reading a novel by Virginia Woolf with the primary aim of learning more about British cultural life in the 1920s. Most of those who do are scholars. What nonspecialist readers are looking for in literature is rather less easy to define: perhaps the best we can do at the outset is to say that they are looking for something to go on with, something that will help them live their lives.

Few resources now exist within the discipline of literary study that can help us to respond to this observation, such as it is. A whole range of mid-twentieth-century critical practices that once tried to put literature into contact with these kinds of vague and capacious terms, the central example perhaps being F. R. Leavis's neo-Arnoldian "criticism of life," now operate within the discipline only in residual, discredited, and nostalgic forms. In their place, today's most influential methodologies for literary study are all, in their various ways, historicist/contextualist, not only in the broad and welcome sense that they see literature in other than transcendental, universalizing, ahistorical terms, but also in the rather more specialized sense that they treat literary texts chiefly as opportunities for producing knowledge about the cultural contexts in which they were written and read. Recent efforts to break new ground—"New Formalism," "Surface Reading," "Distant Reading"—have been, in this sense, repetitions of the same.[4] In contrast to the nonspecialist reader, the majority of today's literary scholarship *is* most interested in Woolf for what she can teach us about her time and place. Thus if one were to try to nominate a single slogan for the historicist/contextualist paradigm in its entirety, one could do little better than by selecting Fredric Jameson's slogan "Always historicize!" which I take as the horizon beyond which the disciplines of literary study have so far been unable to see.

It has certainly proved a very productive slogan. Many of the advances made by the discipline in the 1980s and 1990s were made by those acting in its spirit, if only rarely directly under its banner—the paradigmatic advance being the movement from those mid-century critical practices that treated works of literature as repositories of timeless and universal human values, to our contemporary scholarly practices that treat texts, in the broadest sense of "texts," as deeply embedded in particular histories. Yet it has seldom been noted that our period's governing injunction to historicize is by no means a unitary one, and has in fact concealed within itself two rather different demands, neither of which is logically necessary to the other. On the one hand, it has called on us to demonstrate the historical and cultural contingency of categories elsewhere taken as timeless, essential, or universal; yet on the other hand, it has called on us simply to write cultural history. The two projects are quite distinct, and neither is implied in the other: just as one can, if one likes, write history from a universalist standpoint, one can also critique essentialisms without having to act as a historian.

Where it is understood at all, the turn in the 1980s to the current historicist/contextualist paradigm is generally understood as a political victory for progressives over the relatively conservative criticisms of the mid-century, of which the New Critics (in the United States) and the Leavisite critics (in the United Kingdom) once proved such convenient emblems—open to the charges of universalizing, essentializing, dehistoricizing, depoliticizing, elitism, Kantian idealism, and so on. This view that the turn to our current paradigm was a victory for progressive thought has some plausibility. Certainly, prominent conservatives have, in effect, agreed with it: it was in the 1980s and 1990s that, most notably in the United States, the right wing of liberalism adopted a "culture wars" strategy, taking the discipline of English, in particular, as a central target and decrying its hijacking by progressives, relativists, multiculturalists, postmodernists, and so on, all of whom were taken to have refused their proper role of transmitting, via the study of Great Books, the virtues of traditional Western culture. The left-liberals subjected to these attacks have also agreed, in the sense that they have tended to see the discrediting of mid-century criticism and the turn instead to historicist/contextualist analysis as a sign of liberal progress. Accordingly, in this period, the left-liberal core of the discipline has celebrated the various elements of the historicist/contextualist paradigm—particularly the opening up of the canon, the refusal of the traditional emphasis on the cultivation of aesthetic judgment, the demotion of the category of the "literary," and the consequent proliferation of objects of analysis—as welcome signs of a broader democratization of literary study. Thus both wings of liberalism—in the US lexicon, both "conservatives" and "liberals"—have seemed to agree that the turn to our current paradigm was a victory for the latter.

A victory for left-liberalism, then. Was the turn to our current paradigm also a victory for the left proper: those whose commitment to equality runs beyond the boundaries set by the liberal consensus? We are not without reasons for thinking so. For as we shall see, the turn to our current paradigm was in fact first and most powerfully argued for by those on the radical left, the lines of influence flowing from Raymond Williams, Pierre Bourdieu, and Michel Foucault, respectively, being perhaps the central examples. And indeed, once one steps back for a moment to try to characterize the broader political constitution of the discipline since the late 1970s, one is struck by the fact that it was in this period that, for the first time, a significant proportion of the truly major figures were Marxists of one kind or another: first, Raymond Williams himself, but then also Terry Eagleton, Fredric Jameson, Gayatri Spivak, Franco Moretti. Nor, for the most part, did these radical figures propose an orientation for literary studies fundamentally at odds with that proposed by the liberal mainstream. Rather, the discipline seemed willing to come with them, at least a certain part of the way: in this period, the substantial political differences between Marxist and left-liberal work within the discipline stood out only against the background of a shared commitment to a single paradigm, argued for first and most strenuously by the Marxists, in which the assumed goal of literary study was cultural and social analysis. The liberal center of the discipline holds, of course—there can be no serious suggestion that the field as a whole has embraced Marxism, even in its more academic forms. Yet it remains true that in our period, even while being continually misunderstood, misrepresented, and subjected to stern critique, Marxists nevertheless have managed to secure a fair proportion of the more prominent places in the discipline's imagination: places from which it has been possible for them at least to aspire to guide the work of the discipline as a whole. Searching the annals of intellectual life in the English-speaking world, one struggles to find another discipline, still less another period in the history of the discipline of literary studies, in which this has been true to an equivalent extent, for an equivalent length of time.

Thus when we come to assess the political valence of the "scholarly turn" in the late 1970s/early 1980s, the matter seems entirely clear: it was a progressive turn, and perhaps even in certain respects a turn to the more radical left. But this is strange. For was it not in just this period that neoliberalism established itself as an unquestioned global hegemony, leaving the left in disarray in every sector? How was literary studies able to absent itself from this general movement? More: how did literary studies manage, not merely to hold firm against the tide, but to move strongly against it? Everywhere else, the left in retreat; but within literary studies, a historic advance. If one is a literary academic on the left, this story of a local victory against all historical odds is a cheering one. Is it true?

Jameson's slogan—from *The Political Unconscious* (1981)—comes to us from the turning point: the point at which our current paradigm began to assume its present dominance.[5] We can see something of the complexion of this moment by observing Perry Anderson in 1982, opening his first Wellek Library Lecture at U.C. Irvine.[6] Not without a certain performance of archaism, Anderson begins by looking back to Leavis, reminding his audience that literary criticism, whether "practical" or "theoretical," is typically just that, *criticism*—its irrepressibly *evaluative* impulse spontaneously tending to transgress the frontiers of the text towards the associated life beyond it. Social theory as such paradoxically lacks a comparable discriminatory charge built into it. (9, emphasis in original)

Here at, or perhaps just after, the inception of the new historicist/contextualist paradigm, it was still possible for Anderson to speak in the old way, as if it were generally understood that "criticism" were something distinct from and even opposed to "social theory," and that the former were primarily a matter of forming judgments about the relative aesthetic merits of literary works—judgments that would then be taken to have some bearing on the rest of "life." This was about the last moment in the history of the discipline when one could speak in these kinds of terms and hope to be widely understood. Over the next thirty years, the terms "criticism" and "social theory" would both be absorbed into a single project of historicist/contextualist analysis, making them all but interchangeable. Today "literary critics" read texts in order to understand and theorize the social. The specific sense of "criticism" that Anderson relies on here has vanished from view.

But in the late 1970s and early 1980s, the two categories were still so clearly distinct from one another that it was possible for Terry Eagleton to outline a provocative strategy for turning "criticism" *into* "social theory," or as he put it, "cultural analysis." In 1983, Eagleton wrote that:

Such a strategy obviously has far-reaching institutional implications. It would mean, for example, that departments of literature as we presently know them in higher education would cease to exist. . . . Whatever would in the long term replace such departments . . . would centrally involve education in the various theories and methods of cultural analysis. . . . The genteel amateurism which regards criticism as some spontaneous sixth sense has not only thrown many students of literature into understandable confusion for many decades, but serves to consolidate the authority of those in power.[7]

If one could no longer outline this strategy today, that is because it has succeeded: over the last three decades, departments of literature have indeed exchanged the project of evaluative criticism, with its "genteel amateurism," for the very different project of "cultural analysis." This profound transformation of the field was justified, in the end, on political grounds: "criticism" as a project had merely "serve[d] to consolidate the authority of those in power." Since then, the shift has widely been seen as continuous with a broader democratization of literary study that was felt to have been occurring in the discipline since the mid-1960s. One can then understand why it has seemed to many that the instituting of "Always historicize!" as the guiding injunction for literary study over the last three decades has represented a dramatic success for the left.

Yet even at the outset, the politics of this turn away from criticism and toward historicist/contextualist cultural analysis were not so clear. A year later, Eagleton ran the old distinction in a new way, observing that:

> The problem of the Victorian man of letters is one which has never ceased to dog the English critical institution, and is indeed quite unresolved even today: either criticism strives to justify itself at the bar of public opinion by maintaining a general humanistic responsibility for the culture as a whole, the amateurism of which will prove increasingly incapacitating as bourgeois society develops; or it converts itself into a species of technological expertise, thereby establishing its professional legitimacy at the cost of renouncing any wider social relevance. . . .[8]

From where we now sit, it is possible to see that sometime in the late 1970s or early 1980s, literary studies opted for the second path. For in the Anglo-American world, the literary disciplines are now quite evidently disciplines of professional scholarship, of "technological expertise," much along the lines of the social sciences, and quite as a result of the turn from criticism to cultural analysis that Eagleton himself was calling for. On the whole, those who study literature at the higher levels of the academy no longer try to safeguard or intervene in the "culture as a whole," and they certainly do not define themselves as "amateurs." Instead, they see themselves as specialist scholars, charged with the more obviously professional task of producing historical and cultural knowledge for an audience of other specialist scholars. If the turn to "cultural analysis" was a turn to the left, it was also the moment at which the discipline agreed to transform itself into a discipline of observation, tracking developments in the culture without any broader mandate to intervene in it.

Perhaps we can now see something of the dual political character of our period's governing injunction to "historicize." Insofar as it has led to a critique of the essentialisms and universalisms of an old elite, it has been palpably of the left. Yet insofar as it has also asked literary thinkers to give up the wider social function to which "criticism," for all its many faults, at least aspired, and has taught them instead merely to observe the culture, however "critically," by writing cultural theory and cultural history, it has been a depoliticization: in that sense, of the right. Only the first of these aspects of the historicist/contextualist paradigm has been well publicized. Literary studies was once a discipline that, at least on paper, proposed detailed and intellectually rigorous methods both for analyzing the culture and for taking action to change it. In contrast, the scholarly turn, for all its explicit commitment to politicization, has left us with a discipline of cultural analysis alone. In our period, there is of course no dearth of avowed political commitment, yet even those whose explicit goal is to intervene in the culture seek to do so by providing further and better analyses. A situation of that kind tempts some to claim that cultural analysis itself constitutes intervention. Yet today, it ought to be clear that analyzing the culture through a political lens takes one only so far; a coherent body of techniques and methods by which to change that culture would be something else entirely. Without the second, the first is of little use.

IV

In past decades, many of those who reflected on the history of the twentieth century considered it as falling naturally into two periods, with the crucial break occurring somewhere around its center: a beak between pre- and post-1945, for example; or a break between "modernism" and "postmodernism"; or else, as was once thought, a break to the left in the 1960s. Yet in recent years these two-part periodizations have come to seem less tenable. Now that the century is behind us, it is easier to see that its middle decades were in many ways a period of relative continuity. As a result, the term "postmodernism" no longer answers clearly to present concerns, and the 1960s, for all that they have continued to attract the enthusiasms of a generation, have come to seem merely the prelude to a much more significant crisis, best symbolized by the terminal crisis of Keynesianism in the 1970s and the subsequent turn to global neoliberalism in the 1980s. Thus nowadays thinkers addressing the history of the twentieth century more often tend to break it into three periods: a first period stretching from somewhere around 1914 or 1917 through to the Great Depression of the 1930s—a period continually haunted by the specter of an end to liberalism, riven and confused by the revolution in Russia, the stock market crash of 1929, and the two world wars; a second, more stable period most easily discernible from 1945 to the early 1970s, but with clear roots stretching back to the New Deal politics of the 1930s—a period in which the forces of labor and those of capital reached a Keynesian or welfare-statist compromise not unrelated to the ideological pressures of the Cold War; then a decade of crisis in the 1970s leading into a third or neoliberal period, clearest in its outlines from the late 1970s/early 1980s through to somewhere in or around 2008—after which a further crisis, still to be resolved.[9] Naturally there is much disagreement about the details.

What does this new clarity about the history of the twentieth century mean for literary study? For the most part, the literary disciplines' sense of their own history is still stuck in the older two-period mode, and as a result fails to capture the quality of our present moment. Today, if one asks literary scholars to identify the most significant break in their discipline's recent history, they generally think for a moment and then say "theory": an answer which, when pressed on the central question of historical causation, generally reduces either to "postmodernism" or "1968"—the two favored terms of the older periodization. Our own period is then continually thought through only in the impoverished terms of "after theory," continuing the old line from the 1980s when, in the absence of a compelling analysis of the present, everything was simply designated "post-." Thus the questions asked within literary studies have tended to be of the old two-period kind: what was "theory," really? What were its real politics? How can we proceed in its aftermath? Are not all bonds now broken and all certainties lost? These questions now seem of rather limited interest, deriving as they do from decades in which it seemed impossible to say when we were, only when we weren't. "Theory" names the moment of crisis in the discipline, it is true, but it tells us very little about the character of the neoliberal order that established itself within literary studies in the wake of the crisis. To understand that, we need to reconsider the history of the discipline from the ground up.

Bearing in mind this larger problem of periodization, let me take a moment to outline the structure of the book that follows. In the first chapter, I tell the story of the largely lost project of "criticism." In the second and third chapters, I tell the story of the rise to dominance of the newly singular historicist/contextualist "scholar" paradigm that replaced it. In the fourth and longest chapter, I examine the more recent history of the discipline in an attempt to find there the seeds of a renewed left critical paradigm that might replace, compete with, or simply supplement the presently dominant historicism/contextualism. Considered as a unit, these four chapters track the development of the discipline throughout the twentieth and twenty-first centuries, focusing particularly on what I take to be three of the most important strands within it: first, the project of literary criticism, as distinct from the project of literary scholarship; second, the history of the various positions in philosophical aesthetics that have been thought to underpin that project of criticism; and third, the history of the changing methodologies that have functioned as criticism's "working edge," particularly the various reading methods that have sheltered under the names "close reading" and "practical criticism." When we track these three lines of thinking as they develop through the century, treating them as central to the discipline, something rather surprising emerges: it begins to look as though the history of literary studies since the 1920s falls roughly into three periods—three periods that match rather closely those of what I have called the "new periodization."

An extremely rapid summary of that history may be helpful here. In the first period, I. A. Richards inaugurated all three lines of thinking, putting the project of criticism on a disciplinary footing by developing for it both a philosophical foundation in an incipiently materialist account of the aesthetic and a working tool in the methodologies that came to be called "close reading" and "practical criticism." Today, much of Richards' work is misremembered within the discipline, largely due to our tendency to conflate it with what followed it: in the United States, this has chiefly meant conflating it with the New Criticism; in the United Kingdom, with Leavisite criticism. Against this, I try to recover the distinctiveness of this early critical work. In particular, I show that the methodological innovations Richards proposed in fact derived from his earlier philosophical innovations in the field of aesthetics. For it is not often enough remembered nowadays that Richards first arrived at the methods that would become "close reading" and "practical criticism" as a result of his sweeping critique of the mainstream tradition in philosophical aesthetics: for Richards, the aesthetic was to be understood not in the idealist sense, current since Baumgarten and Kant, as an autotelic repository of final value, but in an instrumental sense, as indicating the whole range of our social practices for encountering value. One might then say that the "critical" tendency within Anglo-American literary studies has its roots in an instrumental or even a materialist aesthetics. Certainly criticism's characteristic methods of "close reading" and "practical criticism," at least, were originally designed as the working edge of such an aesthetics, helping readers, each from their own specific material situations, to use the aesthetic instruments of literature to cultivate their most useful practical capabilities. Yet when Richards' work was taken up by later thinkers, much of this philosophical basis was ignored or deliberately cordoned off, and criticism was then effectively recovered into the mainstream tradition of idealist aesthetics, though its characteristic methodologies continued to bear traces of their origins in an aesthetics of a different kind.

In the second period, extending through the mid-century up to the 1970s, the project of disciplinary "criticism" was taken up by the New Critics in the United States and by the Leavises and their circle in the United Kingdom, and turned to purposes almost directly opposed to those for which it originally had been intended. Specifically, the incipiently materialist aesthetic foundation for criticism was transformed into an explicitly idealist one, and the methodologies of "close reading" and "practical criticism" were redirected so that their emphasis lay not on cultivating the aesthetic capabilities of readers, but on the cultivation of aesthetic judgment, which all too often reduced to the mere ranking of the relative aesthetic values of particular texts. The distinctive emphases of the first period were then forgotten, and the project of criticism, together with its array of tools, came to be associated instead with a more conservative cultural politics. Thus, for example, in the discipline today one can observe the widespread— and, I think, mistaken—sense that "close reading" has its origin in a Southern New Critical renovation of Christian hermeneutic practices. This period continued through the middle of the century: even where they differed in

other ways, the most influential mid-century humanist criticisms largely
accepted the assumptions of this second, more conservative, version of "criticism." In the latter part of the century, this began to lead to the sense that
"criticism" as a project was *necessarily* conservative in its politics, and thus to
the transition to what I am calling the third period—our own.

In this third period, which began in the late 1970s or early 1980s and
continues through to the present, the project of "criticism" was rejected as
necessarily elitist, dehistoricizing, depoliticizing, and so forth; the idea of the
"aesthetic" was rejected as necessarily Kantian, idealist, and universalizing;
and the central methods of "close reading" and "practical criticism" were
transformed into means of producing historical and cultural knowledge on
the basis of small units of text. Viewed as part of the longer history of the
discipline, the most striking feature of this third period is that literary "scholarship," which had always accompanied literary "criticism" within the discipline, gradually came to replace it and increasingly came to define the work
of the discipline as a whole. When the current consensus around a scholarly
historicist/contextualist approach to literature first began to be put together,
it was in large part justified by the argument, offered initially by leftist
thinkers such as Raymond Williams, or (differently) the followers of Pierre
Bourdieu, or (differently again) the followers of Michel Foucault, that critical and aesthetic approaches to literature must be rejected. It was this rejection of the project of criticism, by way of a rejection of the category of the
aesthetic, that cleared the way for many of the most important movements in literary studies that would follow, from the cultural studies and
cultural materialist approaches that explicitly took Williams as their emblem,
through the influential ideology critique of Frederic Jameson and those who
followed him, to other less obviously related movements including the new
historicism, postcolonial literary scholarship, and most recently, much of
"digital humanities" and quantitative literary studies.

One must of course add that, in its day, the discipline's argument against
critical and aesthetic approaches had its merits as a means of showing the
limits of both the Leavisite and the New Critical positions. Yet, as the first
part of this history shows, it was in fact quite wrong to reject the project of
criticism as if its motivating concept, the aesthetic, could only ever be
thought through in idealist terms. What was being elided here was the fact
that modern disciplinary criticism had been founded on an aesthetics of just

the opposite kind. In our own period, this historical amnesia has allowed a programmatic retreat from the critical project of intervening in the culture, back toward the project of analyzing the culture, without any mandate for intervention—an ironic and indeed dialectical reversal, given the fact that the turn to cultural analysis was argued for initially by thinkers on the radical left of the discipline.

Viewed in this way, the history of literary studies finally falls into the same three rough periods as does the history of the twentieth century more broadly. First of all, we have an early period between the wars in which the possibility of something like a break with liberalism, and a genuine move to radicalism, is mooted and then disarmed. Second, we have a period of relative continuity through the mid-century, with the two paradigms of "criticism" and "scholarship" both serving real superstructural functions within Keynesianism. The Keynesian period then enters into a crisis in the 1970s—a crisis registered in the discipline in a famously confused debate over "theory," which in effect acts as cover for the underlying shift from two paradigms to one—and finally, in the late 1970s/early 1980s, we see the establishment of a new order: the unprecedentedly complete dominance of the "scholar" model in the form of the historicist/contextualist paradigm. If this congruence comes as something of a surprise, it is also quite unsurprising: what would one expect to find except that the history of the discipline marches more or less in step with the underlying transformations of the social order?

It would of course be unwise to pretend that the schematic view I offer here is anything other than provisional—like all schematics, it leaves out a great deal. No doubt some of what it leaves out will prove to be important in ways I have not managed to acknowledge—and here, as a warning against mistaking the schematic as a complete map, it is perhaps worth repeating once again that the story I tell here is largely the story of literary criticism, rather than the quite different story of literary scholarship, with which it is obviously closely intertwined. A history that tracked the development of the latter, from its roots in nineteenth-century philology, through mid-century literary history, biography, and bibliography, all the way to our current historicist/contextualist forms, would be very welcome, and no doubt would have much to say that would adjust what I have written. Nevertheless, taken with a due sense of its limitations, it seems to me that the three-part periodization I have offered here at least provides a better heuristic through which to understand the discipline's development than the two-part periodization usually adopted—silently, of course. It certainly brings some of the broader contours of the discipline's history, and thus the particular impasses and opportunities before it in its present situation, into sharper relief.

V

A final rearticulation of the main argument may help to make explicit the stakes of the book as a whole. Historians of literary studies have told us that the central axis of dispute within the discipline since its inception has been that between criticism and scholarship. Against that background, I here suggest that our period has been an unprecedented one in the sense that since the early 1980s, one party has managed to dominate the field. I also suggest that the effaced project of criticism once represented the discipline's strongest line of connection to a longer history of materialist practice, and that the currently dominant mode of historicist/contextualist scholarship, for all that it was argued for by the left, has in its most salient aspects constituted a depoliticizing retreat to cultural analysis as a result of the spread of neoliberal forces in the wider economic and political sphere.

Once one has articulated this, it becomes possible to state further that the absence of the project of criticism in our period—the absence of any programmatic commitment, not just to analyzing and describing the culture, but to taking action to change it—needs ultimately to be seen as a symptom of the broader political situation of the radical left under neoliberalism, struggling, as it has since the late 1970s, to continue in the absence of any broader movement to support it. As Perry Anderson noted in his now-famous editorial on the occasion of the relaunch of the New Left Review in 2000:

> Ideologically, the novelty of the present situation stands out in historical view. It can be put like this. For the first time since the Reformation, there are no longer any significant oppositions—that is, systematic rival outlooks—within the thought-world of the West; and scarcely any on a world scale either. . . . Whatever limitations persist to its practice, neo-liberalism as a set of principles rules undivided across the globe, the most successful ideology in world history. (17)[10]

As Susan Watkins, the new editor of NLR, noted in 2010 on the occasion of the journal's fiftieth anniversary, the events of the ten years from 2000 to 2010—most importantly, in the wake of the 2008 financial crash, the near complete lack of any serious positing of alternatives to neoliberal capitalism by those in power—seemed to confirm this view.[11] No real reform, let alone revolution, seemed on the horizon. Given this situation, the question for thinkers on the left was, as Watkins put it: what can be achieved by intellectual work "in the meantime"? The kinds of projects offered in response should, I hope, strike the reader as both powerful and familiar: our "first commitment must be to an accurate description of the world" (Anderson 14), which is to say, to "attend to the development of capitalism" (Anderson 17), to "attend to the development of actually existing capitalism" (Watkins 23). For the left in this period, everywhere prevented from proceeding into action, further and better analysis has again and again been the answer. It is thus no surprise to find that the 2000 volume also contains Franco Moretti's paper "Conjectures on World Literature," in which the famous argument against the final remnant of criticism, "close reading," first appears, nor that when Anderson and Watkins come to discussing the study of literary and artistic phenomena from a left perspective, both recommend Jameson.

In the face of such a consensus it is a little daunting to observe that for the left today, politics must be a question, not just of taking reckonings in the service of some longed-for victory in the future, but of taking action in the present: of fighting to develop for ourselves and others lives at least minimally rich in capabilities and sensitivities. For we do not live "in the meantime," we live in the now; and it is only from these continually present struggles that any chance of a humane future may someday come. If, when Watkins was writing in 2010, "no real reform, let alone revolution, has seemed on the horizon," the worldwide events of 2011 immediately put this view to the fire: a global echo-chamber of protest and dissent; reforms from above, still no; "revolutions" from below, yes. Naturally these protests and "revolutions" have been of highly problematic kinds, and in many cases have led to results about which one can only weep. Nevertheless, for many on the left, they have seemed among the first of many signs that neoliberalism may have entered a series of cascading crises from which it will not recover— none of them, to be sure, the terminal crisis of capitalism, but considered together perhaps the terminal crisis of its neoliberal phase. It remains to be seen what form capitalism will take on the other side of the crisis. In any case, it seems as if for the first time in a generation there is a chance, however slim, that the left may be able to halt its thirty-year retreat and tentatively begin to advance once again.

How must the academic study of literature reconstitute itself in order to make a contribution in this new era? Not, I think, by continuing in its present mode, for in our new situation the old slogan "Always historicize!" will no longer serve. If the historicist/contextualist paradigm has been adopted locally for the best of political reasons, it has also been pushed into position by more general political, economic, and institutional forces of a much harsher kind. On the one hand, the turn to scholarship has meant a genuine rejection of easy universalisms and essentialisms, as well as, in the best cases, a sophisticated intellectual commitment to the material rather than the ideal. On the other hand, it has also involved a rarely examined and professionally enabling assumption that our immediate task as higher students of literature is the production of new and better cultural analysis, rather than the development of new methods for cultivating subjectivities and collectivities. In this latter respect, its main effect has been to prevent us from taking action. In search of a balanced assessment of "Always historicize!" then, the best we can say is that it has been a very good banner under which to conduct a retreat.

What banner for a truly critical paradigm on the left? This crucial question can only be answered collectively; I will be vastly pleased if the book does anything to make it more widely asked. But I hope readers will forgive me if I offer, as a preliminary thought, a distorted echo of Marx's most frequently quoted maxim: the maxim that everyone quotes but that almost no one in literary studies really seems to believe. Hitherto, literary scholars on the left have tried merely to interpret the world. We are now entering a new situation. Might there not be a case for a systematic attempt to change it?

Chapter One

The Critical Revolution Turns Right

Most of those who have written at length about the history of literary studies have agreed that modern literary criticism was effectively born at Cambridge in the 1920s, at a moment that has come to be called the "critical revolution"—but of course, it did not come entirely out of nowhere. Already at the *fin de siecle* one can observe a discipline split into something like the binary structure it maintained until the scholarly turn of the late 1970s and early 1980s: we have two camps, with the professional philologist the emblem of the first, and the amateur belletrist the emblem of the second. One can get a good sense of the character of these two camps, and the strength of the historical consensus that attests to it, by comparing the terms used by the better historians. Thus Chris Baldick tells us that the key conflict in the period running from 1890 to 1918 was that between "academics" and "aesthetes": between "scholarly and scientific objectivism on the one side, and aesthetic or 'impressionistic' subjectivism on the other; that is to say between a professional Knowledge of literature and an amateur Taste for it."[1] For Gerald Graff, who takes the relevant period as extending from 1875 to 1915, the conflict is between "investigators" and "generalists": between those who stood for "scientific research and the philological study of modern languages" on the one hand, and the "dissenting tradition" of those who "defended appreciation over investigation and values over facts" on the other.[2] Or again, for John Guillory the period extends from 1880 to 1920, and the relevant conflict is that between "philologists" and "belletrists."[3] And so on. The precise terms chosen differ, but the picture they give us is much the same: in both Britain and the United States, we have a discipline divided into two rough camps that already bear more than a passing resemblance to the "scholars" and "critics" of the mid-century. So the scholar/critic divide certainly had its antecedents, and to modern eyes, if they are willing to squint a little, the "critical revolution" can even be read as a moment of continuity rather than rupture.

But in a more important sense, the critical revolution of the 1920s came entirely as a surprise. For whenever we manage to turn off our hindsight and instead consider the institutional battles of the *fin de siecle* with something like the eyes of a dispassionate contemporary observer, it becomes clear that one side—that of the belletrists—is going to lose. They are determined amateurs in a game that is speedily turning professional. They are unscientific: in eschewing the world of "verifiable facts" and instead opting to commit themselves to the world of "interpretations and values," they seem destined to confirm to the wider university that their practices of aesthetic appreciation, in Graff's words, have "no objective basis and therefore [do] not qualify for serious academic study."[4] In Guillory's words, they will have "failed to maintain a link to the scientificity that alone would have assured [their] disciplinary status in the constellation of disciplines."[5] In short, they are clearly, even proudly, unsuited to the twentieth-century research university that is rapidly springing into being around them.

Thus during the 1910s, one would have been hard-pressed to predict that a new paradigm for literary criticism, and one that prioritized aesthetic experience rather than philological learning, was about to enter what many later observers have termed a "heroic age." The critical revolution of the 1920s was a sharp turn away from what seemed the discipline's obvious trajectory. It allowed the distinctive belletristic emphases on aesthetic appreciation, on cultivating the subjectivity of the reader, and on the connection between tastes and values to be taken up and insisted upon in a thoroughly new way, thereby laying the foundations for a new paradigm for criticism: a paradigm rigorous and scientific enough for the modern research university. This methodological revolution is not well understood today, even by those who work in the field, but its scale and importance were quite clear to many of those involved, and remained clear throughout much of the mid-century.

Taking just one example from the many available, in 1947 the American critic Stanley Edgar Hyman was able to open his book *The Armed Vision: A Study in the Methods of Modern Literary Criticism* as follows:

> The literary criticism written in English over the past quarter of a century is qualitatively different from any previous criticism. Whether you call it the "new" criticism, as many have, or "scientific criticism," or "working criticism," or, as this book does, "modern criticism," its only relation to the great practitioners of the past seems to be one of descent. (3)[6]

The drama of this opening did not derive from any novelty of the argument: Hyman was offering a firm restatement of an accepted view. The rupture was widely, and I think quite accurately, understood as a very complete one. The belletristic criticism of the *fin de siecle* had been transformed into something genuinely new.

The effects of the break were felt well beyond the bounds of university literature departments. By the late twentieth century, what might have seemed merely a methodological innovation within the discipline of English, and thus simply a matter for academics, had had significant and even at times transformative effects on so many other institutions, sectors, fields, and spheres of human concern in the English-speaking world that it is difficult to find a term that will encompass them. I will confine myself to a few examples, chosen more or less at random. It is the critical revolution of the 1920s that we must praise or blame for the leftist or leftish character of the adult education movements that were significant features of the cultural landscape of Britain and some parts of its diaspora throughout the twentieth century, and the subsequent birth of a left "Cultural Studies" as an intellectual and institutional movement. The critical revolution is also, at root, responsible for the continuing distinctiveness, in world terms, of high school literature education in much of India, Great Britain, Australia, the United States, Sri Lanka, Canada, South Africa, New Zealand—an education in literature that, at least in principle, still asks students to cultivate something like a "personal" relationship to specific literary texts by means of extended and careful reading, rather than, say, asking them to study the facts of literary history, as do students in many other parts of the world today. Continuing our heterogeneous list, we can trace the direct effects of the critical

revolution on many significant forms of Anglo-American cultural journalism, both "higher" and "lower," from the early twentieth century through
to the present; on a range of effective campaigns, in the second half of the
twentieth century, against disciplinarian pedagogies in primary schools; on
the relative enthusiasm with which, during the 1960s and 1970s, the literary
portions of the US academy imported continental philosophies derived
from the "linguistic turn; also, if you really want to push your luck, on many
of the scripts for *Doctor Who*.[7] Of course lists of this kind fail to do the thing
justice, since the effects that can be traced clearly are naturally less interesting than the subterranean ones—effects less immediately visible, perhaps,
but also deeper—the kinds of wide-reaching effects that the disciplined
training of multiple generations of minds can have on so many fields and
sectors; the effects that a sustained institutional commitment can have,
when that commitment is to a transformation of the culture, of the public,
or of the common. In this regard, one might say that the most important
effects of the critical revolution were at the occluded but profound level of
the idioms, habits, and sensibilities by which the social body creates, under-
goes, and reflects on experiential forms. For the historical materialist, there
are of course levels at which such idioms must be held accountable to deeper
determinations; nevertheless, whatever adjusts them bears quite directly on
the very character of social life. In any case, the break toward the modern
critical paradigm was not merely a matter for academics. It was to have a
range of significant effects on the social order at large.

What was the nature of the break? What made the modern forms of criticism different from the old? In answering these questions, the key point to
observe is that the break required a movement away from subjectivist
impressionism in aesthetic matters and toward exactitude, meticulousness,
and something approaching "scientific" precision. The central innovation
that allowed this movement was the development of the rigorous methodology of textual analysis that soon came to be known as "practical criticism"
or "close reading." The fact that the development of "close reading" was the
central enabling condition for the critical revolution has been noted by
almost everyone who has studied the period: Baldick is typical of the field
here in his declaration that "nothing distinguishes twentieth-century literary
criticism more sharply from that of previous ages than this close attention to
textual detail."[8] Yet I do not think that the full ramifications of this have

really been thought through. For if close reading was the central advance, then the politics of the critical revolution in its early moments look rather different than is usually assumed.

As we will see in later chapters, the discipline's "scholarly turn" to its current paradigm in the late 1970s and early 1980s was in large part justified on the basis of the argument that the modern critical paradigm had been, at root, a conservative one. One can certainly see the plausibility of this reading: the figures most often wielded as emblems of the early critical paradigm are T. S. Eliot ("classicist in literature, royalist in politics, and anglo-catholic in religion"), F. R. Leavis (for whom the target is often coded as "mass civilisation"), and the New Critics (broadly speaking, Christian conservatives defending what they understood as traditional Southern—initially "Southern Agrarian"—values). But if one sees the development of close reading as the founding innovation, then one might expect the politics of the moment to have been otherwise, for the method actually originated in the work of figures who were rather differently placed politically: I. A. Richards and William Empson were both left-liberals with occasional radical leanings, rather than conservatives; both were internationalists rather than localists in the manner of Leavis or, differently, the New Critics; and both were secularist or atheist rather than religious—Empson stridently so. In later chapters, we will observe many of the key thinkers of our own period yoking these quite different figures together as if they were all conservatives, in order to claim that the critical paradigm was conservative in essence. The historical scene being so mixed politically, the yoking together is problematic. The diagnosis of an essential conservatism begins to seem especially problematic once one notices that the specific innovation that did most to define the modern critical paradigm, close reading, was developed initially by the figures farthest toward the left.

Today it ought to be possible to assess the political character of the critical revolution more accurately, as part of a rethinking of the political history of the discipline as a whole. Thus in this chapter, I will emphasize the critical revolution's political ambivalence, especially in its earliest stages, and the ways in which this ambivalence was subsequently captured and determined for conservatism by the right. To see this, one needs to understand more clearly the history of the key innovations "close reading" and "practical criticism"—a history which has become quite muddled. For as we shall see in later chapters, Richards' and Empson's characteristically left-liberal innovations in this field were soon to become conflated with the rather different politics of those who followed them: in the United States, "close reading" was remarked, and is now usually remembered, as a New Critical innovation, and in Britain, "practical criticism" came to be associated most strongly with Leavis. I shall therefore begin this concise tour of the history of criticism by disentangling the left-liberalism of Richards in particular from the relative conservatism of those who followed him, addressing first the New Critics, and then Leavis and the Scrutiny scene. The case of T. S. Eliot is somewhat different, and points us away from our main story; those particularly interested in it can refer to the Appendix.

First Period: Criticism Established

Modern criticism was founded, in large part, on the new methodology of "close reading." But where did it "close reading" come from? Within the United States, debates about "close reading" often proceed as if the method were first developed by the New Critics. More historically sensitive accounts sometimes acknowledge that "close reading" really began on the other side of the Atlantic, with I. A. Richards and William Empson, but often do so in such a way as to assimilate Richards and Empson to those who followed them by treating them as "early New Critics," "Anglo-" New Critics, a "prologue" to the history of close reading, or similar.[9] To understand the origins of "close reading," and with it the origins of the modern critical paradigm as a whole, we have to see that both these kinds of accounts are mistaken. For "close reading" as conceived and practiced by Richards and Empson and "close reading" as subsequently taken up and disseminated by the New Critics were quite divergent methods, directed toward opposed ends. To show this in any thorough way, one needs to examine the history with an eye to the kinds of positions in philosophical aesthetics being proposed, and I will certainly proceed to that in a moment. But to begin with, it is worth pointing out that one can also begin to suspect it simply by considering the nature of the intellectual formations involved. Richards and Empson were, among other things, Cambridge League-of-Nations liberals, internationalist, cosmopolitan, and secularist. The New Critics were, for the most part, Southern US Christian political and cultural conservatives seeking a return to the "traditional Southern values" of family, religion, and an agrarian way of life. Once one reflects on this, the widespread assumption that the New Critics represented a continuous, rather than at best radically dialectical, development out of the work of Richards and Empson comes to seem rather surprising. Can we really expect a method developed by one of these groups to be taken up by the other without undergoing fundamental change? The Southerners claimed Richards and Empson as forefathers, and we have largely believed them—yet Richards and Empson both emphatically disavowed the connection, Richards claiming that he didn't "know much about the Am. New Critics and never wanted to acknowledge any relation, whatsoever, to whomsoever they are," and Empson calling one of their central tenets "dogma" and "absurd."[10] What was really going on?

The real story, in its broad outlines, runs as follows. Richards and Empson put together what might fairly be called an incipiently materialist practice of close reading, based in an instrumental or (loosely speaking) pragmatist aesthetics, directed toward an advanced utilitarian model of aesthetic and practical education. This was taken up and co-opted by the New Critics, who remade and institutionalized it as a thoroughly idealist practice, based in a neo-Kantian aesthetics of disinterest and transcendent value, directed toward religious cultural conservatism. This may seem like an abstruse or minor point, but it is in fact a fairly major one, since, as we shall see in later chapters, lack of awareness about this early reversal in the political and philosophical orientation of what is often celebrated as our most central and characteristic disciplinary practice continues to have some rather unfortunate effects on literary studies today. One of them is the widespread sense that "close reading" has its origins in Christian hermeneutic practices, and that rejecting it may therefore seem something of a progressive act—we will see this particularly in Chapter 3, when we come to address the work of Franco Moretti and the associated rise of quantitative literary studies. The effacement of the origins of the practice has given many the impression that it is somehow, at root, a practice of autonomous or idealist aesthetics, and as such, originally or even necessarily decontextualizing, dehistoricizing and/or depoliticizing. However, once we take a closer look at the history of the discipline, it becomes apparent that close reading is now being critiqued on the grounds of its purported origins in the very kinds of positions in philosophical aesthetics it was built to oppose.

More generally, the effect of the new critical co-opting of "close reading," and the forgetting of the earlier history, has been to motivate the widespread conviction that "critical" and "aesthetic" justifications for literary study must ultimately be rejected, since they can only be made in idealist terms of the kinds favored by the New Criticism and cognate movements. The early history of the discipline shows that this is not so: the case of the early critical paradigm demonstrates, not only that another kind of aesthetics is possible, but that it once existed, and was indeed responsible for the development of many of the discipline's characteristic methods and concerns. Of course, I hasten to add that one would not want to resurrect I. A. Richards' particular brand of aesthetics today, even if one could: flawed in its day in ways that we shall shortly note, it would no doubt continue to fail to serve our needs in the present. But perhaps being reminded of a left-liberal, rather than Christian conservative, version of the aesthetic—and one that in many ways reached beyond liberalism by explicitly trying to break with the idealism that had been the dominant strand in bourgeois aesthetics since Kant— might help us to appreciate the possibility of taking it further, to build instead a genuine aesthetics, and a materialist aesthetic criticism, for more radical purposes within the discipline today.

I. A. Richards, Close Reading, and Practical Criticism

Accounts of the history of close reading that treat it primarily as a New Critical practice often begin with Richards' *Practical Criticism* (1929), on the grounds that there Richards pays attention to very small units of language in short lyric poems in a way that led directly to the New Critics' emphasis on "the poem in itself," and their associated rejection of the analysis of any kind of historical or political context. What is much less often acknowledged is that Richards' methodological innovations were based on, and enabled by, his earlier theoretical innovations: the clearing out of old aesthetic theories that Richards, C. K. Ogden, and James Wood undertook in *The Foundations of Aesthetics* (1922); Richards' and Ogden's systematic study of linguistic misunderstanding in *The Meaning of Meaning* (1923); and, in particular, Richards' development, in *Principles of Literary Criticism* (1924), of a sophisticated answer to the fundamental question of what literature is good for.[11] The last of these is of most direct relevance to us here.

In the simplest terms, we might say that Richards' argument in *Principles of Literary Criticism* was that the most important thing about works of literature was their aesthetic potential, by which he meant not their formal beauty as an end in itself, but their ability to act as means by which readers could cultivate many of their most useful practical faculties. His account of what this signifies for literary study generally is a complex one, but we can catch the general tenor of it as it comes through into *Practical Criticism* in his line: "It is less important to like 'good' poetry and dislike 'bad,' than to be able to use them both as a means of ordering our minds" (327). The work of literature, for Richards, was to be a kind of therapeutic technology, and the critic was therefore to be something like a doctor of applied psychology, helping us to use that technology to improve our minds. It was on the basis of this kind of aesthetic thinking, which sees the aesthetic as a mode of instrumental, rather than final, value that Richards began to develop the practice of close reading.

It is worth taking a moment to examine the philosophical foundations of this view. One of Richards' chief goals in *Principles of Literary Criticism* is to try to develop a general answer to what he takes to be the fundamental question for criticism, and for aesthetics generally, viz.: "What is the value of the arts, why are they worth the devotions of the keenest hours of the best minds, and what is their place in the system of human endeavours?" (3) Clearly, this is a large question, and not a new one. Richards' attempt to answer it begins with a tremendously ambitious ground-clearing exercise: a dismissal of the entire body of writings on philosophical aesthetics since Kant.

The title of Richards' second chapter, *The Phantom Aesthetic State,* sufficiently indicates the main line of attack. Richards thinks that Kant led the whole tradition of philosophical aesthetics into a dead end by positing the existence of a special "aesthetic state" which we might describe, loosely, as a mode of experience radically divorced from practical matters such as inquiring and desiring. In rejecting any such state, Richards' most immediate target is the art-for-art's-sake aestheticism of the 1890s—he cites Vernon Lee's *The Beautiful* (1913); Oscar Wilde and Walter Pater are also clearly on his mind—but his description is also intended to fit a vast range of aesthetic thinking, before and since, that tries to use the Kantian division of the faculties to set up the "aesthetic" as a special or privileged mode of experience, divorced from experience of both intellectual/cognitive and desiring/moral kinds.

In view of the ways his work was later taken up by thoroughgoing Kantians, it is worth dwelling here on the fact that his rejection of this Kantian, idealist aesthetics is made in the strongest terms. He tells us that Kantian aesthetics "has had an influence upon speculation which would be ridiculous if it had not been so disastrous. It is difficult even now to get out of ruts which have been seen to lead nowhere" (8). While he broadly accepts many of Kant's claims *outside* the realm of aesthetics, he informs us that *within* aesthetics, Kantian idealism has led to "calamitous distortions" (9). Whatever the merits of this line of argument as a critique of Kant—and we should, I think, be at the very least suspicious of any thorough critique of Kant's aesthetics that does not understand itself as necessarily undermining much of the other two parts of the system—it is hard to miss the fact that Richards is in earnest here.

Against these idealist philosophies of the distinct aesthetic state, he offers us what it seems fair to call an incipiently materialist view of the aesthetic: a view of aesthetic experience that vigorously insists on its continuity with experience of normal, practical kinds. He insists that:

> When we look at a picture, or read a poem, or listen to music, we are not doing something quite unlike what we were doing on our way to the gallery or when we dressed in the morning. The fashion in which the experience is caused in us is different, and as a rule the experience is more complex and, if we are successful, more unified. But our activity is not of a fundamentally different kind. To assume that it is, puts difficulties in the way of describing and explaining it, which are unnecessary and which no one has yet succeeded in overcoming. (12)

Richards, then, is putting together his theory specifically to oppose any attempt to set up the aesthetic as a self-sufficient category insulated from the rest of life. This becomes most explicit at the end of the chapter, when Richards turns to show that his critique of the art-for-art's sake philosophies of the 1890s is also a critique of the modernist aestheticisms of his contemporaries in the 1920s:

A further objection to the assumption of a peculiar aesthetic attitude is that it makes smooth the way for the idea of a peculiar aesthetic value, a pure art value. Postulate a peculiar kind of experience, aesthetic experience, and it is an easy step to the postulation of a peculiar unique value, different in kind and cut off from the other values of ordinary experience. 'To appreciate a work of art we need bring with us nothing from life, no knowledge of its ideas and affairs, no familiarity with its emotions.' (Clive Bell, *Art,* p25) So runs a recent extreme statement of the Aesthetic Hypothesis, which has had much success. To quote another example less drastic but also carrying with it the implication that aesthetic experiences are *sui generis,* and their value is not of the same kind as other values: "Its nature is to be not part, nor yet a copy, of the real world (as we commonly understand that phrase), but a world in itself independent, complete, autonomous" (A. C. Bradley, *Oxford Lecture on Poetry,* p. 5).

This view of the arts as providing a private heaven for aesthetes is, as will appear later, a great impediment to the investigation of their value. . . . *Art* envisaged as a mystic, ineffable virtue is a close relative of the 'aesthetic mood,' and may easily be pernicious in its effects, through the habits of mind which, as an idea, it fosters, and to which, as a mystery, it appeals. (13; I have tried to reproduce the change of font on "Art" in the original)

If this had been published in the United States in 1983 rather than in the United Kingdom in 1923, it would surely have been unreadable except as a full-scale assault on the lingering legacy of the New Criticism. In direct opposition to the kinds of positions that it will come to be mistaken for, Richards' theoretical project is to break the aesthetic out of the Kantian loop of self-sufficiency and redundancy and instead to put it back into contact with the material concerns of life. For him, this means shifting the emphasis away from the supposedly "objective" aesthetic or formal qualities of the work of art considered in isolation, and onto the nature of the relationship between the artwork and its most important context—its audience. "We are accustomed to say that a picture is beautiful, instead of saying that it causes in us an experience which is valuable in certain ways" (15); "We continually talk as though things possessed qualities, when what we ought to say is that they cause effects in us of one kind or another" (16): Richards' aesthetic theory continually asks us to turn our attention away from the artwork "in

itself" and to focus instead on the nature of the relationship between art-
works and their audiences. Having effected that shift, much of the rest of
Principles of Literary Criticism is devoted to trying to show how much of life
that relationship involves. Morals and capacities for morals; pleasures and
capacities for pleasure; opportunities and capacities for cognition and
analysis—the aesthetic, considered in this contextual and instrumental
sense, comes to overrun all the borders that Kant erects to divide the faculties. Morals and the will, truth and cognition, beauty and the capacity for
pleasure: Richards' account of the aesthetic tries to throw lines out to them
all. If we had thought that Richards was a kind of proto- or Anglo- New
Critic, then reading *Principles of Literary Criticism* should set us straight
fairly quickly: in philosophical aesthetics, at least, Richards holds views of
just the opposite kind.

By the time he comes to write *Practical Criticism* (1929), then, Richards
is doing something rather different to what readings of his work back
through the lens of New Criticism suggest. Famously, *Practical Criticism* is
an account of an experiment Richards conducted in the 1920s, in which he
had his Cambridge English students write commentaries on various poems
without being told anything about them in advance.[12] From the vantage
point of the late twentieth- or early twenty-first century historicist, a cursory
glance over the history of the discipline will all too often light first upon
Richards' removal of the poems' titles, dates of publication, the poets' names,
and so forth, and assume on that basis that it is witnessing the opening salvo
in the New Critical war on context. This reading misses the core of Richards'
project. A more sustained look at the disposition of the forces reveals that
Richards is really firing in the opposite direction: far from trying, in proto-
New Critical fashion, to strip works of their contexts in order to encourage
a close attention to literary language "for its own sake," Richards is in fact
trying to find the most rigorous and precise way he can to put works of literature into a productive relation with their contexts of reception.

His commitment to "context" in this sense is in fact rather deep. Before
anything else, *Practical Criticism* is an attempt to examine as precisely as possible the actual relationships existing between works of literature and their
most important context: their readers.[13] Once we have put aside the idea that
Richards is an early New Critic, we can begin to see that he is concerned
everywhere to put the text into some productive relationship to its context of

reception. For present purposes, it is important to note two parts of this project in particular: what I am going to call the "diagnostic" and the "therapeutic" parts. The first part of Richards' project—the diagnostic part—is to propose the use of works of literature, in concert with readers' responses to them, as sensitive instruments with which to determine the state of feeling in contemporary culture. Or, as he puts it, poetry can serve as

> an eminently suitable *bait* for anyone who wishes to trap . . . current opinions and responses . . . for the purpose of examining and comparing them, and with a view to advancing our knowledge of what may be called the natural history of human opinions and feelings. (5–6, italics in original)

In this capacity, he tells us, *Practical Criticism* should be considered a "record of a piece of fieldwork in comparative ideology" (16). Contemporary historicist/contextualist scholars often overlook this diagnostic aspect of Richards' project, though it is one with which one might have thought they would have some sympathy.[14] Indeed given its strong resemblance to the general project of cultural analysis that the historicist/contextualist approach posits as the main goal of disciplinary literary studies, it is really not at all incompatible with current modes. Later, we will examine Raymond Williams' work as an early example of cultural analysis in the current mode; here, it is worth noting that Richards is proposing, in passing, something not at all unlike Williams' method, in which works of literature are taken as indices of "structures of feeling" operating within culture generally, the key difference between the two being that, where Williams directs our attention to the context of production, Richards directs our attention to the context of reception.[15]

Of course, one needs to say in the same breath that, having once outlined this diagnostic aspect of his project, Richards did not go on to carry it out in any systematic way: nowhere in his work can we find rich and coherent historical and cultural analysis of the kind we find in the best of our contemporary historicisms, from Williams onward. Indeed, from the vantage-point of the best scholarship on the left of the discipline today, it is not hard to see that Richards is naïve about the nature of the political and economic contexts his "fieldwork in comparative ideology" is seeking to analyze, and indeed that this is a naiveté characteristic of the tradition of utilitarian humanist liberalism from which he springs. It would certainly be possible to make much of this failing, which folds a flaw into all of Richards' most useful theoretical and practical tools, from the early analysis of language and meaning, through the science of misunderstanding, the practical aesthetics and the associated method of reading, all the way through to the cluster of work on "Basic English"—a flaw that makes them unable to stand up to the real historical, cultural, and (especially) political and economic forces on which they are designed to be set to work. Indeed, one might then go on to trace the ways in which Richards' Benthamite enthusiasm for technological or "applied psychology" solutions to what are really economic and political problems led directly, in a way that is not often enough remembered, to the development of new and pernicious techniques of mass manipulation in fields such as advertising, marketing, and public relations: precisely those cultural elements of capitalist modernity that much of the later critical paradigm was to react so strongly against.

But this is to take Richards at his weakest. For present purposes, the more important point is that, from the outset, a central part of Richards' project is motivated by a will to use literary texts, together with contemporary readers' responses to them, as diagnostic instruments to determine the state of culture. A more thoroughgoing commitment to cultural and contextual analysis, of much the kind we have today, would thus be consistent with Richards' more general position. In realizing that Richards was proposing the use of literary texts, not as aesthetic objects gloriously isolated from all possible uses and contexts, but as diagnostic instruments for "fieldwork in comparative ideology," we realize that he was a lot more like us than he is generally thought to be. He was, in fact, clearing new ground for historicist/contextualist scholars of culture, though did not yet have the tools to work it.

That much for the diagnostic part of Richards' project. The second part of Richards' project—what I am calling the "therapeutic" part—takes us into rather different territory. For a large part of the interest of Richards' approach to literary studies—and certainly a large part of its difference from otherwise similar approaches today—lies in its commitment to proceeding on from diagnosis and into treatment, as it were: to proceed from "fieldwork in comparative ideology" in the service of a "history of human opinions and feelings," into a full and systematic effort actively to intervene in that history.

Thus *Practical Criticism* was intended to provide "not only an interesting commentary upon the state of contemporary culture, but a new and powerful educational instrument."[16] The larger goal of Richards' study of misunderstanding, his aesthetics, and his method of "close reading" was to improve on the historicisms of his contemporaries by developing a way to use literature, not just to analyze cultures, ideologies, and psychologies, but to improve them. This is a crucial part of what would come to distinguish literary "scholarship" from literary "criticism" throughout the mid-century: where the former tried to use literature as a means through which to analyze culture, the latter tried to set literature to work on the aesthetic sensibilities of readers, with the aim of bringing about some larger change in the culture as a whole.

There had, of course, been "criticisms" of something like this kind before. Since the beginning of aesthetic discourse proper in the late eighteenth century, many had tried, under the sign of "criticism," to call on literature, or else on the aesthetic generally, as a way to intervene in the state of culture. Here one might list again the names of the classic nineteenth-century "moralists" or cultural critics: Mill, Carlyle, Arnold, Ruskin, Morris. Yet until Richards none had yet been in a position to develop for "criticism," to the standard required by the modern university, both a philosophical foundation and a sophisticated practical methodology. Even in his own day, Richards was not alone in seeing the need for a general project of aesthetic education, nor was he alone in seeing that a real commitment to aesthetic education would mean developing a method for teaching aptitudes and sensitivities of the broadest and most general, as well as most unreliable, tenuous, intuitive, and idiosyncratic kinds. He was, however, virtually unique in his insight that this new era, in which the study of English Literature was being institutionalized, could support, and would in fact require, these aptitudes to be taught by a method that was repeatable, reliable, and precise enough to take its place among the disciplines. In this sense, the development of "close reading" was a genuine advance. The effect of Richards' work here was to put literary criticism, considered as an active attempt to use literature as a tool of aesthetic education in the service of broader cultural change, on something like the scientific footing required in order to qualify it as a discipline within the modern research university, alongside—and even sometimes in competition with—literary scholarship, philology, and literary history. Once it crossed the Atlantic, however, close reading, with its foundation in an anti-idealist aesthetics, was to become quite a different thing.

Second Period: Criticism Turns Right

The New Criticism: Close Reading for Kant

When one moves from Richards and Empson to the New Critics, the first thing one notes is a dramatic shift in world-view and ideology. It is worth dwelling on that shift for a moment, since it did so much to determine the fate of "close reading," and thus, in time, of modern criticism itself. The best place to look for an account of the New Critical worldview is probably *I'll take My Stand: The South and the Agrarian Tradition* (1930), the Introduction to which was effectively the manifesto of the Fugitives, the movement of which the New Critics were almost all, in their early days, a part.[17] The guiding question there is: "Just what must the Southern leaders do to defend the traditional Southern life?" This emphasis on the defense of a specific "tradition" leads quickly enough into education: "What policy should be pursued by the educators who have a tradition at heart?" It seems fair to say that the dominant feeling in the manifesto is a frustrated sense of entitlement—the particular kind of frustration, and associated antimodern resentment, that arises when an intellectual formation feels that a new order is denying it rights and privileges that an older, now idealized order would have granted to it as a matter of course. In the case of the Fugitives, the current order is "Industrialism," seen as "Northern" and (somehow) "Communist"; the older order is that of the traditional agrarian South, idealized chiefly through the elision of any serious engagement with the system of slavery on which that order had been based; and the rights and privileges being denied are those due to these men as *men*—as *white* men—or rather, more precisely, as white male Christian property owners brought up as the inheritors of a certain concept of culture. Of course many of the New Critics moved on from this initial position when, for various historical reasons, it began to seem unconscionable, but the traces of the structure of feeling are everywhere in their major work, and must be borne in mind when we evaluate it.

Others have given much fuller accounts of the ideological conditions within which the New Critics first formed their views.[18] I will draw attention to just one element, albeit one that seems to determine much of their position: their very insistent (I am tempted to say obsessive) anti-communism.

> [I]t must be insisted that the true Sovietists or Communists—if the term may be used here in the European sense—are the [Northern] Industrialists themselves. They would have the government set up an economic super-organization, which in turn would become the government. We therefore look upon the Communist menace as a menace indeed, but not as a Red one; because it is simply according to the blind drift of our industrial development to expect in America at last much the same economic system as that imposed by violence upon Russia in 1917. (xli–xlii)

This is a kind of view with which those of us who watch the United States are only too familiar today: "Democrats are communists!" and so on. One of many sad reflections available to us at this point is that the New Critics' best insights occasionally approached those of the communists they so detested: in particular, their quite radical insistence, in the face of conventional educational humanism, on the fact that "the trouble with the life pattern is to be located at its economic base, and we cannot rebuild it by pouring in soft materials from the top" (xliii–xliv). This seems to me something like a good Marxist diagnosis of the chief weakness in the main liberal response to the problems of industrialism—a diagnosis of liberalism's failure to admit the determination of the superstructure by the base. Having made that diagnosis, though, the New Critics did not see the need to proceed to anything like a serious analysis of the "economic base." Instead, they retreated precisely to the kind of localist and individualist positions that had been developed by the dominant liberalism in its most conservative forms: "The responsibility of men is for their own welfare and that of their neighbours; not for the hypothetical welfare of some fabulous creature called society" (xlvi). It is in formulations like these that their defense of "community," which might seem to resemble a Leavisite defense of an "organic community" in England, in fact collapses very quickly into a something very like a libertarian defense of the rights of the individual. In this way, their fixation on the threat of communism ensured that they remained out of touch with the political and economic realities of their time. This lack of political and economic realism made itself felt particularly in the ungrounded optimism of their more constructive assertions, including, crucially, their view that "an agrarian regime will be secured readily enough where the superfluous industries are not allowed to rise against it." They discovered the unrealism of this position soon enough.

This structure of feeling could not but have a profound effect on Richards' project as it was translated across the Atlantic. The easiest way to summarize this effect is to note that, while the New Critics happily took up many of Richards' practical innovations and made them into core components of literary study in the United States, and thence elsewhere, they did so in a way that split them off from their theoretical foundations in an incipiently materialist aesthetics and then reoriented them such that they began to point in the opposite direction—back toward Kant. In shorthand, one might say that the determinedly anti-Kantian theoretical project of *Principles of Literary Criticism* was dropped, and the method prepared for in *Practical Criticism* was kept, the latter text therefore being read in a rather distorting light.

We can see this by considering the case of Cleanth Brooks. His reminiscences about his first encounters with Richards' work—entitled, significantly enough, "I. A. Richards and *Practical Criticism*"—insist on just these distinctions. He was, he said, "happy to give in full measure to the practical critic what I have withheld from the theoretician" (594).[19] He tells us that he found much of Richards' theoretical apparatus, "particularly in *Principles [of Literary Criticism]*," "distasteful" or "difficult" (589). The latter two terms seem particularly significant as markers of the New Critical response to the work of the Cambridge critics. Surely this is precisely what one expects to see when a set of practices developed by one intellectual formation is taken up by a very different one, operating both with a very different ideology ("distasteful") and a very different level of intellectual sophistication ("difficult"). The theory seems somehow at once at odds with and irrelevant to one's own real concerns, and as such is both resisted and misunderstood.

Brooks gives us a more thorough account of this response in the first few paragraphs of the paper. He begins by contrasting *Principles of Literary Criticism* and *Practical Criticism*. After praising the latter, he writes:

With *Principles* I encountered more difficult going. What Richards had to say was exciting, but I resisted the new psychological terminology as well as the confident position of the author. Nevertheless the book could not be dismissed. I had to cope with it—to try to form an adequate answer to it—or else capitulate.

The result was that I read *Principles* perhaps a dozen times during that first year of acquaintance—and profited from the experience. For the kind of reading that I practiced in trying to find a sound basis for rejecting what Richards had written was intense reading, the sort from which one learns. If I did not gain an understanding of Richards' whole system, an understanding so clear that it compelled acceptance, I did at least sharpen my insight, ways of perceiving, and methods of analysis. (586)

Brooks, to his credit, has no qualms about telling us that his difficulties in understanding the work formed no impediment to his rejection of it. On the contrary: it is his "attempt to find a sound basis for rejecting" *Principles*—his sense that to agree with Richards here would be to "capitulate"—that leads him to try to understand it, again and again.

What in Richards' theory struck Brooks, and the other New Critics, as so objectionable? On the surface, the problem seems to have been with something called "psychological machinery." Here, with this much reiterated phrase, we again encounter the symptoms of a situation in which one intellectual formation fails to understand another: Brooks rather disarmingly admits that "my rejection of it sprang from no theoretical sophistication on my part: instead, such machinery simply seemed irrelevant as well as mystifying" (591). "Irrelevant" and "mystifying" here go quite nicely alongside "distasteful" and "difficult" earlier: Brooks strongly dislikes the "psychological machinery," but it is at the same time not quite clear to him why he should care.

But, to pursue the question a step further, what was the problem with Richards' "psychological machinery?" It is tempting to say that the emphasis is on the noun, and that Brooks and the other New Critics were simply rejecting Richards' scientific bent: they were, after all, the source of a great many influential restatements of what we might take to be a traditional Romantic opposition between science and poetry. But this does little to solve our problem: one could just as easily observe that the New Critics tended to call anything they disliked "machinery," and to contrast it with their own more "organic" approaches, even if they were in fact rejecting it for quite other reasons. And there are other aspects of Richards' scientific approach to which Brooks does not repeatedly object: his tight, "scientific" focus on specific details of language in lyric poems being the obvious example. No, surely we must say instead that the emphasis is not on "machine," but on "psychological," and that what is really being rejected here is the *reader,* as a form of context that the New Critics want to insist is strictly irrelevant to the pure aesthetic text.

This is worth examining, since it is largely from this kind of interpretation that we derive our current sense that "close reading" originated in an attempt to focus attention on "the text itself" rather than on the reader of the text, as well as the long-standing characterization of Richards as a "psychological" critic first and foremost—a rather misleading characterization. The most celebrated and derided instance of this New Critical rejection of the reader is, of course, Wimsatt and Beardsley's "Affective Fallacy," which, together with their "Intentional Fallacy," sought to cut off both reader and writer from the literary work; but those texts have been much discussed elsewhere.[20] Instead, let us observe Ransom making the same move in a more sophisticated fashion in *The New Criticism* (1941).[21] For many decades now, this has proved a convenient and popular book for those looking to learn something about this particular phase in the history of the discipline—no doubt in part because the title seems to promise a clear summary. Ransom treats Richards at length in his opening chapter, first claiming him as a founding father for New Criticism, but then moving to offer a rather damning critique. It is in no small measure as a result of Ransom's account of Richards here that many students and scholars, particularly in the United States, have been given the impression that the work of the early critical revolution was reasonably contiguous with that of the New Critics, rather than opposed to it in central respects.

Ransom's main effort in *The New Criticism* was to show that the New Critical effort to sever the text from its various contexts in order to enable it to be treated purely "in itself" had not yet gone far enough. Within this he had two more specific concerns: "psychological" and "moral" considerations in criticism.

Briefly, the New Criticism is damaged by at least two specific errors of theory, which are widespread. One is the idea of using the psychological affective vocabulary in the hope of making literary judgments in terms of the feelings, emotions, and attitudes of poems instead of in terms of their objects. The other is plain moralism, which in the new criticism would indicate that it has not emancipated itself from the old criticism. I should like to see criticism unburdened of these dregs. (xi)

It is to be noted that in both these cases the concern is ultimately to ensure that valid considerations about texts in themselves are distinguished from invalid considerations about their effects, psychological or moral, on their readers. Richards is Ransom's example of the former, and Yvor Winters is his example of the latter, but Richards, with his theory of how literature can be used to cultivate, among other things, richer and more ethical psychological responses, could just as easily have been critiqued as an example of both. The fact that he is *not* critiqued as an example of both errors gives us a preliminary indication of how strangely Ransom construes Richards—he seems to think of Richards' criticism as based in a rather simplistic theory of affective response, which is not the case. Here he is on Richards:

> Probably the most stubborn popular error which aestheticians are agreed upon in fighting is the notion that the work of art deals immediately with the passions, instead of mediately . . . *Richards is well aware of this chapter of aesthetic theory, which begins with Kant and has gone through several equivalent versions since.* His peculiar interest in the attitudes or consequences of the cognitive stimulus takes some of the emphasis off the emotions. What is left is an unfortunate, and, I judge, unconscious evasion of the cognitive analysis. *He employs a locution which is very modern, and almost fashionable, but nevertheless lazy and thoughtless. He refers to the distinctive emotion of a poem instead of to its distinctive cognitive object.* (16–17; my italics)

These—"lazy" and "thoughtless"—are strong terms, made stronger by the fact that the terms that might seem intended to qualify them—"modern" and "fashionable"—are among the most damning in Ransom's lexicon. What is it about Richards' "reference to the distinctive emotion of a poem"— if that is, in fact, what Richards provides—that incites such a reaction? Is Ransom's just a grumpy rejection of the "new-fangled"? Again, it is tempting to pair this with Brooks' resistance to Richards' "new psychological machinery," and put them both down to Southern Agrarian anti-modernism, but once again, this actually tells us rather little.

It tells us more, perhaps, to note the real strangeness of Ransom's invocation of Kant. "Richards is well aware of this chapter of aesthetic theory," Ransom tells us, "which begins with Kant and has gone through several equivalent versions since." Ransom here seems to be saying: "Richards is well aware of what the authorities have said about this issue; why, therefore, does he ignore them?" But this is to proceed as if Richards had intended to bow to the authority of Kant. Given the clarity, explicitness, and ferocity of Richards' assault on Kant in the opening chapters of *Principles of Literary Criticism,* it is difficult to know what to make of this. Is it simply that Ransom has not read *Principles* and is instead proceeding solely on the basis of a reading of *Practical Criticism?* But that seems a serious charge. I think perhaps we must say instead that Ransom, like Brooks, has read *Principles* but found it "mystifying." To say this is not to accuse either of a merely personal failing, for what we are really encountering is a fundamental difference in the nature and ideology of the two intellectual formations. The thinking of a Richards or an Empson develops within a specific milieu, in which it is assumed that to engage with an authoritative text is at least in part to critique it, even if sometimes only for the purposes of intellectual one-upmanship. As a shorthand description of the milieu, we could do worse than simply observing that often enough they could both be found attending meetings of the Cambridge "Heretics Society," a liberal lecture and debate society that particularly sought to host speakers who challenged traditional sources of authority, especially religious authority. In contrast, for thinkers brought up in the Southern United States, who then came to see it as their task to reaffirm and defend a conservative cultural and religious tradition under threat from an encroaching modernity, it was much more natural to assume that one reads a text primarily in order to expound its authority or to come to an assessment of its relation to other textual authorities. Ransom writes as he does here because, for thinkers formed within this very particular structure of feeling, it really is *not quite imaginable* that another thinker in aesthetics, raised within a very different structure of feeling, might set himself the task of questioning the authority of Kant.

So again we observe that the encounter between two very different intellectual formations is resulting in some real confusion—often, at root, of a rather simple kind. For present purposes, the substantive point is simply that, seemingly without knowing it, Ransom effects a complete reversal of the theoretical orientation of the kinds of practice that Richards had initiated: to both the "error" of making literary judgments on the basis of judgments about affective states, and the "error" of "plain moralism," Ransom's response ultimately will be to appeal to the authority of Kant. Ransom's Kant authorizes the famously radical New Critical attempt to secure the autonomy and self-sufficiency of the aesthetic object: which is to say, an attempt to defend precisely what Richards had critiqued as the "phantom aesthetic state." "Close reading" was now being set to work as the practical arm of the very kind of aesthetic thinking that it had been built to oppose.

Consequences for Literary Study

This reversal in the philosophical orientation of what would go on to become the discipline's characteristic method had a range of effects on the discipline as it proceeded. We can see one of the immediate consequences of it by returning briefly to Brooks' reminiscences. There, without false modesty, he tells us that "In my own use I greatly extended Richards' concepts and pressed their implications." What might Brooks be thinking of here? A paragraph later, he tells us:

> It was possible, I believed, to set up a kind of scale: at the bottom, poems that relied heavily on the principle of exclusion, left out too much of human experience, and so were thin and over simple. They tended accordingly toward sentimentality and general vapidity. Toward the top of the scale were poems that used successfully a high degree of inclusion. (590)

With something of the air of a great discoverer, Brooks here unveils a thought that surely would have seemed evident enough to any of Richards' more committed readers: the thought that some of Richards' observations—here, his working distinction between mental states that achieve stability by excluding complexities and contradictions, and those that do so by including and balancing them—could, if one were so inclined, be used to prop up a hierarchy of aesthetic values. Richards himself already had been so inclined: the whole thrust of his project in both *Principles of Literary Criticism* and

Practical Criticism is to try to find a way to assess works of art on the basis of
the potential value of the experiences that they could make available to their
audiences. At times, it is true, this had even led him to make blanket statements about the superiority of some forms or modes over others: his cham-
pioning of tragedy, in the very chapter of *Principles* to which Brooks is referring, being the central example. But the majority of the time, Richards can
be found running a line quite opposed to this: emphasizing instead the great
complexity of the question of the value of different mental states, the tenu-
ousness of our grasp of the nature of the relationship between artwork and
audience, and thus the provisionality of any kind of aesthetic judgment. He
is very chary indeed of any claim to set up once and for all a canon or hierarchy of aesthetic values, even on psychological grounds, and he is explicitly
opposed to any attempt to set one up on somehow "intrinsic," "formal," or
other nonpsychological grounds.

Given this, it seems that Brooks is mistaken in his view that he "greatly
extended Richards' concepts and pressed their implications"; rather, the possibility he glimpses is one that Richards himself had thought through and
largely rejected. For our purposes, the more important point is that Brooks
here is typical of the movement of which he is a part in his enthusiastic
embrace of the idea of a hierarchy, coupled with his rejection of Richards'
characteristically liberal attempt to find a more material justification for it in
the realm of psychological value. For him, as for the other New Critics, the
key move in adopting Richards is to rescue the aesthetic from the realm of
practical, material, and instrumental values, where Richards had tried to put
it, and instead put it back into the Kantian and idealist realm of transcendental value where it seemed to belong. From this point onward, "aesthetic
value" was to be thought of as residing, not in anything the text could be
used to achieve in the mind of the reader, but somehow solely in the text
itself. Thus when Ransom—in what is perhaps his most famous single essay,
"Criticism, Inc." (1937)—came to argue for the establishment of a rigorous
institutional commitment to literary criticism, as distinct from literary
scholarship, he quite naturally spent time defending criticism against the
philologists' claim that aesthetic appreciation was strictly for amateurs,
because insufficiently rigorous—and yet he also saw fit to spend almost as
much time defending "the autonomy of the work itself" against "moralist"
critics such as "New Humanists" and "Leftists" who were seeking to bring

ethical or political considerations to bear on literature, in an effort assess its effects on the minds of actual readers.[22]

This shift of emphasis from an incipiently materialist aesthetics to a thoroughly idealist one, and the accompanying shift from "extrinsic" to "intrinsic" criticism, was to have considerable consequences for literary study throughout the middle decades of the twentieth century. With it, we have arrived at the largely sterile concern with hierarchy and canonicity that will occupy much of Anglophone literary studies throughout the Cold War period: a series of ultimately unresolvable debates about the exact constitution of a universal canon, as if one could determine what was "good" art and what was "bad" art without any reference to what the art might be good or bad *for*. One can only speculate about what literary studies, and literary education more broadly, might have looked like throughout the mid-century if the discipline had instead been able to follow Richards' more liberal, in the better sense, and certainly more materialist aesthetics: the kind of aesthetics that led him to state that "It is less important to like 'good' poetry and dislike 'bad,' than to be able to use them both as a means of ordering our minds."[23] Putting this line side by side with Brooks' claim to have discovered the possibility of "set[ting] up a kind of scale," it is hard to avoid coming to the same judgment as Richards' biographer, John Paul Russo: "In many ways the New Critics sought to cut Richards down to their size."[24]

It is certainly true, and has long been noted, that Richards and Empson on one side of the Atlantic and the New Critics on the other shared a fundamentally Romantic sense that modernity (and particularly industrial modernity) posed a range of threats to the continuity and richness of cultural life—though to the questions of what those threats were, and what a rich and worthwhile cultural life might look like, they had very different answers. It is true, too, that they shared a sense that the scholarly model of literary studies as a discipline of knowledge production, whether "literary-historical" or "philological," was a symptom of, rather than a genuine response to, this kind of negative modernity; and, accordingly, both Richards and the New Critics were particularly alive to the dangers of putting too great an emphasis on the importance of a text's context of production.[25] But surely too much has been made of these similarities. For the Cambridge liberals, the solution to the problem of modernity was education. For the Southern Christians, the solution was piety. The "practical" in *Practical Criticism* had, in Richards' usage, meant something like "directed towards the practical end of culti-vating readers' sensibilities"; later, under the New Criticism, it was to mean "directed towards the 'practical' end of assessing the value of poems against that of other poems." Through the latter, spread far and wide by the cultural force of the superpower of which they were a part, the goal of so much crit-ical work in the discipline became, for a long time, not to educate the reader, but to adulate the text.

Richards' Reception within Britain: F. R. Leavis

So far our story has led us from Richards' Cambridge in the 1920s to the United States in the 1950s. In order to continue our story into the 1970s and 1980s, we must first return to Britain, for in that later period, too, it was from Britain that the really momentous changes in the nature of Anglophone literary studies were to come. Within Britain, Richards' setting up of literary criticism on a disciplinary footing had its most dramatic effects through the medium of F. R. Leavis and the *Scrutiny* critics.[26] Despite the evident differ-ences between Leavisism and New Criticism, this reception led to develop-ments that were in many ways analogous to those we have just traced. For Leavis, despite the fact that he never had any explicit commitment to an idealist or Kantian aesthetics, nevertheless managed to effect a crucial shift of emphasis within the discipline in Britain and much of its diaspora, turning criticism away from Richards' concern with the value *to readers* of the aesthetic experiences that literature could provide, and toward a more hierarchical concern with evaluating and ranking the relative value of the texts themselves. This was despite his saving emphasis on the deep connec-tion between literature and terms such as "Life," the "Living Principle," and similar. Richards' particular innovations, including "practical criticism" itself, were then remarked as Leavisite in a way that concealed their real ori-gins, such that even today the *Johns Hopkins Guide to Literary Theory and Criticism* describes Richards as "Leavis's Cambridge collaborator"—an odd reversal, but typical of a broader pattern of reception, as we shall see.[27]

In Leavis' early work, Richards is clearly the foundational figure. His first truly major work, the pamphlet manifesto "Mass Civilisation and Minority Culture" (1930), begins with an epigraph from Matthew Arnold that is bowed to and then quickly set to one side as the product of a less problematic age. In its place, as a key contemporary articulation of what Leavis takes to be the Arnoldian tradition, he offers us an extended passage from Richards' *Principles of Literary Criticism* (1924)—a passage that Leavis tells us "should by now be a *locus classicus.*" It is worth quoting this passage from Richards in full, so as to see more clearly the particular uses to which Leavis puts it:

> But it is not true that criticism is a luxury trade. The rearguard of Society cannot be extricated until the vanguard has gone further. Good will and intelligence are still too little available. The critic, as we have said, is as much concerned with the health of the mind as any doctor with the heath of the body. To set up as a critic is to set up as a judge of values. . . . For the arts are inevitably and quite apart from any intentions of the artist an appraisal of existence. Matthew Arnold, when he said that poetry is a criticism of life, was saying something so obvious that it is constantly overlooked. The artist is concerned with the record and perpetuation of the experiences which seem to him most worth having. For reasons which we shall consider . . . he is also the man who is most likely to have experiences of value to record. He is the point at which the growth of the mind shows itself. (144)[28]

Much of this language is of course jarring by today's standards, in part because of the confidence with which Richards announces his sense of the social importance of the critic's therapeutic role: to those who know how the story turns out, confidence of this kind is bound to look blithe at best, if not indeed simply elitist in the most obvious sense. For this reason Leavis, who took up just that emphasis and pounded it repeatedly in ever more resounding a fashion, is usually reduced to a caricature in today's literary scholarship, on the rare occasions when one encounters him at all. The reduction is not entirely unfair, since Leavis does much to render himself so reducible. Here, for instance, he isolates a passage in Richards that, taken out of its original context, would seem to propose the idea of an Arnoldian vanguard "extricating" a benighted "rearguard" from moral and intellectual squalor, and he then uses it to authorize his own distinction between a "minority" possessed of true "culture" and a "mass civilisation" that would seek to swamp it. That this emphasis is not typical of Richards at his best ought to be clear—indeed, even in this problematic passage there are other, better emphases, as we shall see when we return to it at the end of this section—yet reading Richards back through Leavis, one cannot help but feel that one is encountering here the root of the later, fundamentally conservative defence of minority "standards." The early critical paradigm then seems an irredeemably elitist phenomenon, and one is tempted simply to dismiss it as reactionary.

At this point it would be possible to move quickly to the task of making firm distinctions between the earlier left-liberal work of Richards and Empson, with its buried, compromised, but still not negligible radical elements, and Leavis' later, more evidently conservative work. This is to say that, if one is trying to recover some of the promise of the early critical paradigm, as I am, then one has a strong urge simply to jettison Leavis entirely as a lost cause—and certainly that seems the approach most likely to convince, since he attracts so little sympathy today. Yet for better or worse I find myself unwilling to take so short a road. For I take it that the widespread reduction of Leavis to a caricature has been a serious collective error on the part of the discipline—Leavis unmistakably represents a turn to the right, but not merely or solely a turn to the right; he also has much deeper emphases. Here it is instructive instead to hold in mind the classic critiques of the Leavisite position offered by the Marxist left, Perry Anderson's and Francis Mulhern's in particular—critiques that knew very well the sophistication of the argument they were dealing with, and were thus unwilling to be simply cavalier. I certainly hold no brief for Leavis, but no one who understands what the demands are can dismiss him lightly. In fact, at the risk of alienating all possible sources of support, I will add that Leavis' work strikes me as fuller of possibilities today than ever before, not because his position has grown more acceptable over time—very far from it—but precisely because time has brought the position down so completely that his deeper, grounding insights now lie intact under the ruins, free of the weight of the old edifice, simply waiting to be found. Among the major early critics, Leavis is distinctive for his tendency to offer both the deepest and the shallowest thoughts in the closest proximity, and the fact that the shallowness of the latter is now self-evident to most serious observers has the odd effect of rendering his fundamental insights more available for use. Moreover, those insights are often of just the kind to which literary studies today tends to be most blind.

For Leavis, the key figure in the longer history of criticism was Matthew Arnold. Let us then observe him articulating his own account of the task of criticism by way of a parsing of Arnold's phrase "criticism of life":

> Pressed for an account of the intention behind the famous phrase, we have to say something like this: we make (Arnold insists) our major judgments about poetry by bringing to bear the completest and profoundest sense of relative value that, aided by the work judged, we can focus from our total experience of life (which includes literature), and our judgment has intimate bearings on the most serious choices we have to make thereafter in our living. (*Scrutiny* 7, 58)

If Leavis sees a path back to Arnold here, it is because the ground around him has been cleared by Richards—the Richards who insisted that, even within the newly professionalizing world of academic criticism, engaging with questions of "relative value" in literature was important chiefly because it would help us to engage with questions of "relative value" in life. In inheriting that conception of the literary, Leavis inherited a whole position on education and on culture more broadly, though of course he changed the terms of it in ways that were to prove very significant later on. If one really wants to emphasise the continuities between the two projects, one can observe, as crucial instances, that Richards' placing of literary criticism on a disciplinary footing enabled Leavis' characteristic insistences on English Literature as a "distinctive discipline of thought" (35); that Richards' conception of literary study as the primary therapeutic wing of liberal education largely enabled Leavis' characteristic insistences on the centrality of the literary disciplines to the university as a whole; and, in turn, that Richards' view of liberal education as one of the primary therapeutic means through which the worst symptoms of modernity could be treated in the wider culture did much to prepare the ground for Leavis' whole position on the central role of literary criticism in society at large.[29] On this note, it is also worth observing that both thinkers shared a commitment to the view that, in another of Leavis' famous phrases, the "constitutive function" of the university is, or should be, "to create and maintain an educated public" (11).[30] I note in passing that this places both thinkers at a significant distance from our modern "progressive" consensus that the university's highest intellectual task, to be defended against the philistines who merely seek profit, is "the production of knowledge."

Perhaps most importantly, Leavis also took up Richards' grounding insights into the nature of language, became inward with them, and then brought them forward into fluency in what can only be called an exceptionally brilliant way. To see this, let us first return to the final line in the quote from Richards above, which posits the artist—and particularly, it turns out later, the literary artist—as "the point at which the growth of the mind shows itself." This may seem merely jargon, but really the phrase points to a more subtle achievement of thought than might first appear. One of the defining (in the end, crippling) weaknesses of the critical paradigm, even in its early form, was its lack of a serious engagement with the philosophy of history, yet there is something like a shade of Hegel here. There is in Richards a deep appreciation of the fact that our capacity for rich experience is not primarily individual, but social and historical. For him, our primary instrument of thought and feeling is the necessarily collective one of language, and this language is itself the sediment of the countless ordinary efforts of practical thought and feeling that make up a whole society's historical life. In the sentence I have just quoted, Richards is telling us that the artist's attempts to articulate the value of experience are historical in nature, regardless of the extent to which the artist understands or acknowledges this, and that to the extent that they succeed, they figure for a moment what is really a collective historical achievement. This is not a position that sits easily with liberal individualism in its cheaper forms. If one wants to make it look conservative, one can call the position Burkean; if wants to uncover its more radical elements, one can call the position collectivist and materialist, and note that it is continuous in important ways with much of Morris, back through Ruskin, to the tradition of the Romantic revolt. In any case it is, I think, quite a deep insight into the necessarily social character of experience, into the role of language in history, and therefore into the essentially collective and linguistic character of worthwhile historical change.

It is this insight that Leavis took up and turned to his own ends in the most sophisticated and demanding manner. Thus Michael Bell, one of the best sympathetic readers of Leavis I have encountered, treats Leavis' sophisticated understanding of language as his strongest claim on our thought, and indeed as the "basis of his whole endeavour." He also notes that the usual critiques of Leavis tend to ignore this: "The fundamental point, and the area in which Leavis *is* a powerful analyst, tends to be passed over as unproblematic or as if it were not there" (133). He accordingly goes on to show that Leavis' conception of language is a kind of native English equivalent to the "linguistic turn" that determined the course of so much continental philosophy, and that is often taken as the line of demarcation between Anglo-American and continental thought. It seems to me that Bell is right about this; I only want to add that, in view of the longer history, one needs to see the sophistication of Leavis' view of language as one of the foundation stones of the critical paradigm itself. This is too large a point to be demonstrated concisely, but as a way of pointing toward it, let me simply take one of Leavis' formulations about language: a phrase that Leavis utters in passing, as it were, on the way to other things.

The phrase I have in mind appears in the essay "Thought, Language and Objectivity," where Leavis refers to language as "the heuristic conquest won out of representative experience" (44). This is only part of a much longer sentence, but it is a part worth dwelling on since, both in its density and in the casualness with which it is uttered, it shows how fluently Leavis was able to render Richards' insights. In saying this, I do not mean to reduce the one to the other—my point is that the new fluency is itself a kind of advance. As Leavis uses it, "heuristic" gives us the instrumental view of language that Richards had developed with C. K. Ogden: a view that characterised language as an always provisional means by which human beings pursue particular ends in in specific contexts, as distinct from a view that would characterise language primarily as an attempt truly to mirror the world, or as a mere vehicle for meaning in any simple sense.[31] "Conquest won out of . . . experience" gives us Richards' account of language as the sediment of a collective historical effort to come to terms with the world. And "*representative* experience" gives us Richards' account of the particular character of that collectivity, a character that I am even tempted to call—with great caution when speaking in Leavis—democratic, since the underlying insistence is on what is shareable in that experience and on what is therefore at least potentially common to all.[32]

This is just one way of observing that, even at some of the deepest levels of his thinking, Leavis was an inheritor of Richards' project, though of course in certain crucial respects he carried it further, with effects that were felt around the globe. But having observed that, we need to go back and note also the specific ways in which Leavis redistributed Richards' emphases. Here it is instructive to return to the passage with which Leavis opened "Mass Civilisation and Minority Culture": the passage from Richards that began "But it is not true that criticism is a luxury trade. The rearguard of Society cannot be extricated until the vanguard has gone further." Leavis uses this as a starting point from which to launch his own defense of "standards," yet when one reads the passage in its original context—a chapter of Richards' *Principles of Literary Criticism* entitled "Art and Morals"—one finds that it is not really an attempt to distinguish between the enlightened elite and the benighted masses, but is rather a step in a quite different argument: an argument against traditional and religious views of morality, which Richards sees as an obstacle to the construction of a modern society. Richards' argument in this chapter is for a "naturalistic morality": one that understands the problem of morality in earthly terms as the "problem of how we are to obtain the greatest possible value from life," and understands "value" in psychological or behaviourist terms, such that the "most valuable states of mind are those which involve the widest and most comprehensive co-ordination of activities and the least curtailment, conflict, starvation, and restriction" (53–54). This, he claims, is where the artist helps us, because the experience of art, rightly undergone, helps us to cultivate co-ordination of that kind. The argument is democratic in spirit: against those who would ask us to be content with society as it is, Richards insists that it is possible to create a society in which "no man should be so situated as to be deprived of all the generally accessible values" (54). For Richards, our failure so far to achieve this in the realm of morals is owing to the fact that, "instead of recognizing that value lies in the 'minute particulars' of response and attitude, we have tried to find it in conformity to abstract prescriptions and general rules of conduct" (55). For him, the achievement of a decent society would require "the clearing away from moral questions of an ethical lumber and superstitious interpolations" (54). Only by moving beyond these traditionalist moral dogmas could we extend the value of art to all.

Thus when we come to the passage Leavis quotes, Richards' opening declaration that "criticism" is not a "luxury trade" is distinctive for its democratizing flavor. The strongest emphasis in the passage is on the idea that "such apparently 'unpractical' activities as art or criticism," which may seem irrelevant to the broader project of constructing a decent society in liberal terms, are in fact central to it (54). As a point of comparison, it may help those more familiar with the American scene to think of Dewey here, rather than of Leavis—or at least, rather than of Leavis as he is usually received. In any case, Richards is showing the deep role art might be taken to play in a utilitarian or consequentialist morality, and setting it against what he takes to be art's ultimate irrelevance in a Kantian or deontological one. Or if you prefer, the argument is for a secular materialism, and the enemy is religion and superstition. In any case, it is by no means a nostalgic or anti-modern call for a return to "organic community," such as some of those associated with Leavis (notably Denys Thompson) were wont to make.[33] Quite the contrary, the authority being appealed to is modernity itself, in the form of a kind of materialism; the emphasis is on the value of ordinary experience made accessible through art and unencumbered by traditional conceptions of duty and morality; and the goal is to find a way to extend that value as widely as possible throughout the society as a whole. When Richards writes that "The rearguard of Society cannot be extricated until the vanguard has gone further," Leavis reads "rearguard" as "mass civilisation," but what Richards means is something closer to religious conservatism. To be clear, Richards' argument here obviously has its problems, perhaps first among them its complete elision of politics *per se*, and I certainly do not defend it. I merely emphasise that in its early forms, the argument for criticism is that of a modernising left-liberalism in a democratic mood, whereas later, in Leavis' hands, the argument takes a profoundly antidemocratic turn.[34] Once again, the liberal ambivalence of the early critical paradigm has been determined for the right.

These are all questions of professed cultural politics, and they have their importance. Just as important, however, are the more buried politics that reside at the deeper level of method—in effect, here, the politics of one's theory of the aesthetic. Here, too, Leavis turned the project of criticism to the right. One can see this by returning to Leavis' parsing of Arnold's phrase "criticism of life." "[W]e make ... *our major judgments about poetry* by bringing to bear the completest and profoundest sense of relative value that ... we can focus from our total experience of life"; "[O]*ur judgment* has intimate bearings on the most serious choices we have to make thereafter in our living." Here, the question of "relative value" has undergone a shift

closely analogous to the shift it underwent in the United States in the same
period. Richards had tried to encourage us to compare the relative value of
the different psychological states made available by poems. Leavis here wants
us to make a similar comparison, this time between the relative value of the
different modes of "Life" that the poems testify to and instantiate, but his
new emphasis on the scene of critical judgment threatens to turn this into a
comparison simply between different *poems*. For Richards, it was reading,
engaging with, and being acted upon by texts that enabled them to influence
our living; for Leavis, it is *judging* them. "[O]ur judgments . . . the work
judged . . . our judgment." Where the emphasis had once been on the value
of the reader's experience, now the emphasis is on the scene of judgment that
allows the reader—or rather, ideally, the critic—to assess the relative value of
literary works. There is a great risk, then, of losing the initial emphasis on the
instrumental value of literary works, their value as means to further ends,
and coming to see them instead in idealist terms, as ends in themselves, as
repositories of final value. This, in turn, threatens to override the saving
emphasis on education. Crudely put, the critic's task, which had once been
envisioned as the use of works of literature as instruments of aesthetic education, is all too often reduced simply to the ranking of works.

In Leavis, and in the tradition that followed out of and reacted against
him, this emphasis on criticism as a scene of judgment rather than of education can at times become very pronounced. Leavis' most positive endorsement of Arnold's work as a critic runs follows:

> [W]hat has to be stressed is his relative valuation of the great Romantics:
> Wordsworth he put first, then Byron (and for the right reasons), then Keats,
> and last Shelley. It is, in its independence and its soundness, a more remark-
> able critical achievement than we can easily recognise today. (63)

What can one say about this reduction of criticism to facile questions of
rank?[35] It is awfully tempting to joke that it has some deep relation with the
peerage, except that the mid-century American critics do it too. Certainly
this is a particularly egregious example, though it is hardly an isolated one,
as anyone who has read much criticism of this period knows. More importantly, the sense of the project of criticism being taken for granted here,
together with the position in aesthetics implied, make themselves felt

throughout Leavis' work. Responding to critics who approach Wordsworth's poetry from a biographical perspective, Leavis tells us that he is "interested in explanation and genetic accounts only insofar as they enable one to appreciate more intelligently and fully the creative achievement and to realise the importance of the poet"; which is to say, he supports biographical accounts of Wordsworth only insofar as they promise to lead us to "a better perception of the nature of his genius and so to a fuller realisation of the value of what he achieved" (25, 30; my italics). These formulations may seem more acceptable, but are really quite akin to his tables of precedence: we are here dangerously close to the kinds of sterile circularities which will come to encumber so much of mid-century humanist criticism, in which the work is important chiefly as a testament to the genius of an author who could write such an important work, and all that is left to the critic is the task of sorting out, on some mysterious basis, which works and authors are really of the highest rank.

Relatively secure in the intellectual space carved out for him by Richards' aesthetics, Leavis famously refused to enter into debates about philosophy, preferring instead to insist on the autonomy and independence of literary study as a discipline.[36] As a result, he nowhere felt the need explicitly to engage with Richards' aesthetic claims, and certainly never consciously took up the mantle of Kant in the manner of the New Critics. In the end, though, the effect was not dissimilar: in Britain, as in the United States, Richards' early attempt to put criticism on something more akin to a materialist basis by way of an aesthetics of instrumental value—an aesthetics of means—is co-opted by a later notion of criticism that largely reverts to an idealist aesthetics of final value—an aesthetics of ends. In Britain as in the United States, "criticism" was to move in a direction precisely opposite to that indicated by Richards' guiding injunction that "It is less important to like 'good' poetry and dislike 'bad,' than to be able to use them both as a means of ordering our minds."

Chapter Two

The Scholarly Turn

With the benefit of hindsight, it is not hard to see that once the idea of "criticism" had been taken up by forces of this kind—the idea of criticism, together with the philosophical aesthetics that underpinned it and the methods of "close reading" and "practical criticism" that were its working tools—a critique from the left was bound to come. When that critique did come, it came on multiple fronts. Powerful and life-changing feminist analyses; brilliant and damning insights into the workings of race; trenchant reassertions of the worth of the colonized in the face of colonial oppression; and also, in time, fundamental dissent from the far-reaching dominion of reproductive heteronormativity—the aggregate effect of these was a broad critique of a wide range of elitisms, essentialisms, and false universalisms, amounting in the end to a collective rejection of the mid-century mode. In search of the means by which to make this critique, many in the discipline ended up turning to continental thinkers who had been trained in quite different traditions, and thus all these forces were at once flanked and out-flanked by continental "Theory," especially in its various poststructuralist forms. Existing accounts usually identify the proximate cause of this break with the old mode as the entry of the generation of 1968 into the academy, and it is certainly true that much of the spirit and many of the key terms in these critiques were provided by the various left and left-liberal social movements of the late 1960s and 1970s, in concert with wider decolonial struggles. In fact, as many have noted, the discipline's rejection of mid-century criticism was part of a more general shift to the left in Anglo-American intellectual life throughout the period—a broad current running in a progressive direction in many disciplines, decried by the right as the tenuring of '60s radicals, celebrated by the left as a "Culture in Contraflow."[1] For all the many complexities of the period, there seems little doubt that the general tendency was a democratizing one, at least in the short term. An obvious sign of this was that, for the first time, many of the primary questions being asked within literary studies were political ones.

Even today, one has only to intone the best-known names—taking a random sample from across the relevant generations, without much claim to representativeness, say Millett, Showalter, Moi on gender; Morrison, Hall, Gates Jr. on race; Achebe, Said, Ngugi on colonialism; Rich, Butler, Warner on sexuality; Lacan, Foucault, Derrida on textuality *tout court*—to summon a storm of explicitly political questions. What were the origins of patriarchy, and what was its relationship to capital? What was "whiteness," and how had it come to acquire its brutal force? How precisely had imperialisms managed to re-present their violence as the advance of civilization? Was the question of gender oppression even thinkable without the question (the *prior* question?) of sexual preference? And in what ways was our thinking on all these questions necessarily bound up in the particular texts, idioms, norms, and socialities in which it was being thought? Questions of these kinds were not new, of course, but in the 1960s and 1970s they were substantially new to the research program of Anglo-American literary studies. Their arrival at the center of the discipline was understood by many as a cyclonic force, throwing all the old assumptions into disarray.

How are we to keep our bearings in such a storm? It seems best to declare at once that I am not going to try to assess each of these lines of critique on its own terms. To any reader who would have preferred an extended treatment here, I apologise: the discipline's history having been told in the way it usually has, it is perhaps only natural to expect that a book of this kind would center itself on the various political critiques that were born out of the 1960s. I am afraid this is an expectation that I can only disappoint, since my argument is precisely that many of the mistakes which mar the discipline's sense of its present political character derive precisely from its continued insistence that it is *these* critiques on which the historian ought to remain

focused; that it was *these* critiques, born out of the 1960s and clearly progressive in their general character, that determined the trajectory of the discipline that followed—as if there had been no later reorientation and retreat.
The magnetic appeal of the 1960s still throws compasses out. For in fact the
foundations of the discipline's current paradigm were really laid much later,
under the pressure of quite different circumstances—circumstances that
many have misrecognized. Today, with the benefit of hindsight, it is perhaps
easier for us to see the real gains of the period—nothing less than civil rights
locally and decolonisation globally—not simply as victories for the left, but
also, and at the same time, as deeper reconfigurations in preparation for a
subsequent, and much more decisive, turn to the right.

Thus it seems better, when confronted with this new storm of political
questions, simply to step back out of it, so as to read it entire against the sky.
For in the longer view, the whole tempest reveals itself as a symptom—a
symptom of the crisis of mid-century criticism, breaking out in precise synchrony with the crisis of the Keynesian liberalism that had underpinned it.
The symptom is interestingly doubled. In the first place, the fact that questions of this order—political questions—were being asked in such an insistent manner, across multiple fronts, was a new development within the discipline in the late 1960s and the 1970s, and was noted as such by many,
whether in praise or blame. From a left perspective, one can only celebrate
the fact that the depoliticizing deadlock of mid-century criticism had finally
been broken, and perhaps one may then go on to read this breaking of the
deadlock as a guarantee of the progressiveness of the tendency as a whole.
That has certainly been the dominant reading.

And yet, having read the symptom in this way, one must then return to
read it again, for if the questions being asked were important ones, there
were also other new and important questions, not *within* the research program, but *about* it: questions about the political character of the new
critiques themselves. To what extent were second-wave feminist critiques of
the welfare state likely to secure basic structural changes, and to what
extent were they working to replace a materialist politics with a mere politics
of recognition, thereby serving, albeit often inadvertently, as the "hand-
maidens of neoliberalism?"[2] Which of the new race critiques were genuinely challenging to the existing racial order, and which were in fact
expressions of that racial order in its newly "diverse," "multicultural," and

US-expansionist form?[3] When did the critique of past colonialisms lead to a break with colonial oppression in the present, and when did it instead etherealize or render merely "representational" what ought to be materialist concerns?[4] If queer theory had obviously raised itself above mere "identity politics," largely on poststructuralist foundations, had it not sometimes thereby left itself floating above deeper structural determinations, too?[5] For as so many observers noted, poststructuralist "Theory" itself was by no means simply or uncomplicatedly progressive in its politics. Was deconstruction activist or quietist, and what political weight ought we assign to the so-called "ethical turn"? To what extent was the turn to Foucault a turn to the left and to what extent a shift to the right—specifically away from Marxism? Was Foucault a radical, really—or merely a neoliberal in disguise?[6] And so on. There was reason to suspect each of the new forces in the field of serving more than a single master. If nothing else was certain, one can nevertheless say with confidence that the crisis of mid-century criticism was a confusing one.

Thus even from the outset the politics of the supposed turn to the left in the late 1960s and 1970s were not so clear: if there were radicalisms of many different kinds, there were also liberalisms, and in each case it had yet to be determined which would gain the upper hand. Mid-century criticism had certainly entered into crisis—that much was clear—but the political character of the new regime that would come to replace it was not yet apparent. Here I am tempted to venture a general principle for cultural analysis, which would state that in order to perceive the true contours of any historical crisis, it is necessary to examine not only the features of the crisis itself, but also the character of whatever new order establishes itself in its wake. The crisis of the 1970s was important, of course—indeed, for a long time now histories of literary studies have treated it as virtually all-encompassing—but when one views it in relation to the longer history of the discipline, it becomes apparent that its primary significance lies in the fact that it effectively masked and enabled a more epochal change: the collapse of the discipline's central structuring principle. For now, for first time since the 1920s, the discipline seemed to be moving into a world beyond the "scholars versus critics" debate. By collapsing and obscuring the old distinctions, the crisis of the 1970s was eventually to clear the way for the rise to dominance, in the early 1980s, of a singular, scholarly, historicist/contextualist paradigm.

The question of continental "Theory" is perhaps the central example here, and it may therefore justify a short digression. In the late 1960s, and then even more clearly throughout the 1970s and 1980s, many debates within the discipline began to be framed in terms, not of "critics" versus "scholars," but of a hazily defined "Theory" versus an even more hazily defined "everything else." Today most observers still tend to assume that "Theory" was what debates in that period were really about, and yet I would ask those who are strongly committed to this view at least to consider the possibility that it is mistaken. Could it not be that this assumption obscures the real lines of development within the discipline? The extraordinary vagueness of the battle lines drawn by the parties marching under and against the banner of "Theory" seems to indicate the plausibility of this. One obvious indicator here is the fact that, throughout the period, the key term "literary theory" could be used in any number of different, and often opposed, senses. It might refer, for instance, to historical or cultural analysis of a basically scholarly kind (indeed, we will see Raymond Williams using the term in this way in just a moment). Or else it might refer to the newly sophisticated structuralist approaches to poetics that tried to consider literary genres as forming a coherent system in their own right. Or it might perhaps refer to archive-based cultural analysis in a Foucauldian vein. Or again, it might refer to deconstructive practices of setting the text to work that had more in common with the project of "criticism" than they did with any "scholarly" historicist approach. And so on. No serious observer has failed to note this confusion, which is characteristic (even constitutive?) of the "Theory" debate—yet it has not been so easy to offer a serious account of the broader historical transformations that this confusion served.[7]

It is at this point that the difference between older two-period accounts of the twentieth century and newer three-period accounts becomes so telling. For if one believes, as so many once did, that the 1960s represented a historically decisive break to the left, then it makes sense to tell the story of literary studies in the second half and the twentieth century as it is usually told: as a continuous democratization or liberalization of literary studies from the 1960s to the present, beginning in the dark days of the new criticism, or else of Leavis-ism, and then breaking outward into a glorious heterogeneity of progressive modes. As I noted in the Introduction, this is a very pleasing story for those on the liberal left of literary studies, yet it seems to me that as time has gone by, the justifications for believing it have worn keep getting thinner and thinner. *Was* the twentieth century really split in two by a decisive break to the left in the 1960s? Surely not. Now that we are able to survey the century in its entirety, the brief step to the left in the 1960s and early 1970s reveals itself as the prelude to a much more decisive break to the right in the late 1970s and early 1980s—a break so decisive that it was to inaugurate a whole new period.

To illustrate this point, let us briefly compare two moments in the work of Perry Anderson. In 1990, Anderson's seminal essay "A Culture in Contra-flow" had identified a range of left and leftish forces newly active in British intellectual life in the 1970s and 1980s, making parallel advances across a wide range of key disciplines. His diagnosis, in its essentials, was that fires of 1968 were now being carried, torch-like, into the academy—the same diagnosis that many were making with respect to contemporaneous developments in the United States. So far, so left. Yet to understand the wider historical significance of this observation, one must read it in the context of Anderson's subsequent declaration, ten years later, that forces more basic than "culture" had proved decisive: in the year 2000, he famously announced that the "only starting point for a realistic Left" was a "lucid registration of historical defeat."[8] Both observations have their truth, but the local truth of the first must be measured against the more general truth of the second. As Anderson's initial metaphor already suggested, an oppositional intellectual culture can flow counter to the wider current only for a time—and in fact, as it happened, it did not take very long in historical terms for the more general shift to the right to prove irresistible.

Accordingly the story I shall be telling in both this chapter and the next is the story of a local break to the left that is rapidly and inexorably dragged to the right. Though stories of that kind are familiar enough, this one will have its unfamiliar elements, largely because it avoids the usual reference points. For one can see the broader pattern of the discipline's development much more clearly if one is willing to take full advantage of the benefit of hindsight by setting to one side the whole tangled crisis of the late 1960s and 1970s—all the movement figures, activist scholars, and continental theorists who are so often presumed to be the proper objects of our attention—thereby focusing instead on the birth of the new paradigm itself. Naturally there are many ways to document the birth of that paradigm: I have chosen to examine a single figure in depth, taken as an emblem for the rest. This is a dangerous course—can any single figure really be taken as representative? Only with many provisos. But the obvious alternative—to survey many figures, schools, or tendencies, but each more briefly—carries the danger of a superficial treatment that would miss the complexity and ambivalence of the moment, and it is precisely the ambivalence of the moment that I am seeking to demonstrate.

Which figure, though? Save perhaps queer theory, which arrived on the scene somewhat later, each of the main lines of progressive critique offers many candidates. Thinkers on gender, race, and colonialism all played important parts in the critique of mid-century criticism and of the idealist aesthetics and universalizing humanism on which it was based—and as we have just noted, it is difficult to overstate the role played here by poststructuralist theory, both within and without the more overtly political camps. Yet we see the real lines of development much more clearly, and certainly more concisely, if we bracket for a moment the continental critiques that were imported from quite a different context and focus instead on immanent critiques: critiques of the discipline's functioning that were made in terms largely developed within the discipline itself. And to my mind, the most sophisticated and influential figure who came forward with a critique of that kind, and certainly the most instructive for our purposes, was the British socialist thinker Raymond Williams.

Raymond Williams

Though he seems often to have understood himself as marginal, Raymond Williams is better thought of as exemplary, in two senses: both the sophistication and the representativeness of his work have been underestimated. His thinking thus provides us with a uniquely illuminating case study of what was really a much broader tendency. Trained at Cambridge when the influence of Leavis was approaching its postwar peak, Williams' initial positions were labeled, by both admirers and detractors, a "left-Leavisism."[9] The story of his origins in that particular formation is not well-known in the United States, where he is remembered mostly for his later work as a founding figure in cultural studies, but this is a pity, since William's inheritance from Leavis and, through him, from Richards remains a determining one throughout his

work, even if he eventually came to critique key elements of it in the strongest terms.

There are really two stories we need to tell about Williams' intellectual
development out of the Leavis tradition and into the figure who did so much
to shape the discipline in our period. The most important is the story of the
radical break with that tradition which he effected through his wholesale
rejection of the task of "criticism," his sweeping critique of the category of
the "aesthetic," and his attempt to replace both with a practice of fine-
grained historicist/contextualist scholarship. For our purposes, the key
point here will be that by the time Williams came to make that break, the
strident anti-Kantianism of Richards' aesthetics—what I have called his
"incipient materialism"—had been buried under a weight of New Critical
Kantianism and Leavisite idealism-in-effect, encouraging Williams to try to
sweep the field of aesthetics entirely clear, instead of differentiating between
idealist and more materialist forces within it. This allowed an argument
against a specific strand of aesthetic thinking—admittedly, the dominant
strand since Kant—to pass for an argument against aesthetics *tout court,* and
thus paved the way for the rejection of criticism and its wholesale replacement by scholarship, leading in turn to the dominance of the scholarly
model that we see in the discipline today. But in order to appreciate the
subtleties of that story, it is necessary to tell also the rather more complex
story of the largely hidden continuities between even William's later positions and the Richards/Leavis tradition that did so much to form his
thinking. Let us begin there.

Continuities between Leavis and Williams

One of the best sources we have for understanding Williams' intellectual
development is *Politics and Letters,* a book-length interview with him conducted by the editorial board of the New Left Review in 1979.[10] A brief
warning to begin with: the title of the book creates the potential for some
confusion, since Williams had also been a cofounder of a journal of the same
name in the late 1940s. In *Politics and Letters,* the book, Williams summa-
rized the attraction that Leavis had held for the founding editors of *Politics
and Letters,* the journal, as follows:

The immense attraction of Leavis lay in his cultural radicalism, quite clearly. That may seem a problematic description today, but not at the time. It was the range of Leavis' attacks on academicism, on Bloomsbury, on metropolitan literary culture, on the commercial press, on advertising, that first took me. You must also allow for the sheer tone of critical irritation, which was very congenial to our mood.

Secondly, within literary studies themselves there was the discovery of practical criticism. That was intoxicating, something I cannot describe too strongly. . . . At the time we thought it was possible to combine this with what we intended to be a clear Socialist cultural position. In a way the idea was ludicrous, since Leavis' cultural position was being spelt out as precisely not that. But I suppose that was why we started our own review, rather than queuing up to become contributors to *Scrutiny*.

Finally, there was Leavis' great stress on education. He would always emphasise that there was an enormous educational job to be done. Of course, he defined it in his own terms. But the emphasis itself seemed completely right to me. (66)

Cultural radicalism, practical criticism, and stress on education: is it too much to say that this could pass for a description of the key elements of Leavis' inheritance from Richards? Perhaps. Certainly the "tone of critical irritation" seems distinctive of Leavis: when anticipating opposition, Richards was always more likely to seem by turns earnest, superior, and amused. But it seems fair to observe at least that positions which, in Cambridge in the 1930s, would have seemed the particular innovations and emphases of Richards were now, by the late 1970s, being remembered and responded to as Leavisite. This refiguring was to have significant consequences. "Practical criticism" in particular, and then through it "criticism" generally, came to be seen as marked with Leavis' distinctive brand.

We can see this clearly later in the same book-length interview, when Williams describes the influences to which he was responding when he wrote his first book, *Drama from Ibsen to Eliot* (1952).[11] Here Williams remarks on a common tendency within and around literary studies simply to equate "practical criticism" with Leavis, on the grounds that Leavis' work was the "most powerful exemplar" of the method. Williams calls this a "crucial mistake" and rightly reminds us that the method began with Richards' work in the 1920s. But we might be forgiven for wondering whether

Williams was not, in fact, making a version of the same mistake, and so underestimating the effect of Leavis' influence in this period, on him as well as on others. "Why do people close-analyse within the main practical-critical tradition?" he asks himself. "In order to clarify their response *as evaluation*" (193, my italics). The emphasis here is the distinctively Leavisite one on practical criticism as the staging of the scene of aesthetic judgment, and the same emphasis returns whenever he discusses the method. This is perhaps clearest in Williams' paper "Literature and Sociology: In Memory of Lucien Goldman," and particularly in the section entitled "The Limits of Practical Criticism," where practical criticism is clearly equated with Leavis and critiqued accordingly. So many of the main elements of Leavis' position appear in Williams' description of practical criticism here: the appeal to "sincerity" and "vitality" via an invocation of Lawrence; the "informed critical minority"; the attack on "scientism"; the refusal to enter into philosophical debate about key concepts. Most importantly, there is the distinctive emphasis on judgment: on making the "distinction of good literature from the mediocre and the bad." It is interesting to ask whether Williams would be able to dismiss "practical criticism" in this way were it not possible to characterize it in these specifically Leavisite terms. In any case, it seems fair to say that, his provisos notwithstanding, Williams is reading the history of "practical criticism" back through the lens of Leavis.[12]

In this respect, Williams is not an isolated case, but the clue to a more general tendency. Moreover, the Leavisian emphasis was seen as attached not just to the particular method of "practical criticism" or "close reading," but to the project of criticism more generally. For in fact, throughout so much work in this period, references to the project of "criticism," whether in the mode of praise or blame, carry just this emphasis on aesthetic discrimination and judgment. One of Williams' interviewers in *Politics and Letters* expresses the common assumption succinctly when he refers to "the process of discrimination and evaluation that has traditionally been thought to be the central function of criticism" (334). No one demurs from this, yet as we have seen, Richards' initial account of the central function of disciplinary "criticism" had carried a very different emphasis: an emphasis precisely not on "discrimination and evaluation," if by that we mean learning to distinguish "good" works from "bad," but instead on education toward "better ordering our minds." By 1979, though, that earlier project had been effaced: instead,

Leavis' emphasis on the staging of critical judgment was simply accepted as the necessary emphasis of *any* project of "criticism."[13] This is to say that the general project of literary "criticism" has become for all intents and purposes fused with Leavis', and then also the New Critics', idealist and ultimately conservative emphasis on judging the relative merits of literary works with a drive toward establishing some sort of final hierarchy of aesthetic values.[14] Williams, in his critique of these positions, demonstrably shared the same set of starting assumptions, his typically scrupulous reminder that it was a "crucial mistake" to equate "practical criticism" with Leavis notwithstanding.

Williams' Break with Leavis

We see then that the main line of continuity between Williams and the mid-century critics who preceded him was this emphasis on the idea that criticism was necessarily a matter of staging the scene of critical judgment. Observing this emphasis puts us in a better position to understand the real significance of Williams' break with those critics—the break that was such a turning point for the discipline as a whole. For in fact it was this particular set of assumptions about the necessary conservatism and idealism of the project of "criticism" that eventually led Williams to feel it was necessary to reject it entirely, together with the whole field of aesthetic thinking on which it had been based.

To observe this in action we have to turn to Williams' classic work *Marxism and Literature* (1977), one of the most important of the works that we in the discipline today are often, whether knowingly or unknowingly, relying on when we assume that aesthetic justifications for literary study have been discredited as merely ideological.[15] Here we can see how Williams' powerful and necessary critique of the idealist strand of aesthetic thinking, dominant since the coining of the term in the late eighteenth century, is marked and even, one might say, deformed by his felt need to respond to the more local history of criticism within the discipline. Or rather—to put the matter perhaps more bluntly than it deserves—we can see that in *Marxism and Literature* Williams purports to make what is really a local critique of the Leavisite and New Critical models of criticism, and of the associated Kantian or neo-Kantian model of the aesthetic, stand as a rejection of "criticism" and "aesthetics" *tout court.*

Overtly, Williams' was an argument against the concept of the aesthetic in its entirety. The core of the argument is the claim that any attempt to draw a clear distinction between "aesthetic" situations and "other" situations is deeply problematic, since it involves us in the positing of a suspect "aesthetic state," "aesthetic response," or "aesthetic function." For Williams, the positing of any such state or function is an unwarranted abstraction and specialization from the multiplicity and variety of actual social practices. The fact that this idealization from material practice is ultimately ideological in nature should lead us to reject the term "aesthetic," and the associated tradition of thinking, entirely:

> [Under capitalism] Art and thinking about art have [had] to separate themselves, by ever more absolute abstraction, from the social processes within which they are contained. Aesthetic theory is the main instrument of this evasion. (154)

These are broad terms, so it is worth noting that what Williams really means when he says "aesthetic theory" is *idealist* aesthetic theory—or rather, we might say more precisely that Williams' argument is that there can be no other kind. Why does Williams feel the need to reject all aesthetic theory as idealist? We can approach an answer by observing the terms in which Williams articulates the idea of an "aesthetic response":

> Art, including literature, was to be defined by its capacity to evoke this special [aesthetic] response: initially the perception of beauty; then the pure contemplation of an object, for its own sake and without other ("external") considerations; then also the perception and contemplation of the "making" of an object: its language, its skill of construction, its "aesthetic properties." (150)

These are indeed the approximate terms of the idealist mainstream of aesthetics, but the emphasis here is being derived from threats in Williams' more immediate environment—from the New Criticism and cognate movements. This is at its clearest in the case of formulations like "the pure contemplation of an object, for its own sake and without other ('external') onsiderations." As we shall see, it is with arguments of this kind that Williams takes care of the idealist core of aesthetic thinking—arguments that derive many of their terms, and certainly much of their force, from a local need to reject conservative forces active in the discipline during the period. This local argument is then offered as an argument against aesthetic thinking *per se,* as if the aesthetic could not be thought through in other terms than those the period offered.

Yet as we have seen, the aesthetic can be thought through in other terms, and was in fact thought through in other terms at the origin of the discipline. Further, now that we have traced at least the broad outlines of the early history of the discipline's treatment of the category of the aesthetic, we are in a position to observe that Williams is repeating an older move here. For though he would not have liked us to say so, what Williams is offering us here is something very much akin to Richards' critique of the aesthetic, and in particular Richards' critique of the "phantom aesthetic state."[16] When we note the differences between the two projects, we must do so against the background of this more basic similarity: both figures inaugurate a new period in the history of the discipline by way of a sweeping rejection of idealist aesthetics. It is only against this background that we can appreciate the real significance of their coming to very different conclusions about aesthetics in general. For Richards the critique of idealist aesthetics was to be considered a clearing operation, on the way to a reconstruction of the aesthetic in other, more materialist, terms. In contrast, for Williams—or at least for Williams as he has been received in the discipline ever since—the critique of idealist aesthetics ended with a wholesale rejection of aesthetics, and its replacement with a thoroughgoing historicism. The political difference between the two thinkers is, of course, very evident: Williams transposes the terms of the critique of idealist aesthetics from liberalism to socialism, with all the losses (close attention to the specific contours of individual psychological states) and gains (a more sophisticated account of the economic and political order in which individual psychologies take their place) which that shift so often implies. If one is on the left, then once one has noted this political difference, it is perhaps tempting to conclude that Williams' more complete rejection of the aesthetic is the more politically advanced. This, I think, would be a mistake. For seen in the context of the longer history of the discipline, Williams' move to reject the aesthetic in the name of contextualist/historicist cultural analysis acquires quite a different political significance.

To see what is really at stake in that movement toward a specifically scholarly historicism, we need to begin by noting that Williams, unlike Richards, encountered the problem of aesthetics, not essentially as a problem of critical praxis, but as a problem of description or analysis. If for Williams it is a problem that the concept of the aesthetic involves an abstraction from real social processes, then this is because such abstractions make it difficult to perform accurate cultural analyses. Williams' project has become so thoroughly our own that it is difficult even to remark on this without risking redundancy, but here we should: as a student of literature he is trying, first and foremost, to produce knowledge about culture. This in itself represents a proposal for a fundamental shift in the orientation of the discipline. In many places, we must read his moving and character- istic emphasis on the analysis of "actual practices" as an attempt to negotiate this shift.

Few remark on it, but from our present perspective it seems that the insis- tence on literary study as cultural analysis, in the face of perceived or actual threats from other possible orientations, is one of the central themes of Williams' later work. Thus, for instance, Williams concludes his critique of the aesthetic by drawing the principle that:

> The key to any analysis, and from analysis back to theory, is then the recogni- tion of precise situations in which what have been isolated, and displaced, as 'the aesthetic intention' and 'the aesthetic response' have occurred. (157)

The task is "analysis," following which one proceeds, not forward into action—whatever that might mean—but "back to theory." The "practice" being assumed *is* analysis. It is specifically in his capacity as a literary *scholar*, then—a cultural historian, cultural theorist, and sociologist—that the aes- thetic strikes Williams as such a powerful and pernicious source of obfusca- tions. He rejects idealist aesthetics not in the old way—on the basis of its lack of utility for the purposes of training readers, cultivating sensibility, creating and maintaining an educated public, or similar—but on the basis of its inaccuracy as a tool for cultural analysis. His argument for a more thor- oughly historicized version of literary studies is primarily an argument for literary scholarship.

With this in mind, we can begin to see that much of Williams' critique of the whole tradition of philosophical aesthetics is in fact directed toward a target much closer to home: "criticism."

> The replacement of the disciplines of grammar and rhetoric (which speak to the multiplicities of intention and performance) by the discipline of criticism (which speaks of effect, and only through effect to intention and performance) is a central intellectual movement of the bourgeois period. (149)

The charge that "criticism" is complicit in capital is clear enough. It is perhaps less clear exactly what is at stake in Williams' invocation here of the replaced "disciplines of grammar and rhetoric." It helps if we realize that, though he would not have used these terms, Williams is calling our attention to these "disciplines" precisely as forms of scholarship—here, forms of inquiry that take as their goal the production of accurate knowledge about language and language use—and trying to remind us of the losses literary and cultural study sustained when these properly scholarly forms were replaced by criticism, which, by speaking only of "effect," has tended to obfuscate the conditions (and especially the political conditions) under which the literature was first produced.[17] Moreover, his critique of criticism, like his critique of the "aesthetic," is here being offered as a broad one even though it is really being made in more local terms. Williams critiques "criticism" as a long-standing historical phenomenon ("a central intellectual movement of the bourgeois period"), but he is really thinking about the term in a much more local sense: specifically, he is thinking of criticism of an early-to-mid-twentieth century Cambridge kind, with its programmatic insistence on "speak[ing] of effect, and only through effect to intention and performance"—the kind of criticism in which he was trained. Williams' sense that this kind of criticism is characteristic of the whole bourgeois period really derives from Leavis—specifically, Leavis' backdating of "criticism-as-judgment" to Matthew Arnold.

All these emphases become telling in an oft-overlooked passage in *Marxism and Literature.* Here Williams tells us that potentially liberating creative forces were "specialized" and thus "contained" in the concept of "literature," and that this process was:

> decisively reinforced by the concept of "criticism": in part the operative procedure of a selecting and containing "tradition"; in part also the key shift from creativity and imagination as active productive processes to

categorical abstractions demonstrated and ratified by conspicuous humanistic consumption: criticism as "cultivation," "discrimination," or "taste."

Neither the specialization nor the containment has ever been completed. . . . But each has done significant harm, and in their domination of literary theory have become major obstacles to the understanding of both theory and practice. It is still difficult to prevent any attempt at literary theory from being turned, almost *a priori,* into critical theory, as if the only major questions about literary production were variations on the question 'how do we *judge?*' (146, emphasis in original)

In light of the previous chapter, it is I hope a little easier to observe that what Williams is most immediately objecting to here are Leavis' particular emphases: first on "tradition"; then on "cultivation," "discrimination" and "taste"; and last on the centrality to literary study of this question "how do we *judge?*," here taken as the founding question of criticism *per se.* But we also need to notice, in that second paragraph, the ways in which the basic terms of the inquiry have changed. For what is at stake in Williams' claim that criticism's dominance over "literary theory" has become a major obstacle to "to the understanding of both theory and practice"? When we encounter formulations of this kind, it is all too easy for us to note only that Williams, in the face of those who would emphasise "theory" alone, is making a typically careful attempt to give equal weight to both "theory" and "practice." We think, perhaps, of the figures that appear so often as targets of critique in Williams' work—figures like the ideological Oxbridge don, or the airily theoretical academic Marxist, both of whom, for Williams, are divorced from any actual "practice"—and then, depending on our own views on the matter, either we feel the force of the critique or we reject it. But what we need also to notice here is that this careful balancing, which seems an argument for a kind of "practice," is in fact being performed in the service of a rather different argument: the argument that the work of the cultural scholar is the analysis of, rather than intervention in, culture. Earlier, we saw that William's own scholarly "practice" is a practice of analysis. Here, for Williams, the task of literary study is "the *understanding* of both theory and practice"—in other words, precisely not practice, but the understanding of practice, which all too easily reduces to the production of knowledge about practice. This is the crucial break he makes with the tradition that began with Richards, but was then co-opted by Leavis and the New Critics: the break with literary study as a direct intervention in culture; the break toward literary study as the mere analysis of culture. It is Williams' characteristic and repeated emphasis on the importance of "practice" that allows him to negotiate this difficult turn.[18]

We can observe this argument becoming explicit in the next line, in which Williams warns us that "literary theory"—which for him really means literary study as cultural analysis—is still being threatened by the regressive force of "critical theory"—which for him means literary study as a training-ground for the faculty of judgment. Williams is worried that his attempts to make literary study into a practice of cultural diagnosis may even now, at this late stage, be hijacked by those who still see literary study in the old way, as a form of liberal/conservative cultural treatment. He does not make use of the opposition between "scholarship" and "criticism" to understand this, but this is what he means. The key argument in the book, though it never appears as such, is that the whole project of criticism, together with its foundation in philosophical aesthetics, needs to be rejected as bourgeois, and replaced by a thoroughly scholarly historicist/contextualist model of literary study. The force of the argument derives from the assumption, bred into the discipline by long decades of relative conservatism, that neither criticism nor the aesthetic can be thought through in other than idealist terms. The fact that Richards had founded the discipline on a criticism and an aesthetics of rather another kind has been forgotten. The force of Williams' critique of conservative forces in his immediate environment had the effect of bringing forward into a new period the assumption that the therapeutic, as opposed to the merely diagnostic, function of the discipline could only be thought through in idealist terms—ultimately, a conservative assumption. The project of "criticism" did not survive it.

An Unfinished Project of the New Left

Yet it would be misleading to tell the story of the demise of criticism as if Williams were the villain. It is more accurate to say that Williams, in a genuine attempt to grapple with conservative forces around him, overemphasised his critique in ways that were then seized upon by later thinkers—seized upon, indeed, by the very political forces that he had done so much to teach us how to understand, if not exactly to confront. This is a key turning point in our story: Williams' rejection of criticism is both an instance and an emblem of the "scholarly turn" that inaugurated the current period of literary study. For this reason, it is worth pausing for a moment to reflect on the broader intellectual milieu in which Williams' move toward scholarship took its place. Doing so will help us to read the history that followed with a better sense of what was really at stake in it. What I will be suggesting is that Williams, and then the "scholarly turn" more generally, represents a missed opportunity—and yet an opportunity that we can see opening up around us again today, as a result of the crisis of neoliberalism. Whether we manage to take it this time remains to be seen.

Let us then briefly set the story of the demise of criticism in a new context: that of the intellectual work of the British New Left. One of the foundational projects of the New Left, especially as it initially coalesced around the work of Raymond Williams, E. P. Thompson, and Richard Hoggart, was to bring together, on the one hand, the aesthetic tradition of Romanticism, with its emphasis on the value of human experience, and on the other hand the more strictly political and economic insights of Marxism, socialism, and cognate movements on the radical left. In many ways, the key figure for this aspect of the project was William Morris, who seemed to represent the point at which these two streams of critique converged.[19] But within literary criticism, the more local battle with Leavis and the New Critics—the need to clear the ground of this sort of criticism—led to a change of emphasis and, ultimately, we might say, to a deforming of this project. Williams' wholesale dismissal of criticism and too-sweeping critique of the aesthetic led, in the work of those who followed him, to a near-complete replacement of criticism by scholarship, with unfortunate results for literary studies generally—and for literary studies on the left, in particular. As we shall see in the next chapter, Williams' local critique of Leavisite and New Critical versions of the project of criticism and of the aesthetic continues to be repeated by later scholars in very different and indeed quite opposite situations, long after the threat it was formed to deal with has passed away.

Yet Williams himself was a much subtler thinker than many who came after him. Characteristically, he was far-sighted enough to anticipate, at least to a certain degree, the danger of his critique being taken up in other circumstances in such a way that it would become a hindrance, rather than a help, to the left. "Criticism" was to be offered no quarter, and here I would respectfully fault his foresight, but with respect to the aesthetic he offered two "saving clauses," as I shall call them—two qualifications, both too often forgotten, to temper the force of his otherwise sweeping critique. The first was this, which opens his chapter on "Aesthetic and Other Situations":

> Yet it is clear, historically, that the definition of 'aesthetic' response is an affirmation, directly comparable with the definition and affirmation of 'creative imagination,' of certain human meanings and values which a dominant social system reduced or even tried to exclude. Its history is in large part a protest against the forcing of all experience into instrumentality ('utility'), and of all things into commodities. This must be remembered even as we add, necessarily, that the form of this protest, within definite social and historical conditions, led almost inevitably to new kinds of privileged instrumentality and specialised commodity. The humane response was nevertheless there. (151)

I must say I find this rather a moving passage, and not because I agree with the terms in which it holds up the aesthetic for praise. One cannot read Williams' early work—particularly his classic *Culture and Society* (1958)—without feeling that he has thought his way very deeply through what one might, as a shorthand, call the tradition of the Romantic revolt: he feels the force of it deeply, "in his living," as he might have put it, and by a constant effort of thought and feeling he has marshalled and championed it when others would have given it up.[20] Now, with characteristic even-handedness, he celebrates a crucial part of that tradition as a prelude to letting it go. He celebrates the aesthetic, that is, in the Kantian terms offered by the Romantic revolt—as a "protest against the forcing of all experience into instrumentality"—but only as a prelude to dismissing it in the same terms.

If there is a certain joy and even exultation in his embrace of something more akin to a traditional Marxism here (in his introduction, he tells us that "this book is the result of [a] period of discussion, in an international context, in which I have had the sense, for the first time in my life, of belonging to a sphere and dimension of work in which I could feel at home") there is also a real ambivalence: he is pushing away a set of beliefs that were once, for him, deeply held (4–5). Perhaps this partly explains the force with which he rejects the aesthetic here. At any rate what he does not do—and this was to prove crucial in the subsequent history of the discipline—is to reserve a space for any "protest against the forcing . . . of all things into commodities" that would see the aesthetic precisely in instrumental terms.

This is unfortunate, because the clues that could have led him to such a view were there to be found. For there had in fact been those who had tried to break with this idea that the aesthetic must always be only a protest against instrumentality, and for the New Left, they were very close to home indeed: William Morris, for example. It would of course take us too far out of our way to examine Morris' thought in depth here, but it is well worth pausing for a moment to reflect on one of its characteristic tendencies, since doing so will shed light on some of the features of Raymond Williams' own thinking, and thereby illumine the face that literary studies has borne since. Morris was no more fooled than Williams was by the grand claims of idealist aesthetic theory: having learned first from Ruskin and then from the Marxist tradition to recognise the ways in which culture was materially determined, Morris happily condemned bourgeois aesthetics as "the numerous schemes by which the quasi-artistic of the middle classes hope to make art grow when it has no longer any root."[21] Yet this rejection of bourgeois approaches to art did not lead him to surrender the field of aesthetics entirely. Instead, it led him to try to construct a new approach to art: one that would take into account the economic realities of working life. For him, this meant rejecting any claim that the aesthetic realm was to be understood as a standing critique of utility and instead insisting on it precisely as a *deeper kind* of utility—thus "Nothing can be a work of art which is not useful."[22] In Morris' best thinking, this deeper kind of utility would itself be part of the "root", since it would be inseparable from the material production of "utilities" normally so called. Thus the society Morris felt he was fighting for was one in which:

> we should have so much leisure from the production of what are called 'utilities,' that any group of people would have leisure to satisfy its craving for what are usually looked on as superfluities, such as works of art, research into facts, literature, the unspoiled beauty of nature; *matters that to my mind are utilities also.*[23]

This argument is so consistent with Raymond Williams' general emphasis that it is hard, if one forgets for a moment the actual conditions under which his thinking developed, to believe that he did not make it himself. Within historical materialism, Williams was once most controversial for his critique of the base/superstructure model—famously, he tries again and again to demonstrate the ways in which the highest elements of the superstructure (say, as a very imprecise shorthand, "culture," and similar) end up underpinning some of the most fundamental elements of the base (say, again very imprecisely, "economy" and similar). With this in mind, could there be a more Williams-esque argument than Morris' claim here that supposed "superfluities" like "works of art, research into facts, literature, the unspoiled beauty of nature" and so on are all actually "utilities"? It strikes me that this view of the aesthetic is precisely what the New Left's running together of the Romantic and Radical streams of revolt ought to have achieved in the field of aesthetics: on the one side, an aesthetic confrontation with the Marxist critique of political economy, which would force it toward a wider and more open engagement with the deepest and richest forms of human life; on the other, a confrontation with bourgeois, idealist aesthetic thinking which would force it to grapple with the fact that processes in the "higher" cultural sphere are largely determined by the blunt facts of material production, and therefore by the historical development of a class society. Morris should have been recognised as the clue to the fact that the latter project needed to be carried out, not by dismissing the aesthetic entirely, but by reframing it in instrumental and materialist terms.

That clue had been taken up by others. Across the Atlantic, the pragmatist tradition had managed to take up Morris' emphasis on the instrumentality of art, after a certain fashion.[24] And of course, we have already seen that I. A. Richards, another admirer of Morris, had built disciplinary literary criticism on the basis of an aesthetic theory of something like this kind. But though these thinkers went on to develop aesthetic positions that were much more sophisticated than Morris' in other respects, both were liberals rather than leftists, and neither would prove capable of addressing the problem of material production as seriously as he had—seriously enough, that is, to break aesthetics from the main line of bourgeois liberalism within which it had originated. Williams, if only he had followed this path, would have been capable of that.

So the clue was there to be taken up—and was in fact taken up, but not by socialists. Morris' breakaway aesthetic insights were re-gathered into the mainstream of bourgeois thought, and the trail he blazed was not followed by any major figure within the socialist tradition. The question then becomes why? Why did the New Left, for which Morris was such a crucial figure, not seize upon this possibility—the possibility of developing an aesthetic theory that emphasized the usefulness, rather than the glorious uselessness, of the work of art? It would have been entirely characteristic of Williams to argue for a version of the aesthetic that would posit it, not as a protest against instrumentality, but as a deeper form of instrumentality. Why did he instead feel it was necessary to reject the whole field of aesthetic inquiry, as if the questions posed there could only ever be answered in liberal terms? Why did he not carry through his general emphasis into the field of aesthetics, which was ostensibly the field with which he was most directly concerned?

In the context of the history we have outlined, it seems clear enough that the explanation lies precisely in the fact that aesthetics *was* the field with which he was most directly concerned. Williams felt so strongly the need to respond to pernicious aesthetic arguments within his immediate purview—which is to say, within disciplinary literary criticism—that he was unable to carry through his general emphasis there, and instead moved to reject the discourse in its entirety. Speaking more broadly, we might say that the felt need to reject the Leavisite and New Critical positions then dominant within the discipline was simply too strong for the New Left to be able to carry its distinctive emphasis through into this crucial area. Instead, the New Left's general position on aesthetics became deeply marked by the need to respond to that specific threat, and it remains so marked even today when the specific threat has long since passed. Putting this differently, one might say that the New Left, and after it the discipline as a whole, learned how to assault idealism in the field of aesthetics, but did so without learning how to occupy the territory so cleared.

There is a final point to be made about Williams, and it is perhaps the most important one. It is that Williams was farsighted—or should we say ambivalent?—enough to anticipate many of the problems that were bound to arise as a result of his sweeping dismissal of the aesthetic. In *Marxism and Literature,* and then again more explicitly when pressed in *Politics and Letters,* he softened his critique by offering a crucial qualification—what I shall call his second saving clause for the aesthetic. His initial version of it runs as follows:

[W]e cannot rule out, theoretically, the possibility of discovering certain invariant combinations of elements within this group [of intentions and responses that have traditionally been clustered around the term "aesthetic"], even while we recognise that such invariant combinations as have hitherto been described depend on evident processes of supra-historical appropriation and selection. (156)

This is not Williams at his clearest, and indeed the retreat into abstraction might itself be read as a sign of the ambivalence to which I am trying to draw attention. Ambivalently, then, Williams is telling us that even though he rejects the aesthetic in all the terms in which it has so far been articulated— idealist terms—he nevertheless does not rule out the possibility of one day discovering a properly materialist account of it. In *Politics and Letters* he makes the point again in somewhat clearer language, and combines it with a projection of future work. The interviewers have pressed him, questioning his (seeming) argument in *Marxism and Literature* that the allied concepts of "literature" and "the aesthetic" must be abandoned. They suggest instead that in rejecting those, Williams is surrendering too much valuable ground. Williams responds:

> Well this is difficult. What I would hope will happen is that after the ground has been cleared of the received idea of literature, it will be possible to find certain new concepts which would allow for special emphases. Otherwise there is obviously a danger of relativism or miscellaneity, of which I am very conscious. That will have to be done—it will be a necessary stage. Even with the category of the aesthetic, I say it is wholly necessary to reject the notion of aesthetics as the special province of a certain kind of response, but we cannot rule out the possibility of discovering certain permanent configurations of a theoretical kind which answer to it—as we certainly don't rule out conjunc-tural configurations of a historical kind in which the category effectively obtained. . . . The mistaken assumptions which lie hidden in the old concepts have to be cleared away for us to be able to begin searching again for a more tenable set of emphases within the range of writing practices. (325–326)

Williams' second saving clause for the aesthetic, then—and it is a large one—is that his wholesale critique of it, together with his insistence on tearing down the distinction between the "literary" and the "non-literary," is ultimately to be considered a clearing operation, and that once the field has been cleared of the influence of Leavis and the New Critics, a new aesthetics, together with a new model of the "literary," will have to be constructed along more properly materialist lines. This proviso has been forgotten, presumably because it does not sit at all easily with the discipline's current consensus that "aesthetic" justifications for literature necessarily serve conservative purposes—indeed, it has presumably been forgotten in large part because *Marxism and Literature* is so often assumed to offer a justification for just that consensus. But Williams was right to offer it, even in the course of a necessary critique of idealist aesthetics, and he was also right to reiterate and confirm it when pressed. He was also, I think, right to foresee that there would come a time when we would again need the thing he was so anxious to reject in the late 1970s.

In making what has proved to be an extremely influential critique of idealist aesthetics, Williams was tearing the "criticism" of his day up by its philosophical roots and planting in its place the seeds of what would become a whole tradition of historicist and contextualist scholarship. I hope that by this stage, it is also clear that he was at the same time repeating the very ground-clearing exercise that founded "criticism" in the first place. For once we appreciate Williams' full position, in which the critique of idealist aesthetics is to be seen as a clearing operation on the way to a more materialist reconstruction of the term, we can see that it is in fact rather startlingly congruent to Richards.' The differences that remain between the two are those between liberalism and socialism on the one hand, and those between criticism and scholarship on the other—differences that do not line up in the way that the left of the discipline in recent times has believed. If in Richards' hands the aesthetic was only partly reconstructed, and then was used as a foundation for a liberal model of criticism, relatively naïve about the broader economic and political determinants that were eventually to make it impossible to achieve even in its own terms—a model that was thus easily recovered by the main tradition of bourgeois aesthetics—we should not therefore dismiss aesthetic criticism entirely. Even that flawed liberal model gave us "close reading," which is still, in its various forms, the most useful tool in the discipline today. More importantly, what the example of

Richards demonstrates, I think, is that contrary to the common assumption that "criticism" and "aesthetics" are necessarily creatures of the right—an assumption bred into the discipline throughout the middle part of the twentieth century—another kind of criticism, based on another kind of aesthetics, is possible. If Williams' initial project—to "unite radical left politics with Leavisite literary criticism" was, as he later put it, "ludicrous," then this was because of Leavis, not because of literary criticism. Seeing this, one sees something like a path toward a left aesthetic criticism today.

Chapter Three

The Historicist/Contextualist Paradigm

LET US THEN return to our story proper by addressing the third and most recent period in the history of literary studies—our own. The central point to be made here is that much of the most important work performed by the discipline over the last three decades, particularly by the left, has really amounted to a working-through of the initial critique of criticism—the critique for which I have offered Williams as an emblem. Observing this allows one to see more clearly the complex character of the discipline's current paradigm. To the extent that Williams' critique, and others like it, remains a welcome corrective to idealist tendencies within the discipline, this working-through has been a productive one. Yet for the most part today's historicist/contextualist paradigm has neither taken into account Williams' saving clauses, nor tried to correct for his overlooking of the incipiently materialist aesthetics that lay at the roots of the discipline. Truly to demonstrate the extent of the range over which this generalization holds would no doubt require a whole new book; I will make the point more concisely by focusing on the work of just four key figures/movements on the left of the discipline: Terry Eagleton, the New Historicism, Fredric Jameson, and Franco Moretti. Again, I do so with some misgivings, since this small sample of key figures hardly covers the field—and yet even so, it seems better to examine a few figures in depth, rather than risk the superficiality of a wider survey. I will have more to say on the question of their representativeness at the chapter's close.

Terry Eagleton

Terry Eagleton, Williams' student, offers us our first and earliest example of what was quickly to become a general tendency. One may summarize the position he took in the 1980s and 1990s by saying that he critiqued the categories of "literature" and the "aesthetic" as elitist mystifications, rejected the associated practice of "criticism" as necessarily Leavisite or New Critical, and recommended the restructuring of departments of literature around the central goal of "education in the various theories and methods of cultural analysis" (186).[1] In other words, his position was that of Williams in *Marxism and Literature*, without the rider that all of this was to be seen as a provisional clearing operation on the way to a reconstruction of "literature" and the "aesthetic" in more materialist terms. We might say that Eagleton's version of the argument was the more successful: as I noted in the Introduction, today's departments of literature are indeed largely structured, not around the concept of "literature" in the old aesthetic sense and the seemingly idealist project of its "criticism," but around "cultural texts" and the seemingly more materialist project of their analysis, without any general sense that this structure should be considered merely a temporary phase in a longer plan.[2]

One sees how thoroughly the story of the origins of "criticism" had become muddled by this point when one reads Eagleton's chapter on "The Rise of English" in his influential *Literary Theory: An Introduction* (1983), or his treatment of the same in his subsequent volume *The Function of Criticism* (1984).[3] In both of these works, Eagleton's discussions of the origins of "practical criticism" and "close reading" assume that we understand Leavis as the dominant figure, with Richards introduced belatedly as a kind of follower of Leavis, and a "link between Cambridge English and the American New Criticism."[4] In other words, by this stage in the discipline's history the refiguring of "criticism" as Leavisite or New Critical in essence had proceeded to such a degree that it amounted to a simple mistake in chronology. The mistake is understandable: as we have seen even Williams, who had been nuanced enough to warn us of the error of conflating "practical criticism" with Leavis, had nevertheless fallen into that error in effect.

Having offered influential restatements of Williams' arguments against both the concept of "literature" and the project of "criticism," Eagleton went on to elaborate Williams' primary argument against the "aesthetic." His *The*

Ideology of the Aesthetic (1990), a commodious work that ranges through a heavy list of aesthetic thinkers from Baumgarten and Kant onward, might seem to have been offered as a break with Williams—as a kind of *defense* of the aesthetic against sweeping attacks by historical and cultural materialists:

> I . . . have in my sights those on the political left for whom the aesthetic is simply 'bourgeois ideology,' to be worsted and ousted by alternative forms of cultural politics. The aesthetic is indeed, as I hope to show, a bourgeois concept in the most literal historical sense, hatched and nurtured in the Enlightenment; but only for the drastically undialectical thought of a vulgar Marxist or 'post-Marxist' trend of thought could this fact be an automatic condemnation. (8)[5]

Yet the continuity with Williams' argument soon becomes clear, for Eagleton's central positive claim for the aesthetic is the same in all its major elements as what I have earlier called Williams' first saving clause. Eagleton:

> This concept of [aesthetic] autonomy is radically double-edged: if on the one hand it provides a central constituent of bourgeois ideology, it also marks an emphasis on the self-determining nature of human powers and capacities which becomes, in the work of Karl Marx and others, the anthropological foundation of a revolutionary opposition to bourgeois utility. The aesthetic is at once, as I try to show, the very secret prototype of human subjectivity in early capitalist society, and a vision of human energies as radical ends in themselves which is the implacable enemy of all dominative or instrumentalist thought. (9)

This is precisely Williams' account of the aesthetic as that element in bourgeois thought that functions as a "protest against the forcing of all experience into instrumentality." Considered as a defence of the aesthetic, it really only ever amounts to a reminder that, in Eagleton's words, "From *The Communist Manifesto* onwards, Marxism has never ceased to sing the praises of the bourgeoisie" (8). One might be forgiven for finding this kind of praise a little underwhelming. What is missing here is any real sense that it might be possible to break with the bourgeois tradition of aesthetics without surrendering the category entirely: to clear away the idealist emphasis on "autonomy," "self-determination," and opposition to "utility," and rebuild the aesthetic on something more like materialist—which here would mean instrumental—grounds.

In a wider sense, such critiques drew their force from a feeling that the concepts of "literature," "criticism" and "aesthetic value" were, at root, hierarchical and elitist ones, each serving an important legitimating role for many of the most hierarchical and elitist elements of the bourgeois order. In Britain in 1988, Eagleton could put it as bluntly as this: "Departments of literature in higher education, then, are part of the ideological apparatus of the modern capitalist state" (174). This is true, of course, and important to note, but the crucial question is as to the *extent* to which it is true. For considered as a question of strategy, it is crucial to know, on the one hand, when and in what kinds of contexts the disciplines of literature function as legitimating institutions for oppressive forces, and on the other hand when and in what kinds of contexts they function as means by which we are able to resist those forces. Only rarely has this kind of claim been made with the necessary degree of historical specificity. One might take for example Eagleton's comments in the 1996 preface to the second edition of *Literary Theory:*

> What is truly elitist in literary studies is the idea that works of literature can only be appreciated by those with a particular sort of cultural breeding. There are those who have 'literary values' in their bones, and those who languish in the outer darkness. One important reason for the growth of literary theory since the 1960s was the gradual breakdown of this assumption. (viii)

It is perhaps too "nice" a critical point to note here that the shift from present to past tense is of considerable interest: what "is" truly elitist today, in 1996, "was" an assumption that began to break down in the 1960s. More important is the question that this observation allows us: were these particular forms of literary elitism, which, we are told, began to break down in the 1960s, really still the most salient target for critique in 1996, when Eagleton was writing? In 1996, was the distinction between the literary and the nonliterary, the cultivated and the uncultivated—in effect, the category of the aesthetic—still the chief means by which literary studies served a role in the ideological apparatus of the modern capitalist state?

I think the answer is no, and here of course there is a great deal to be said that would take us away from our main story. Yet it seems worth at least noting this: that surely if the last three decades have taught literary studies anything about its relationship to the capitalist state, it is that the capitalist state in its current phase of development does not want us around. Under a Keynesian funding regime, it was possible to think that literary study was being supported because it served an important legitimating role in the maintenance of liberal capitalist institutions. The steady and now nearly complete withdrawal of state funding for literary studies during the period of neoliberalism should convince us that we are now in quite a different situation. Returning to Eagleton's argument, and trying to be generous to it, it seems fair to allow that, specifically within Britain, a certain kind of cultural conservatism still takes refuge behind something like the terms under critique here—and yet one must then add that this is decreasingly the case, and that today, any serious analysis surely would have to conclude that the dominant forms of legitimation are now elsewhere.[6] At any rate, whatever view we form about the situation either at present or as it stood in 1996, the salient point is that, within the discipline as it stood in the late 1970s and early 1980s, it was evidently still possible to feel that these kinds of large-scale assaults on the concept of "literature," on literary study as "criticism" and the associated methods of "practical criticism" and "close reading," and on the concept of the "aesthetic" more generally, were being directed at a genuine target on the right—namely, the last vestiges of the Leavisite and New Critical forces of the 1950s, as they continued to spring up in all sorts of less precise forms of humanistic criticism over the decades that followed. In the context of a discipline that continued to feel the influence of these conservative movements, it was easy to feel that the advancing of critiques of this kind was a politically progressive act.

But as the critique spread to other times and places, these conditions, such as they were, no longer obtained. If class exploitation in Britain was still, in the 1950s and—residually—in the 1970s and 1980s, legitimated in part by pernicious forms of elitism about "cultivated" and "uncultivated" classes, a liberal insistence on a hierarchy of aesthetic tastes, and so on, the same could not be said of the United States in the 1980s and 1990s, where pretended attacks on "elite" regimes of taste were the very stuff of right-liberal discourse, as indeed they remain. With the turn to finance capitalism and full neoliberalism, the terms of the cultural debate shifted: the dominant classes within capitalism were now being legitimated, not by their pretensions to highbrow taste, but precisely by their miming of a critique of highbrow taste. More broadly, and across many different regions, it is true that the old mid-century liberalisms had often sought to justify themselves by appealing to their aesthetic sophistication, on the assumption that the aesthetic high ground and the moral high ground were the same; yet after the crisis of the 1970s, the situation largely reversed itself, the new liberalisms instead tending to pose as democratic levellers of aesthetic distinctions. From the early 1980s onward, the democratic, enlightened, free-market view, operating at many levels of the new liberal sensibility, was that any recourse the idea of aesthetic value was to be dismissed as simple snobbery; instead, it was insisted, we ought to acknowledge that what we were really dealing with were individual consumer preferences—mere "matters of taste." In this changed historical context, Williams' critique of the aesthetic, repeated again and again, assumed quite a different political character.[7]

The New Historicism

It is instructive here to turn to a tendency that held a significant sway over the discipline in the late 1980s and 1990s, and that continues to influence much of what goes on in it under other names at present, though most often in the sense that scholars understand themselves (often wrongly, I might add) to be reacting against it. The New Historicism was a very varied tendency, and so of course much of what I say about it here will have to be qualified when dealing with specific cases. Yet without attempting to come to an assessment of every figure important to the tendency, we can at least trace some of the broad outlines of its treatment of the category of the aesthetic, and in so doing arrive at some sense of its political character, in its context. In particular, it is important to observe the ways the New Historicists took up Williams' critique of the aesthetic, in a context in which the political effect of that critique was bound to be very different. One could go to the early work here, but I think perhaps the most concise way to make the point is by referring to Stephen Greenblatt and Catherine Gallagher's *Practicing New Historicism* (2000), the closest thing to a manifesto the movement produced—albeit a manifesto produced, somewhat oddly, in the wake of the victory, rather than as an initial call to arms.[8] In this connection it is worth recalling that Greenblatt had been Williams' student for a time, though for both Greenblatt and Gallagher, the more central inspiration was Foucault. In any case, what seems most salient about the text is the way in which the left critique of the aesthetic—which had begun to develop in the 1950s and 1960s, but achieved its most coherent and radical form in the 1970s—came through into the New Historicism of the 1980s and 1990s in a mediated fashion, as a reservation about canonicity: a reservation that is really very mild in comparison with the critique's much more forceful early forms.

Nevertheless, Greenblatt and Gallagher wrote of it as if it were a striking innovation. When reading the manifesto, one is immediately confronted by lines like this one: "Having impetuously rushed beyond the confines of the canonical garden, we stand facing extraordinary challenges and perplexing questions" (14). What is the tone here? One tries to read generously, and these are obviously fine writers and deep thinkers, yet I must admit that I am at a loss when trying put myself into a positive relationship to it. If one takes the note of rapture seriously, the line becomes a New Historicist paean to New Historicism, and is thus hard to accept as other than embarrassing; if one instead treats it as coyness—or, in Greenblatt and Gallagher's terms, "half facetiousness"—then one is left wondering what, beyond self-dramatization, it is meant to achieve. Trying to be fair, the best I find myself able to say is that the tone suggests, while being prepared if necessary to deny, that the New Historicist "rush beyond the confines of the canon" really was radically new, exciting, and transgressive (even a little bit titillating, since this is the garden of Eden, after all, and there is presumably nudity involved). So far, so good. But then we must go on to ask: *was* it in fact radically new, exciting, and transgressive? And if it was, then what was really at stake?

With regard to the question of stakes, we could do worse than to take a closer look at the chosen topos: an escape (not expulsion) from Eden. Given the history that we have traced in this chapter, it is tempting to say that the move here to frame the New Historicist critique of the canon as a daring escape from a theocratic authority is being made available by the equation between aesthetic approaches to literature and New Criticism that by now had become almost reflexive. Indeed, as we shall see later, in this respect it lines up quite nicely with Moretti's claim, also made in 2000, that close reading should be rejected because "at bottom, it's a theological exercise," and that now "what we really need is a little pact with the devil." Noting this implied equation gives us our first hint as to what Greenblatt and Gallagher might see as the stake here. Perhaps they are on their way to making a kind of political claim: the claim being that, if policing the boundaries of the canon, and insisting on an aesthetic distinction between the literary and the nonliterary, makes one a stodgy old Christian conservative, then "rush[ing] beyond" those "confines" might be thought properly secularist, liberal, and perhaps even bit progressive.

The most explicitly political moment in the introduction to *Practicing New Historicism* is an implied analogy between the New Historicist "impetuous rush beyond the confines of the canonical garden" and the radical political movements of the 1960s. Let us examine each part of that analogy in turn, in an effort to determine the precise kinds of political claims on offer. In the first part of the analogy, Greenblatt and Gallagher expand on their claim to have gone beyond the boundaries of the canon in a new and exciting way. They begin with the rhetoric of left radicalism, but quickly shift to a celebration of liberal pluralism:

> There has in effect been a social rebellion in the study of culture, so that figures hitherto kept outside the proper circles of interest—a rabble of half-crazed visionaries, semiliterate political agitators, coarse-faced peasants in hobnailed boots, dandies whose writings had been discarded as ephemera, imperial bureaucrats, freed slaves, women novelists dismissed as impudent scribblers, learned women excluded from easy access to the materials of scholarship, scandalmongers, provincial politicians, charlatans, and forgotten academics—have now forced their way in, or rather have been invited in by our generation of critics. (10–11)

The initial phrase "social rebellion" gives something of a radical cast to this, but this is corrected for by that last shift from "forced their way in" to "or rather have been invited in by our generation of critics" which reminds us that *actual* political struggles—the kind that involve a group, or class, "forcing" its way into something—do not take place within the world of scholarship, where the agency remains, sadly but necessarily, with the scholars. In this structure of feeling, it would be very naive indeed of us to assume that a "social rebellion in the study of culture" would have any direct relation to events normally thought of as political: on the contrary, "the study of culture" is conceived of as a project that goes on entirely within the academy. Once we have rejected naiveté of that kind, however, we can begin to make more reasonable political claims: the implied claim here being that, in "inviting" these figures into the study of culture, the New Historicist scholar is at least acting in a democratic and inclusive spirit; the kind of spirit that we might find acceptable for political reasons.

This particular view of the political stakes of academic work becomes more explicit in the second part of the analogy, when Greenblatt and Gallagher go on to claim that there really *is* a relationship between, on the one hand, New Historicism as a movement within the academy and, on the other, actual political struggles outside the academy, feminism in particular—a *historical* relationship:

It is hardly an accident that this broader vision of the field of cultural interpretation, which had been mooted for more than a century, took hold in the United States in the late 1960s and early 70s. It reflected in its initial period the recent inclusion of groups that in many colleges and universities had hitherto been marginalised, half hidden, or even entirely excluded from the professional study of literature: Jews, African Americans, Hispanics, Asian Americans, and, most significantly from the point of view of the critical ferment, women. Women's studies, and the feminism that motivated its formation, has served an important, if little acknowledged, model for new historicism in that it has inspired its adherents to identify new objects for study, bring those objects into the light of critical attention, and insist upon their legitimate place in the curriculum. It has also served to politicise explicitly an academic discourse that had often attempted to avoid or conceal partisan or polemical commitments, and it unsettles familiar aesthetic hierarchies that had been manipulated, consciously or unconsciously, to limit the cultural significance of women.

This unsettling of the hierarchies does not seem revolutionary—we are not inclined to confuse a change in the curriculum with a fall of the state—but it does feel democratising, in that it refuses to limit creativity to the spectacular achievements of a group of trained specialists. (11)

The last note here sounds in the same key as "have been invited" earlier: it insists, against the perceived threat of other, more explicitly political views, that it would be naive to think that academic work can effect political change in anything like a direct fashion. To think that it could would be to "confuse a change in the curriculum with the fall of the state." This sentiment has much to do with the political mood of the 1980s and 1990s, the decades in which New Historicism rose to prominence. Again, the claim is that once we have seen the naiveté of those ("revolutionary") kinds of views, we can move on to a more modest, but more realistic ("democratising") political project—the project of "unsettling hierarchies" by "refus[ing] to limit creativity to the spectacular achievements of a group of trained specialists."

In a moment, I shall return to ask what kind of historical relationship is being posited here, and how it sits with the much more evident historical relationship between views of this political tenor and the political tenor of the period in which they came to light. For now, though, let us simply try to understand the argument being offered us, starting with the quote's final phrase, "trained specialists." To whom does it refer? If we are to understand and celebrate the New Historicists' new "democratising" political project, then we must first find out what kind of "hierarchies" they are claiming to "unsettle," what kind of "trained specialists" it is to whom "creativity" was previously seen as "limited." And we will have to try to parse this quite carefully, because it is by no means obvious. At first it might seem as if we are still talking about the entry into the academy of previously marginalised groups: "Jews, African Americans, Hispanics, Asian Americans . . . women." In that case, the claim would be that the New Historicism brought about a new democratization of *scholarly* work, and the "group of trained specialists" who resisted this would then be the stodgy old gentile white male scholars who previously dominated the academy. But this would be rather a strange way to put it, first because one does not immediately associate stodgy old scholars with "spectacular achievements" of "creativity"—that sounds as if we are talking about literary or "creative" writers, rather than scholars—and second, since, while the opening up of the academy to new groups was certainly a challenge to entrenched prejudices of many kinds, it is not normally thought of as a challenge to scholarly specialization per se. People from marginalized groups who entered the academy and became scholars were, in time, no less "trained specialists" than the gentile white men who had tried to keep them out.

Our first attempt to parse the political project having resulted in a certain incoherence, let us try a second. Perhaps we should instead read these lines in relation to the paragraph we read a moment ago—which is to say, we should understand the New Historicist project of "democratising" and "unsettling hierarchies" by "refus[ing] to limit creativity to the spectacular achievements of a group of trained specialists" as a further reference to the "invitation" that the New Historicists claimed to have extended to "figures hitherto kept outside the proper circles of [academic] interest." The "hierarchies" being unsettled would then be, specifically, the hierarchy of aesthetic judgements that previously determined the curriculum, keeping it canonical in a narrow sense by restricting the range of objects of study, and the "unsettling" would be a "change in the curriculum," namely the "impetuous rush beyond the confines of the canonical garden" that invited in the new objects of study: the "rabble of half-crazed visionaries, semi-literate political agitators, coarse-faced peasants" and so on. This would certainly provide a referent for this phrase "spectacular [creative] achievements"—the New Historicists would be claiming to have broken a monopoly on creativity previously held by dead white male authors of canonical literature. But again, this would be very strange way to put it, for the claim is that the New Historicists have refused "to limit creativity to the spectacular achievements of a group of trained specialists," and surely one does not normally think of Shakespeare and Wordsworth, say, as "trained specialists." The claim remains very puzzling. Just who *are* those "trained specialists"?

It seems very difficult to determine what the claim to be acting as a "democratising" force really consists of, unless we conclude, as I think we must, that the claim is in fact a rather hazy one, useful for rhetorical rather than intellectual purposes, and that the anxiety about "trained specialists" is intruding on it from somewhere else entirely. The hazy claim lies somewhere in the analogy being draw here between the list of heterogeneous figures we just discussed—the "rabble" "invited in" to academic research by "our generation of critics" in the 1980s and 1990s—and the list of marginalized groups who were "recently included" in the academy in the 1960s and 1970s. In the 1960s and 1970s, many marginalized groups were able to enter the academy for the first time; in the 1980s and 1990s, a new and heterogeneous range of figures were made available as objects of study within literary studies; the manifesto superimposes one on the other, the palimpsest seeming to imply something like a causal connection. This rhetorical manoeuvre allows the scholarly movement to associate itself with earlier progressive struggles, thereby seeming to deliver a political mandate for this form of scholarship, but the argument that would support such an association never appears.

Were such an argument to appear, what would it look like? We could perhaps phrase it as follows: since feminist activists fought for, and then secured, the establishment of Women's Studies within the academy, and Women's Studies in turn "served as a model" for the New Historicism, the New Historicism can claim descent from progressive forces in the political sphere. It is not at all clear to me how New Historicism gets to take part of the credit for radical feminist activism here, but it seems to do so. But even if we accept the argument in this form, we find that it gives us no reason to accept the idea that New Historicism functioned as a "democratising" force in its own political context, decades later. Here we can return to the question of the precise kind of historical relation being proposed. For what is at stake in this kind of periodization, which claims that the political context of the 1960s and 1970s is the most important one for understanding a movement that grew to dominate the field in the 1980s and 1990s? Is this not a rather curious move for such careful historical and contextual thinkers to make, to try to identify the external political factors that gave impetus to their movement by focusing on the decades of progressive radicalism that preceded it, rather than on the decades of conservative hegemony in which it actually appeared? Perhaps there is a case to be made that the sensibility of the scholars who built the New Historicism was formed in the earlier, more progressive period. But surely any analysis ought then to go on to consider how that structure of feeling later either changed, or changed its valence, when the surrounding circumstances changed so completely. In the absence of any genuine historical analysis of this kind, it is difficult not to suspect that Greenblatt and Gallagher were eager to get the benefit of an assumed association with the past radicalisms of the 1960s, while turning attention away from any attempt to account for the real political character of the tendency in its present.

Once we start to feel this way about the New Historicism, the pressing question becomes as to the specific contemporary circumstances that

conditioned, and even to a certain degree determined, the real political character of the movement, and here I am afraid that the particular range of
styles and emphases employed begins to appear quite problematic. It begins
to seem, for example, that the coyness of the Greenblatt and Gallagher's
tone—the faux naiveté, the "half-facetiousness" (124)—may exist, both here
and throughout much of the work of the movement's central figures, chiefly
to manage a problem derived from the wider context: the problem faced by
scholars who, for complex reasons, explicitly disavow themselves of any
commitment to the idea of academic work as radical political praxis, but
who nevertheless want to try to get ahead in a discipline where grappling
with live, as opposed to merely analytic, political questions, and thus the
making of political claims for one's own work, has become a necessary
requirement for advancement. The claim that the stakes are genuinely political is implied constantly, but whenever that claim threatens to break out in
the direction of actual political practice, the coy tone returns to imply that
we shouldn't take it all so seriously. Appreciating this helps one to understand the popularity of the movement. A rhetoric of this kind, which by
turns avowed and disavowed intentions that could be described, or critiqued,
as "political," must have seemed appealing to many in the academy who
were nominally on the left but whose material interests, and associated real
commitments, in fact lay with the newly neo-liberalized institutions that
seemed to promise to support them.

Returning to the specific history we have been tracing, we can observe
that Greenblatt and Gallagher were able to imply that their methodological
priorities had a progressive political valence only by relying on the assumption, ironed into the discipline over the preceding decades, that challenging
the aesthetic privileging of literary texts over nonliterary texts, and of some
literary texts over others, somehow amounted to a challenge to "privilege"
more generally. As we have seen, that assumption had once been an argument, and the argument had been formed as a genuine response to a very
different set of circumstances. Williams, for his part, had been confronting
an entrenched form of social conservatism in Britain that took refuge behind
the term "culture," the spectrum "cultivated/uncultivated," and their associated abstractions and elitisms. At least in the Britain of the 1940s, '50s,
and early '60s, this form of social conservatism was very much a live one,
and much of its intellectual justification was being provided continually by

a set of views associated with the disciplinary and paradisciplinary study of English Literature. Williams' stern critique of the project of "criticism," together with his associated critiques of the "aesthetic," the category "literature," and the method of "practical criticism," was born out of this felt need to confront active conservative forces within his immediate political environment. No analogous circumstances obtained in the United States in the late twentieth century. It is this kind of recognition that we must set beside our acknowledgment of the charisma, the real rhetorical excitements, of much New Historicist work. The results of such a weighing seem clear enough: it is simply very hard, from our present standpoint, to see the New Historicism in other terms than as a repetition of Williams' project that sought, in an ambiguous but unmistakable response to specific local conditions, to put on its progressivist trappings while systematically emptying it of real political force.

At this point, no doubt, many of the old guard will protest; it therefore seems important at least to point to some of the more detailed considerations that might lead one to take this view, though of course one does not want to spend the rest of the book debating about the political valence of the New Historicism. I will simply provide three quick examples. First, it seems to me that the much-vaunted New Historicist claim to have rocked the foundations of materialism by bringing to bear on it poststructuralist insights into the all-pervasiveness of representation was, to a considerably larger extent than they were usually willing to acknowledge, a continuation of Williams' well-known critique of base and superstructure—in his words, his attempt to "replace the formula of base and superstructure with the more active idea of a field of mutually if also unevenly determining forces."[9] The figuring of this continuation as a break had important political implications, since it meant that Williams' critique, which had been advanced in unequivocally political terms, in the name of a committed socialism, could now be re-presented as a relatively apolitical act of professionalized scholarship, or, at best, in the name of a much less demanding left-liberalism.

This leads me to my second example, which centers on just this question of professionalization, institutionalization, and the relationship between the increasingly specialized work of the scholars and the nonspecialist public on whose behalf it was ultimately being produced. Here again the New Historicism reiterated a key element of Williams' project—in this case, his repeated warnings about the dangers of academic specialization—while tending to empty it of its live political content. Williams had everywhere insisted on the central importance of a well-theorized practical resistance to the worst effects of academic specialization, disciplinarity, and professionalization, and he had traced this strand of his argument back to the origins of cultural studies in the specific para-academic, and even para-institutional, context of workers' and adult education in Britain. I will quote at length, since the great distance between the situation Williams describes and our situation within the neoliberal university today threatens to render this crucial argument nearly incommunicable:

> [T]he local self-educating organisations of working people and others . . . had been based . . . on [the] principle . . . that intellectual questions arose when you drew up intellectual disciplines that form bodies of knowledge in contact with people's life-situations and life-experiences. . . . Academics took out from their institutions university economics, or university English or university philosophy, and the people wanted to know what it was. This exchange didn't collapse into some simple populism: that these were all silly intellectual questions. Yet these students insisted (1) that the relation of this to their own situation and experience had to be discussed, and (2) that there were areas in which the discipline itself might be unsatisfactory, and therefore they retained as a crucial principle the right to decide their own syllabus. . . . [People] have far more than a right to be tested to see if they are following [disciplinary norms] or if [their views] are being put in a form which is convenient . . . in fact they have this more basic right to define the questions. These people were, after all, in a practical position to say "well, if you tell me that question goes outside your discipline, then bring me someone whose discipline *will* cover it, or bloody well get outside of the discipline and answer it yourself." (156–157)

Much could be said about this passage; for present purposes, its significance is simply that it indicates the extent to which Williams' project was one that strove to remain at a distance from the specializing and professionalizing demands of the higher education system, with which it nevertheless had to work in close proximity.[10] The New Historicism eagerly took up something like this rhetoric of resistance to specialization—in so many places in the work of the main figures, one finds repeated (and often curiously out-of-place) critiques of "trained specialists," one of which we have already examined—but this rhetoric was never advanced into an active critique, for the simple reason that by this stage in the history of literary study they *were* the "trained specialists." This was politically uncomfortable but, the key New Historicists often seemed to feel, sadly inevitable, since for scholars who wanted to function in the new academy, there could of course be no question of actually mounting a *challenge* to that kind of specialization. Their repeated rhetorical attacks on "trained specialists" are, I think, the sign of this discomfort. To this end, what in Williams had been an attempt to operate simultaneously both inside and outside the academy, for expressly political purposes, was reduced, in the New Historicist miming of that rhetoric, to a celebration of "interdisciplinarity"—which is to say, a resistance to specialization *within* the academy.

Within that narrowed space for critique, the distances crossed were not perhaps as large as they could have been, since within the academy, the New Historicists most often chose to celebrate an interdisciplinarity between literary history and . . . disciplinary history. Only in quite thoroughly professionalized terms could this be seen as a live challenge to academic specialization. Meanwhile, the real and ongoing advance of specialization at other levels—from the general movement by which academic work was hived off from those on whose behalf it was nominally being produced, to the much more local hardening of distinctions between specific intradisciplinary fields and subfields—was simply accepted as an unavoidable part of modern scholarship. Thus, for example, it is only in passing that Greenblatt and Gallagher, in their introduction to *Practicing New Historicism,* refer approvingly to their own "conservative interest in periodization (for each of us had been trained to be a specialist in a given area and to take its geographical and temporal boundaries seriously)" (7). It seems that amidst all the rhetoric of rejecting specialization, there was never any felt need to produce an intellectual justification for specialization of *this* kind: they were specialists simply because they had been trained that way. There could never, in these terms, be any question of mounting a challenge even to this kind of intradisciplinary specialization, let alone confronting, in the way Williams had tried to do, the related but more intrinsically significant form of specialization that continually divides intellectual work from the people on whose behalf that work is nominally being produced.

But my third example is the most crucial for present purposes: the way in which Williams' critique of the aesthetic itself was taken up by the New

Historicists in a manner, and in a context, in which its political character was bound to be very different. As we have seen, in 1977 Williams had already offered a wholesale critique of the aesthetic that sought to strike at the very root of the ideology of canonicity. Two decades later, Greenblatt and Gallagher claimed that the New Historicism had led to a "drastic broadening of the field" in which

> [w]orks that have been hitherto denigrated or ignored can be treated as major achievements, claiming space in an already crowded curriculum or diminishing the value of established works in a kind of literary stock market. (10)

What had begun, in Williams, as a wholesale rejection of the traditional basis of canonicity—a wholesale rejection of the category of the aesthetic, and with it the idea of a special aesthetic value or aesthetic state—is here recoded as the promise of a mere reshuffling of the canon; or more precisely, to follow Greenblatt and Gallagher's metaphor, the promise of a new and exciting volatility in the aesthetic market. The intellectual poverty of the market metaphor, together with its inescapably political valence, is a clue to the fact that what we are witnessing here is the rolling back of what had been, in its time, a profound reform.

At an intellectual level, the difference between the two responses really stems from the difference in their depths of engagement with the history of philosophical aesthetics, a difference that can in turn be traced back to forces operating in the wider political and cultural spheres. Williams, because his scholarly work was being put together as a clarifying response to the various pressures of his vexed disciplinary and national situations, had felt the need to engage seriously with the tradition of philosophical aesthetics, with results that we have seen. Eagleton, residually, had felt the need to devote a book to continuing that engagement. The fact that nowhere in the key works of New Historicism can we find any similar engagement is an indication of the fact that, within the United States, by that stage in the history of the discipline, the specific forms of liberal ideology that had traditionally been seen to cluster around the term "aesthetic" were simply no longer being employed by any forceful agent. The dominant forms of legitimation were now elsewhere. The corollary of this within the discipline was that, for US literary scholars such as Greenblatt and Gallagher, there was no felt need to develop

a significant response to the problems posed by idealist philosophical aesthetics, for there was no one to force a deeper engagement. This explains the
curious inertness of the New Historicist treatment of the term. The force of
their critique of the aesthetic, such as it is, was really derived from the spectre
of New Criticism:

> The risk [of our opening-out of the canon], from a culturally conservative
> point of view, is that we will lose sight of what is uniquely precious about high
> art: new historicism, in this account, fosters the weakening of the aesthetic
> object. There is, we think, some truth to this charge, at least in relation to the
> extreme claims routinely made by certain literary critics for the uniqueness of
> literature. Works of art, in the more perfervid moments of celebration, are
> almost completely detached from semantic necessity and are instead deeply
> important as signs and embodiments of the freedom of the human imagina-
> tion. The rest of human life can only gaze longingly at the condition of the art
> object, which is the manifestation of unalienated labor, the perfect articula-
> tion and realization of human energy. The art object, ideally self-enclosed, is
> freed not only from the necessities of the surrounding world (necessities that
> it transforms miraculously into play) but also from the intention of the maker.
> The closest analogy perhaps is the Catholic Eucharist . . . . (11–12)

The version of the "aesthetic" under critique here assumes an "art object"
that is self-enclosed, free from instrumental and contextual concerns,
divorced from authorial intention, and cast in religious terms. This is to say
that, though a generation has passed, once again the critique of the aesthetic
in general is actually a critique of idealist aesthetics in particular: specifically,
the neo-Kantian aesthetics of the New Criticism, here offered, perhaps necessarily, in something of a caricatured form. But if the general form of the
critique has remained the same for twenty-five years, the historical context
in which it is being offered has not: we are long decades past the New Critics
here. Where Williams' critique of the aesthetic had been an attempt to confront powerful conservative forces active in the culture around him, the New
Historicists' "weakening of the aesthetic object" was, in their own words, an
attempt to confront "the extreme claims routinely made by certain literary
critics . . . in [their] more perfervid moments of celebration." It seems fair to
observe that by this stage in our history the significance of the target has
been reduced.

I do not want to press this point endlessly, but it is an important one. "Routinely made" nevertheless seems to imply that, if this target was small, at least it was a live one. But *were* aesthetic positions of this New Critical or pseudo-New Critical kind still a serious threat to the discipline in 2000—or even in the 1990s, when the influence of the New Historicism was at its height? In the 1980s, perhaps, when many of the later New Historicists were trained? The answer, by and large, is no. In this respect, we might compare the chronology offered by Frank Lentricchia twenty years earlier, in his widely influential *After the New Criticism* (1980): "By about 1957, the moribund condition of the New Criticism and the literary needs it left unfulfilled placed us in a critical void" (4).[11] This may be too early a date for some, and there were, of course, residual formations, but in the main, the scientization of the humanities, at an institutional level, and Williams' critique and others like it, at an intellectual level, had long since effected the shift away from such forms of criticism. By the mid-1990s, the historicist/contextualist paradigm had been the dominant mode for at least a decade.

In fact, by 2000, the "aesthetic" seemed to pose so little threat to historicist scholarship within the discipline that the central New Historicists could even demonstrate their inclusiveness by inviting it back in, albeit in an impoverished sense. To see this, let us observe the phrases in which the term is deployed in the introduction to *Practicing New Historicism*. Most are positive: "aesthetic pleasures," "aesthetic polish," "[aesthetic] wonder," "aesthetic pleasure," "aesthetically gratifying," "aesthetic appreciation." An ungenerous reader might observe that in none of these cases does the phrase mean much more than "good looking."[12] These kinds of formulations are available to thinkers of this caliber only because, in the absence of any engagement with a live enemy using the term, the term "aesthetic" can be deployed in an impoverished way. The contrast with Williams' sophisticated use of the term is then quite stark.

To summarize, Williams' sweeping critique of the project of "criticism" and of the associated categories of "literature" and the "aesthetic," which at least in its early stages had been directed at a genuine target to the right, was turned to quite different ends when it was taken up in the very different environment of the United States in the 1980s and 1990s, at a moment when neoliberal forces within the university were systematically favoring the scholarly over the critical model of literary studies. In this newly professionalized and scientized context, the scholarly model of intellectual inquiry—intellectual work as knowledge-production, now usually con-ceived of within the discipline as the production of historical knowledge—was simply assumed to constitute the central task of literary study. For if it was true that the New Historicism felt no need to engage with the long history of aesthetic thought, it was also true that it felt no need to produce a sustained critique of the project of "criticism." As we have seen, both Williams and Eagleton had found it necessary to attack Leavis and the New Critics *as critics,* by way of explicit critiques of the project of criticism itself. These arguments had cleared the ground for the establishment of a newly historicized, and newly scholarly, model of literary study. But in the rapidly neoliberalizing university system of the United States in the 1980s and 1990s, this model of scholarship as the production of knowledge for special-ists no longer needed an explicit defense. The New Historicism could estab-lish itself as the dominant force in the discipline without it.

Returning to our broader history, it is then of much interest to try to reg-ister the changes that occur in the critique of the category of the aesthetic in this period, now that the critique of the project of criticism no longer needs to be made alongside it. For what begins to occur rather often is that within the discipline aesthetic thinking is critiqued on the grounds that it treats as universal things that ought to be treated as particular, and thereby leads to inaccurate, because ideological, knowledge. In the context of the longer his-tory of the discipline, this critique seems curiously to miss its mark, since the critics who originally had maintained a commitment to the aesthetic had never seen their task primarily as one of knowledge production. The fact that the critique is nevertheless advanced as if they *had* is a new and intriguing development, and one that cannot finally be separated from changes in the institutional conditions under which the disciplinary work is taking place.

Fredric Jameson

This is an appropriate moment to turn our attention to the dominant figure of the discipline's more thoroughly politicized wing in this period: Fredric Jameson. Unlike the New Historicists, he certainly registered the need to engage with philosophical aesthetics—or at least the need to justify refusing the engagement. Yet the pressures of his situation were never such as to require from him a critique of the project of criticism. In this sense, he is typical of our period. There is a great deal to be said about the utility and intelligence of Jameson's particular analyses, the most central of which have been his methodological innovations in the field of ideology hermeneutics and his identification of the postmodern as the cultural logic of late capitalism, but I will not be able to do justice to either of these here: our story requires a different emphasis. For while Jameson's major analyses gain much of their force and interest from having been developed in explicit opposition to other work within the discipline, his critique of philosophical aesthetics is of most interest to us precisely because it articulates so precisely the set of assumptions on which the discipline in this period was able to proceed. In this sense Jameson's critique of the aesthetic is no less central to his work for being left implicit. On the contrary, it is central just as one of the most important enabling assumptions, common to all the major contemporary figures within the discipline, that allowed even work as radically iconoclastic as Jameson's easily to be recognizable as disciplinary.

What follows are perhaps his clearest and most succinct comments on the matter of philosophical aesthetics, made in the context of a lecture on the concept of "World Literature":

> One of the problems that misleads us [in our attempt to understand the idea of "World Literature"] is the philosophical problem of aesthetic value—in my opinion, a false problem. It masks, indeed, a far more thorny philosophical problem—a real one this time—which turns on the opposition between the universal and the particular. For when humanist critics raise the question of 'value,' what they really have in mind is 'universal value,' and it's out of the notion of 'universal value' that an antiquated and unserviceable notion of 'World Literature' has always come. I think this emphasis on universal value is wrong, and misguided; it is unproductive even within the Western Canon, giving rise to all kinds of false questions and problems, like the following: is Faulkner greater than Halldór Laxness, or vice versa? Is either greater than Tolstoy? Which is more universal, *I Promessi Sposi* or *Red Chamber Dream*?
>
> I won't pursue these silly questions any further. . . . [T]he question of value is itself a historical one, which arises only after the fact, and does not involve classification according to *a priori* categories.[13]

Here, casually put, we have the principled critique of neo-Kantian aesthetics, idealist modes of criticism, and empty humanist pieties that has been one of the most valuable contributions of radical leftist thought to disciplinary literary criticism, side by side with the reflexive turn to the project of analysis, description, and classification that again and again has crippled it. As should be clear by now, this is Williams' critique—his critique of Leavis and the New Critics, whose repeated restaging of the scene of critical judgment had taught the discipline its obsession with hierarchy and canonicity, and thereby hobbled so much of its mid-century work. It is therefore also in a certain sense Richards' critique, as well as Eagleton's critique: this critique of idealist aesthetics that the discipline keeps repeating and repeating, though each time for different purposes. Though it cannot be said that Jameson's version of the critique is inherited from Williams—any serious attempt to trace the major influences on Jameson's thought would have to head into very different territory, beginning perhaps with Sartre and Marcuse—Williams' version of the critique is the most directly relevant for us here. As we have seen, that version had first taken shape in the 1950s and 1960s, and had achieved its most developed form in 1977 with *Marxism and Literature*. Three decades later—Jameson made these comments in 2008—it has become reflexive. Notably, both of Williams' saving clauses have now been dropped. There is little sense here that the aesthetic has been an important element in the bourgeois protest against the turning of all things into commodities; nor, more importantly, is there any sense that for the left, the critique of the aesthetic should be considered a clearing operation, on the way to a materialist reconstruction of the term.

Williams' critique of the aesthetic had been made in the context of a critique of the project of criticism, and had done much to allow its replacement by cultural analysis. To understand the terms in which Jameson is now making the critique, we need to see that, for him, at a later time and in another national context, literary study *is* cultural analysis—there is no longer any live question of literary studies as criticism in the older sense. Jameson proceeds as most of those in literary studies do today: by assuming that his task as a scholar is the analysis of culture, by which is meant—putting things now in bluntly positivistic terms—the production of accurate knowledge about our cultural history and present cultural situation, together with the development of methods and theories to aid in the production of that knowledge. It is in part a mark of his disciplinary affiliation that he thinks of his role as an intellectual of the left in the same way: the role of the

Marxist theorist of culture is, for him, a diagnostic one, and the actual treatment, if or when it comes, must take the form of political praxis guided by, but not itself a part of, the more strictly academic endeavour.[14] We see this readily enough when we ask ourselves what more positive sense of the term "value" Jameson is encouraging us to prefer by so roundly rejecting the "universal value" of the humanists. His positive claim is that "the question of value is itself a historical one, which arises only after the fact, and does not involve classification according to *a priori* categories." At this particular point in Jameson's position, the term "value," which he is able to think through very deeply elsewhere, is effectively reduced to diagnostic value: speaking loosely, evidentiary value—value for the purposes of accurate analysis. In other words, value to scholarship in the special sense in which I am using that term here.

Armed with this observation, we can then return to his critique of the old aesthetics to ask: *is* the "problem of aesthetic value" really reducible to the "opposition between the universal and the particular"? What would this mean? To understand this argument, we need to take into account the fact that, when Jameson looks at the earlier humanist critics' model of "universal aesthetic value," he is really thinking of "value" in this new, specifically scholarly sense. Against the background of this new set of disciplinary assumptions, the materialist critique of the aesthetic now runs as follows: "aesthetic value" must mean "universal value," because that is what it meant to mid-century humanist critics; and in turn "universal value" is unacceptable because it elides historical particularities, and thereby obstructs the production of accurate knowledge about culture. But *were* the critics who invoked the "aesthetic" as a grounding concept for their particular model of literary study really trying to produce knowledge? The answer is largely no: at least as the position was formulated initially, the goal was not to produce knowledge but to train readers. From this perspective, the "problem of aesthetic value" is not a false problem but a real one, and one that cannot in fact be reduced to an "opposition between universal and particular," since in principle it would be possible to develop, for instrumental purposes, an aesthetics that had no commitment at all to the idea of "universal aesthetic value."

Part of what is being missed here is something Williams knew, in his projection of an eventual reconstruction of aesthetic thinking on a materialist basis. The other part is something that even Williams overlooked: the fact that there exists no necessary connection between the project of aesthetic criticism and idealist universalisms—in fact, as we have seen, Richards launched the former precisely as a critique of the latter. When Jameson rightly excoriates the old humanist line of questioning ("Is Faulkner greater than Halldór Laxness, or vice versa? Is either greater than Tolstoy?") it is easy enough to agree, for he is really excoriating the idealist, mid-century aesthetic criticisms that follow out of Leavis and the New Critics, with their obsession with staging the scene of critical judgment. But surely it is quite wrong to reject the whole project of aesthetic criticism as if it were reducible, in principle, to exercises in establishing the relative rank of various canonical figures. Disciplinary criticism was founded on the basis of a much better response to these kinds of aesthetic questions. To see this, one has only to think back a little further than the mid-century. If a middling humanist of the kind Jameson is excoriating were indeed to ask "Which is more universal, *I Promessi Sposi* or *Red Chamber Dream?*" would the early critical answer be such a bad one? That answer being: "It is less important to like 'good' poetry and dislike 'bad,' than to be able to use them both as a means of ordering our minds."

What about Close Reading?

Our history, then, has led us to a stage where two of our three lines of thinking are in disarray. The project of criticism, initially left-liberal, was co-opted by conservatism, and then dismissed as irretrievably conservative by the left. As our story stands, it has been largely forgotten: now even defunct critics are assessed as if they had been simply bad scholars. In its place, we have a broad consensus built around the idea that the proper project of literary studies is the scholarly one—a consensus so influential as to remain generally unremarked upon. The aesthetic, too, has been dismissed, if not entirely forgotten. First appearing within the modern discipline as a radical break with idealism, it was soon regathered into the mainstream of idealist thought, and then critiqued as irredeemably idealist by the left. At present, the critique of it, where it appears, has become reflexive. Richards' early version has been effaced; Williams' two saving clauses—particularly the second, which specified that the critique of the aesthetic was to be considered a clearing operation on the way to an eventual reconstruction of it in materialist terms—have been lost.

What, then, of the third line we are tracking—what of the methodologies that were developed as the practical arm of the project of criticism: "close reading" and "practical criticism"? We have seen that they began, in our first period, as methods for the practical training of the aesthetic faculties of readers. We have seen, too, that the early reversal that took place in the philosophical and political orientation of the project of criticism led to a significant change in these methodologies: where once they had been intended as tools for helping us to "better order our minds," as opposed to learning to judge works "good" and "bad," in the second period, they tended instead to become theaters in which to stage the scene of critical judgment. What about the third period? If this period really did begin with an epochal shift from literary-studies-as-criticism-and-scholarship to literary-studies-as-scholarship-alone, has this not led to some fundamental methodological change?

I have two answers to this question, both of them, though in different ways, amounting to a "yes." The first "yes" runs as follows. As we have seen, the new consensus on scholarship has made for a profound change in the orientation of the discipline's reading: a change from reading for the purposes of aesthetic education, in whatever meaning of the term aesthetic we might choose, to reading for the purposes of historical and cultural analysis. In the light of this, it is interesting to note the different fates of the two terms we have been tracking. If the term "practical criticism" has been generally abandoned outside of the exceptional (should I say odd?) enclave of Cambridge, this is presumably at least in part because of the ease with which it can be associated with "criticism" in its now objectionable mid-century sense, as the staging of expert aesthetic judgment. In contrast, the term "close reading," which is easier to dissociate from "criticism" in the old sense, has been retained. Yet just this severing of the association between "close reading" and "criticism" has led to an impoverishing generalization of the former term, which is now usually used simply to designate any reading practice that attempts to derive nontrivial meanings from small units of text. This does much to mask the fact that what early and mid-century critics called "close reading" and what the discipline now calls "close reading" are in many ways quite different practices: broadly speaking, earlier modes of criticism saw "close reading" as a focus on small units of text for the purposes of relating to the text as an aesthetic object, whereas today "close reading" usually means a focus on small units of text for the purposes of understanding what the text has to teach us about histories and cultures. It may help to make the point if we observe, perhaps too schematically, that today close reading is a way to focus one's attention on small units of text, whereas for the early critical paradigm, close reading was a way to use small units of text to focus one's attention. Of course, having said this, one would need to go on to observe also that for the major early critics, aesthetic education meant the cultivation of much more than mere "attention": even a basic account would have to include the cultivation of affect, of self-awareness, psychological insight, capabilities relating to value, and so on. The retaining of the old term to designate a substantially new practice has done much to mask the scale of the shift that inaugurated our period.

Observing this helps us to notice that, of all the interesting moves made in the course of recent debates about "close reading," one of the most useful has been Jonathan Culler's call for the discipline to think more deeply about the range of different reading practices that shelter under the name.[15] The periodization I offer here adds something to this debate by suggesting that, historically, we may want to distinguish between three main types of close reading: the initial form, posited though never fully developed as a tool with which to cultivate readers' aesthetic sensibilities in something approaching a materialist sense; the second form, in which the emphasis passed onto the making of critical judgments about the universal or final aesthetic value of the thing being read; and a third form, where the goal has been to use small units of text as diagnostic tools for the analysis of historical and cultural phenomena, in the absence of any aesthetic considerations whatsoever—or indeed, more often, in implicit opposition to aesthetic considerations. In each case, careful attention is being paid to small units of text, but that is about as far as the similarity goes.

One could make a different point to similar effect by observing that if "close reading" involves focusing on small units of text at least partly in order to practice paying certain kinds of attention, then we need to go on to ask, in each case, what kind of "focus" is being directed onto the text, and therefore what specific kind of "attention" is being practiced. To note just one fairly obvious example, the New Critical version of the method sought to train readers to pay a particular kind of attention to the text as a unified whole in a way that our contemporary historicist/contextualist versions usually do not; the latter sometimes claim to be training us to pay attention to the ideological content of texts in a way that the New Critical practice did not; and so on. One could easily multiply these distinctions. Again, the retaining of a single term for these very different practices masks not only the great variety of methods potentially on offer, but also the real historical changes that have taken place in the discipline in our period, chief among them the shift from a model of literary study that includes both literary scholarship *and* literary criticism to a model that tends to limit literary study to literary scholarship alone.

Taking this next step would allow one to build on the position outlined by some of the defenders of close reading. A good example here would be Jane Gallop, who, in the late 2000s, made an argument for close reading premised on the perceptive observation that the greatest threat to the method over the three decades previous had been the ongoing historicization of literary studies.[16] I cannot help but cheer when she observes, dolefully, that close reading "has been . . . tarred with the elitist brush applied in our rejection of the New Critics' canon, and . . . thrown out with the dirty bathwater of timeless universals." In this connection, it is hard not to endorse her turn to the question of radical pedagogy in the last section of the paper, and her claim that we have chiefly the practice of close reading to thank for the fact that the "literature classroom has represented a real alternative to the banking model" of education, in which the teacher simply deposits knowledge in the mind of the student.

Having acknowledged the perceptiveness and power of all of this, we need then to go further to try to rethink many of the elements of this position, which seems marked in important ways by the institutional forces that are supposed to be under critique. This is where it helps to think the method of close reading through its central relationships with the project of criticism and the category of the aesthetic. Gallop is typical of many recent defenses of close reading in that she shares the foundational third-period assumption that the project of criticism and the category of the aesthetic need to be rejected, but tries nevertheless to defend the method that was their working edge. Yet it is the rejection of the first two that has led to the rejection of the last; one cannot, I think, have "close reading" in any sophisticated form without some version of the others. Thus when Gallop tells us that "my point here is not to argue about the relative merits of historicism and close reading as methods for studying literature; I have no doubt that both produce worthwhile knowledge," it seems telling that the defense of close reading, even against the "historicization" of literary studies, needs now to be made in these specifically scholarly, rather than critical, terms (183). If we accept the production of knowledge as our goal, how are we to have close reading in its capacity as an alternative to the "banking" or knowledge-transfer model of education? Responding that close reading allows the students to produce their own knowledge only gets us halfway there; it strikes me as better to say that close reading is a practice of cultivation—or enculturation, if you like—rather than knowledge production per se, and proceed on that basis.

Similarly, Gallop's argument for the value of close reading is in sympathy with the tendencies she is trying to critique in that it rests on a thorough rejection of any aesthetic justification for literary study. She offers us close reading as a defense and a justification for literary studies, but justifies close reading in turn by appealing to its usefulness as a way of approaching political, historical, and theoretical texts, rather than literary ones. Is it too naive, given our investigation of Williams' cunning critique of the category of the literary, to object that the justification for literary studies surely has to rest, at some stage, on the concept of literature? In saying this, I am not defending the category of the literary in its traditional form. Rather, I am simply observing, at a more basic level, that a discipline needs to be able to justify its object of study, not just its method for studying it. Unless literary studies can do this, then even among those who are convinced of the value of close reading the correct institutional response would, and surely will, be to say that students in law, political science, philosophy, and so forth should simply be taught to read more closely in their own disciplines. One can imagine the kind of ideological reading practices that would result—indeed, one does not have to try very hard to imagine them, since to a certain extent they exist already.

Truly responding to arguments of this kind means going back to ask what we really mean by "close reading," beyond paying careful attention to small units of any kind of text. Our questions then must be of the order: what ranges of capabilities and sensitivities is the reading practice being used to cultivate? What kinds of texts are most suited to cultivating those ranges? Putting the issue naively, it seems to me that the method of close reading cannot serve as a justification for disciplinary literary study until the discipline is able to show that there is something about literary texts that make them especially rewarding training grounds for the kinds of aptitudes the discipline is claiming to train. Here again the rejected category of the aesthetic proves indispensable, for of course literary and other aesthetic texts *are* particularly rich training grounds for all sorts of capabilities and sensitivities: aesthetic capabilities, in the materialist and instrumental sense of aesthetic I have been attempting to gesture toward throughout. I ought perhaps to read into the record, at points like this, how very *merely* gestural these gestures have been; the real task of developing claims of this kind is of course philosophical and methodological rather than historical, and thus has seemed to me to belong to a different book.

In any case, the answer to the broader question is "yes": the scholarly turn that inaugurated the current period of literary studies has indeed led to a profound reorientation of our central methodology, in that "close reading" now functions as a scholarly practice, rather than a critical one. That much for my first "yes"; now for my second. For it might be noted, and fairly, that this account, in which "close reading" becomes quite a new thing in practice, but is nevertheless proudly retained in principle, rather troubles the symmetry of my model of the discipline's history. If the shift to scholarship in this period has really been as important as I claim, then should not "close reading" have gone the way of "practical criticism," "criticism," and the "aesthetic"? The story of the demise of criticism and the aesthetic in our period should lead us to expect that the method that was originally developed as their working edge would also come under critique from the left on the grounds that it is irredeemably compromised by its purported origin in New Criticism, Leavism, and similar, and this in turn should lead to calls for its rejection and replacement by more properly scholarly methods. Why has this not happened? In fact it has happened, though somewhat belatedly. For of course Franco Moretti, one of the most interesting and iconoclastic of contemporary literary scholars, has famously made an argument of just this kind.

Franco Moretti

Moretti's work, like Jameson's, has led to more specific innovations than can easily be named. For present purposes, it is enough to note that Moretti's most famous and challenging argument has been a methodological one: his critique of "close reading" in favor of what he has called "distant reading." In the context of the longer history of the discipline, it is of some interest that this critique and rejection of "close reading" has been made in the name of a more general commitment to reforming the discipline by making it more objective, quantitative, and therefore properly "scientific."

Moretti first made his claim for "distant reading" in the paper "Conjectures on World Literature," which originally appeared in 2000 in the *New Left Review*.[17] There, his argument was that the only way literary studies would be able to cope with the massive increase in jurisdiction, as it were, required by its new commitment to the study of "World Literature" would be to eschew close reading in favor of "distant reading." Moretti starts by posing the problem as follows:

> What does it mean, studying world literature? How do we do it? I work on West European narrative between 1790 and 1930, and I already feel like a charlatan outside of Britain or France. *World* literature? Many people have read more and better than I have, of course, but still, we are talking of hundreds of languages and literatures here. Reading 'more' seems hardly to be the solution. Especially because we've just started rediscovering what Margaret Cohen calls the 'great unread': I work on West European narrative, etc., etc. . . . not really, I work on its canonical fraction, which is not even one per cent of published literature. And again, some people have read more, but the point is that there are thirty thousand nineteenth-century British novels out there, forty, fifty, sixty thousand—no-one really knows, no-one has read them, no one ever will. And then there are French novels, Chinese, Argentinian, American . . . Reading 'more' is always a good thing, but not the solution. (45–46)

The problem is that there are too many texts to read, and Moretti's bold solution is to give up reading and do something else instead. Noting this helps us to see from the outset that the term "distant reading," when it later appears, will prove to be something of a misnomer, since the method it describes is not really reading at all: rather, it is a method that, when it appears elsewhere as the uncontroversial stock-in-trade of many scientific or social-scientific disciplines, is unproblematically labeled things like "data analysis," "data mining" (if using specialized search engines), or similar. But then, if one can say this politely, when we call it by its ordinary name it starts to sound a bit less novel, and a bit less like what many of us feel, if vaguely, that we came to the humanities to do. Once we have noticed this, it becomes interesting to ask why exactly the term "distant reading" has been chosen.

In his new preface to this essay in the *Distant Reading* volume, Moretti claims (or rather, claims without claiming, as it were) that the term arose as an accident or a joke:

> That fatal formula had been a late addition to the paper, where it was initially specified, in an allusion to the basic procedure of quantitative history, by the words 'serial reading'. Then, somehow, 'serial' disappeared, and 'distant' remained. Partly, it was meant as a joke; a moment of relief in a rather relentless argument. But no one seems to have taken it as a joke, and they were probably right. (44)

The phrase arose "somehow"; to the extent that he is willing to speculate about the intentions of its author, he tells us that it was partly meant as a joke, though no one seems to have taken it as such. "They were probably right," he concedes, and yet a suspicion has been raised that Moretti's critics rather lack a sense of humor. In all seriousness, I hope that this unfortunate series of misunderstandings will soon come to an end, and that Moretti will no longer to have cause to complain of our dourness. Certainly this new protestation of innocence is a little difficult to take at face value, in a fresh volume not entitled, for example, "Collected Essays on Method," "Quantitative Literary Studies," or "Serial Reading," but, inevitably, "Distant Reading." Wanting to test this claim that the phrase was (perhaps) just an accident after all, and thus returning to reread the original essay, we find that in fact the "fatal formula" is repeated many times, and at key moments, and indeed that it is provocative in just that mode characteristic of Moretti when he makes arguments that are seriously intended. Without wanting to be aggressive, then, it seems to me that the author's attempts to deflect the question really succeed in giving it a new urgency. What is really at stake in the coining of this phrase "distant reading"? Why decide on it, highlight it, and then keep using it again and again? Why did the phrase catch on so readily? Why then would its author move to disavow it, without really disavowing it? What kinds of interests does the underlying analysis serve?

The phrase seems to be offered as a kind of antonym to "close reading," but as Jonathan Culler has noted, the two terms are not opposites at all, because they do not refer to the same order of thing: the real opposition here is that between data analysis and reading per se.[18] Our question then becomes as to what is gained by framing an argument against reading-in-general as an argument against "close reading" in particular. To find out, let us look closely at Moretti's famous critique of "close reading":

> [T]he trouble with close reading (in all of its incarnations, from the new criticism to deconstruction) is that it necessarily depends on an extremely small canon. This may have become an unconscious and invisible premise by now, but is an iron one nonetheless: you invest so much in individual texts *only if* you think that very few of them really matter. Otherwise, it doesn't make sense. And if you want to look beyond the canon (and of course world literature will do so—it would be absurd if it didn't!) close reading will not do it. It's not designed to do it, it's designed to do the opposite. At bottom, it's a theological exercise—very solemn treatment of very few texts taken very seriously—whereas what we really need is a little pact with the Devil; we know how to read texts, now let's learn how *not* to read them. Distant reading: where distance, let me repeat it, is a *condition of knowledge*. (48)

This phrase "close reading (in all its incarnations, from the new criticism to deconstruction)" certainly sums up the received view of the history of the method. By this stage in our history, I hope it is evident that this received view is quite misleading, since it both misdiagnoses the origin and unduly limits the range of the practice. As we have seen, the method was developed well before the New Critics, for ends that were in important ways opposed to those later pursued by them; and the method continues to be used even today, albeit in a radically different form, by historicist scholars who have little or no relation to either "new criticism" or "deconstruction." So we need to think rather more carefully than this about what "close reading" has been and could be.

But by now all this should be clear enough. What matters more here is that, though Moretti's emphasis rests squarely on the *methodological* insufficiencies of close reading, his argument seems in many respects to be a residual version of what was originally a political one. Moretti tells us, of close reading, that "[a]t bottom, it's a theological exercise—very solemn treatment of very few texts taken very seriously—whereas what we really need is a little pact with the Devil." Once again what we are really talking about here is the New Criticism, and much of the force of the argument derives from our presumed opposition to that old "theological exercise"—an opposition which, as we have seen, has always had a political rather than strictly methodological cast. Here we can observe that much of the persuasiveness of Moretti's argument derives from our residual sense that positions of a New Critical kind are somehow still, in 2000 and then again in 2013, a potential political threat to the discipline, and are thus still worth reacting against. This is a big part of what is gained by framing a critique of reading-in-general as a critique of "close reading" in particular: it gives what is really a turn to a scientistic model of scholarship something of a leftist political valence, as a critique of the old idealisms. If the argument for data analysis is an argument against close reading, and close reading is, "at bottom," New Critical and hence idealist, then data analysis comes to seem the proper materialist method.[19] This kind of move should make us uncomfortable, given the fact that the New Criticism is long dead as a significant force in literary studies, and given also the fact that the particular economic, political, and cultural situation that had once allowed it to function as a significant form of conservatism has long since been replaced by a situation of a very different, and in many ways, quite opposite, kind.

Here we can start to see how much of Moretti's position is actually laid out for us, not by Moretti, but by the system of assumptions that gained ground with the scholarly turn of the late 1970s and early 1980s, and that is now the discipline's paradigmatic mode. For surely it is the discipline's earlier rejection of criticism that enables Moretti to assume that his task is to use literary texts as a route to knowledge about larger social and historical forces, and surely it is the discipline's earlier rejection of the aesthetic that enables Moretti to assume that his task is to deal, not just with the "canonical fraction," but with the whole of the "great unread." The phrase—which, as Moretti notes, was originally Margaret Cohen's—seems to imply that the drawing of aesthetic distinctions automatically involves us in the drawing of class distinctions, and in an elitist way. Both this buried assumption and the assumption that lies beneath Moretti's rejection of close reading as "theological" were, in their day, good political arguments from the left: the critique of idealist aesthetics and the critique of idealist criticism, respectively. It is, I think, characteristic of the contemporary scene in literary studies that these explicitly political arguments appear here only, but precisely, in residual form. It is then worth asking what has happened to these good arguments, and others of their kind; why they are no longer being made in explicit terms, but instead must be left to remain as implications beneath the surface of a debate that seems to concern itself with methodology in some more politically neutral sense; and whether, were they to become explicit, they would still seem politically desirable to us in our very different situation today.

One way to suggest an answer to questions of this kind is to ask: what account of the project and value of literary study is being assumed by thinkers who can write, or read, the following sentences, without a profound sense of disjunction? Close reading, Moretti tells us, is insufficient as a methodology because

> it necessarily depends on an extremely small canon. This may have become an unconscious and invisible premise by now, but is an iron one nonetheless: you invest so much in individual texts *only if* you think that very few of them really matter. Otherwise it doesn't make sense. (48; emphasis in original)

In critique of this, would it not now be *undisciplinary,* as it were, to bring up the example of—reading? Even "having a favorite book"? If we are prepared to think in these kinds of nonprofessionalized terms for a moment, Moretti's claim here starts to seem rather remarkable, for it is obvious enough that people invest a great deal in individual texts all the time, without feeling it at all necessary to claim that those texts are the only ones that "really matter." To say otherwise is to fail to imagine that people may come to literature for reasons other than mastery of the entire literary field. Or rather, to put it more precisely, in saying otherwise here Moretti is proceeding on the basis of an "unconscious and invisible premise" of his own: that the only way in which literature can "matter" for disciplinary purposes is as a total system, which in turn matters as a diagnostic instrument for the analysis of the total system of historical and cultural forces. By this stage in the discipline's history, any other approach just "doesn't make sense."

This is the kind of disciplinary logic that Moretti's work so brilliantly extends. Specifically, it is the logic of the scholarly turn's critique of "criticism" and the "aesthetic"—the critique we saw in Williams—and Moretti extends it by pointing out to us, in effect, that once we have jettisoned both of these on the grounds that they are irredeemably Kantian, idealist, and New Critical, we have little reason to hang on to close reading—or even reading per se—at all. He sees, in a way that many others have not, that criticism, the aesthetic, and close reading must be thought through—and thus must be defended or critiqued—together. The whole project of "quantitative literary studies," as currently constituted, is really founded on this insight: that the three lines of thinking we have been tracing cannot be untangled, and that severing the first two commits us to severing the third. When we read his claim that the study of World Literature will "of course" look beyond the canon, because "it would be absurd if it didn't!" we must, I think, detect the exasperation of a vibrant thinker who has wholeheartedly accepted the scholarly ideal of literary study as a discipline of knowledge production, ideally of a "scientific" kind, but who nevertheless continues to find himself in a discipline which has not yet realized what a truly thoroughgoing commitment to that ideal would entail. It is, if you like, the problem of the little boy in the story of the Emperor's New Clothes: Moretti is the only one who has been willing to point out the "absurdity" of our situation, in which we justify literary study by appealing to standards of scholarship—the production of knowledge, ideally of a scientific kind, about history and culture—but continue to use tools and concepts—close reading, as well as, residually, the aesthetic distinction between the canonical and the noncanonical—that were originally built for the very different task of criticism.

Thus if Moretti's argument against close reading has seemed controversial, it is only because we are not used to seeing anyone so enthusiastically follow to its natural conclusion the central logic that has dictated so much of the last three decades of literary study: the rejection of the project of criticism—aesthetic education for something resembling, in aspiration if not in fact, a general audience—and the embrace of the project of scholarship—the production of cultural and historical knowledge for an audience of specialists. In fact one might be tempted to say that the iconoclasm of Moretti's argument lies precisely in the lack of hesitation with which he commits himself to the current orthodoxy. One cannot but admire this commitment to embracing the full consequences of a position, this refusal to be held back by disciplinary inertia, which is surely here the mark of a genuine thinker at work. Yet, having acknowledged this, we need then to go on to ask whether something rather crucial has not been missed—whether, in fact, the position being committed to is not one designed to respond to a situation very different from our own.

Moretti's seminal work *Graphs, Maps, Trees* (2005) takes as its epigraph the following lines from Robert Musil:

> A man who wants the truth becomes a scientist; a man who wants to give free play to his subjectivity may become a writer; but what should a man do who wants something in between? (1)

In its way, it is a version of the question that the belletrists faced at the start of the twentieth century: the question of how a concern for the literary, in its aesthetic and subjectivity-forming capacity ("free play"), ought to be pursued within the rigorous and scientistic terms of the modern research university. Moretti's answer is "quantitative literary history," and it is an answer that is very much in line with the central logic of literary studies in our period.[20] That answer amounts to a newly scientized version of Williams' answer, Eagleton's answer, Jameson's answer, the answer of so many others on the left: the critique of ideology. Further to the right, the answer given by so many others from the left-liberal mainstream of the discipline, from Greenblatt and Gallagher onward, has been to write literary and cultural history by tracking the embeddedness of texts. In all these cases, the answers offered find their intellectual grounding in the basic character of the historicist/contextualist paradigm: that the task of literary studies is the analysis of culture. Yet it is possible to answer Musil's question rather differently. For instance, we could proceed from our attempt to document the history of subjectivity rigorously and scientifically, and into a more active attempt to develop rigorous and scientific methods for the cultivation of subjectivities. To establish such a project within literary studies, we would need to begin by developing both a philosophical account of how subjectivities come to be cultivated and a rigorous methodology of reading. But then here we are with I. A. Richards, back at the start of our story.

The Breadth and Richness of the Paradigm

These are just five figures—six, if you count my hasty comments on Gallup— and I suppose one could argue that my analysis of them proves little about the discipline at large. Obviously, in some crucial respects, they are quite unrepresentative—four of the six are the proverbial "white men," for instance. Yet I do not think anyone would deny that they have been among the more important figures in literary studies over the last few decades, nor that they have functioned as figureheads for broader tendencies. Others could easily be added. For instance, I have made no mention at all of those new lines of work that are so obviously "scholarly" in character that little more needs to be said. An example here would be the field of "book history" or "bibliography," which has prospered in our period: to point out that the field understands its task as the production of knowledge about culture would be no revelation at all. Or one could add Edward Said, another scholar, deeply influenced by Williams, who served as the inspiration for a crucial tendency of the period. Again, to call Said's work, and the work of those who followed him, part of the dominant paradigm is no revelation, for the central range of work in postcolonial studies has very evidently been conducted in classic historicist/contextualist fashion. In this connection it is worth noting in passing that, toward the end of his career, Said had thought his way around to a position from which it seemed to him best to call explicitly for a "return to philology": the effects of the victory of the scholarly paradigm could hardly be clearer. In any case, I believe the figures we have discussed here provide enough points with which to mark out the rough shape of the current paradigm in a preliminary way.

For the benefit of readers who are unfamiliar with the texture of the paradigm as it extends beyond these figures—or who *are* familiar with it, but might need a gentle reminder simply as to the scale of the consensus it represents—it may be worth providing here a rapid roll call of significant examples. Below I have reproduced a key sentence or two from a series of major works of literary scholarship produced in the last thirty years: sentences that I take to express the character of the larger project. This is odd practice— normally one does not reproduce a long series of quotes without performing at least some analysis of them—but it seems to me a useful way to provide, albeit in a ruthlessly concise way, some sense of the breadth, richness, and ultimate coherence of the paradigm. It helps also as a way of recalling that any functioning intellectual paradigm requires work of a wide range of different kinds: the examples assembled here include many attempts to use the literary as an occasion for writing cultural history more or less directly, of course, but also analyses (often "theories") of particular cultural processes, histories and analyses of more obviously literary or aesthetic phenomena, supporting proposals for new critical vocabularies with which to address specific media, attempts to historicize specific genres—and so on. It is, inevitably, a rich and sophisticated intellectual scene, with interlocking and often opposing projects being carried out at many levels. My point is that behind this complexity, one can discern the shape of a common set of assumptions as to what kind of work the literary disciplines are supposed to perform.

A final note before proceeding: I realize that many readers will be tempted to skip these quotes, or else merely skim them, but if you've stuck with the book this far, I urge you to take the full plunge by really reading them through. My own argument aside, the sentences assembled here provide an index to a small sample of some of the finer scholarly thinking of our period. You will have taken my point, which really is a simple one, once you are able to sense the mass of the common body around which all these differently weighted projects revolve.

> [W]hen we studied women's achievements in radically different genres we found what began to seem a distinctively female literary tradition, a tradition that had been approached and appreciated by many women readers and writers but which no one had yet defined in its entirety. . . . Seeking to understand the anxieties out of which this tradition must have grown, we undertook a close study of the literature produced by women in the nineteenth century. . . .
>
> Sandra M. Gilbert and Susan Gubar, *The Madwoman in the Attic*
> (New Haven: Yale University Press, 1979) xi

> In this study I shall explore some of the ways in which evolutionary theory has been assimilated and resisted by novelists. . . . The book is concerned with Victorian novelists. . . . But evolutionary ideas are even more influential when they become assumptions embedded in our culture than while they are the subject of controversy. . . . That process of naturalisation is the other major topic of my enquiry. . . . Precisely because we live in a culture dominated by evolutionary ideas, it is difficult for us to recognize their imaginative power in our daily readings of the world. We need to do so.
>
> Gillian Beer, *Darwin's Plots*
> (Cambridge: Cambridge University Press, 1983) 2

This book argues that in his sonnets Shakespeare invents a genuinely new poetic subjectivity and that this poetic subjectivity possesses special force in post-Renaissance or post-Humanist literature because it extends by disrupting what until Shakespeare's sonnets is the normative nature of poetic person and poetic persona.

Joel Fineman, *Shakespeare's Perjured Eye: The Invention of Poetic Subjectivity in the Sonnets*
(Berkeley: University of California Press, 1985) 1

As I hope to show, the point of the [Victorian novel] . . . is to confirm the novel-reader in his identity as "liberal subject". . . . I further assume that the traditional novel . . . remains a vital consideration in our culture. . . . The "death of the novel" . . . has really meant the explosion everywhere of the novelistic. . . . To speak of the relation of the Victorian novel to the age of which it was . . . the mass culture, is thus to recognize a central episode in the genealogy of our present.

D. A. Miller, *The Novel and the Police*
(Berkeley: University of California Press, 1988) x

I have made no great discoveries of undeniable links, constructed no new "proofs," or found heretofore lost manuscripts showing the West's indebtedness to medieval Arabic culture. I recount no facts that have been unknown or have remained unadduced by many in previous discussions. I will attempt merely to show why the texts, facts, and discoveries of others have seemed negligible or ignorable to so many Romance literary historians and to sketch out a perspective that would render them significant, that would bring them in from the cold and the oblivion to which they have so long been relegated.

María Rosa Menocal, *The Arabic Role in Medieval Literary History*
(Philadelphia: University of Pennsylvania Press, 1990) xiv

Epistemology of the Closet proposes that many of the major nodes of thought and knowledge in twentieth-century Western culture as a whole are structured—indeed, fractured—by a chronic, now endemic crisis of homo/heterosexual definition, indicatively male, dating from the end of the nineteenth century.

Eve Kosofsky Sedgwick, *Epistemology of the Closet*
(Berkeley: University of California Press, 1990) 1

A study of Chaucerian subjectivity thus seems worth undertaking not only for its own intrinsic interest, and not only in order to recover a past too easily misrepresented . . . but because it can perhaps contribute to understanding of the issues involved in the dialectical process of self-construction per se. And while historical knowledge may be a frail instrument with which to confront the vast economic and social forces that are shaping and misshaping our world, it is not finally to be scorned.

> Lee Patterson, *Chaucer and the Subject of History*
> (Madison: University of Wisconsin Press, 1991) 12

Regardless of their affiliation to the right, left, or centre, groups have fallen back on the idea of cultural nationalism. . . . Against this choice stands another, more difficult option: the theorisation of creolisation, métissage, mestizaje, and hybridity. . . . This book addresses one small area in the grand consequence of this historical conjunction—the stereophonic, bilingual, or bifocal cultural forms originated by, but no longer the exclusive property of, blacks dispersed within the structures of feeling, producing, communicating, and remembering that I have heuristically called the black Atlantic world.

> Paul Gilroy, *The Black Atlantic*
> (London: Verso, 1993) 2–3

While scholars generally agree that the systematic use of copyrights, or signs of authorial ownership, in France and England dates from the eighteenth and nineteenth centuries . . . a nascent consciousness about literary ownership in the sixteenth century has been noted, albeit in rather vague terms. . . . I present here evidence of a sustained effort on the part of vernacular writers to protect their works through lawsuit, the use of privileges, an early form of copyright, and the supervision of their publication and distribution as early as the first decade of the sixteenth century.

> Cynthia J. Brown, *Poets, Patrons, and Printers*
> (Ithaca: Cornell University Press, 1995)

Why care about poetic form and its intricacies, other than in nostalgia for a bygone era of criticism? My purpose in *Formal Charges* is to refresh this interest for criticism today by focusing "an historically formed formalist criticism" on Romantic aesthetics. . . . My argument is that Romanticism's involvement with poetic form . . . participates in central discussions of its historical moment. . . .

Susan J. Wolfson, *Formal Charges: The Shaping of Poetry in British Romanticism* (Stanford: Stanford University Press, 1997) 1, 30

The readings which compose *Family Frames* use the photographic imagetexts that are its subjects to forge a theoretical vocabulary that will allow us to talk about specific elements of family photography. . . . What we need is a language that will allow us to see the coded and conventional nature of family picture—to bring the conventions to the foreground and thus to contest their ideological power. . . . In *Family Frames* . . . I examine the idea of "family" in contemporary discourse and its power to negotiate and mediate some of the traumatic shifts that have shaped post-modern mentalities, and to serve as an alibi for their violence.

Marianne Hirsch, *Family Frames: Photography, Narrative, and Postmemory* (Cambridge: Harvard University Press, 1997) 10, 13

If a single claim stands at the heart of this book, it is that Anglo-American modernism is centrally animated by a tension between an urgent validation of production and an admiration for an object world beyond the manipulations of consciousness. . . .

Douglas Mao, *Solid Objects: Modernism and the Test of Production* (Princeton: Princeton University Press, 1999) 11

As I'll argue, the novel rose less by challenging the esthetic and social hierarchies which had kept it down than by projecting those stratifications onto its own audience. Far from leveling class or gender distinctions . . . the novel has internalized and even reinvented them.

Leah Price, *The Anthology and the Rise of the Novel* (Cambridge: Cambridge University Press, 2000) 7

How could domesticity be key to preserving the diet, rituals, and methods that constituted English culture but also be the abject realm to be disavowed in the name of progress? . . . *Staging Domesticity* isolates such contradictions as they surface in early modern plays so as to make visible the contradictory but powerful identifications they offered to audiences.

> Wendy Wall, *Staging Domesticity: Household Work and English Identity in Early Modern Drama*
> (Cambridge: Cambridge University Press, 2002) 5

Domestic interiors . . . rarely appear in the high-level hierarchies of poetry or prose until later in the eighteenth century, but then dominate nineteenth-century novels and poetry. This book will try to account for the historical and cultural change in the status and use of description. . . .

> Cynthia Wall, *The Prose of Things: Transformations of Description in the Eighteenth Century*
> (Chicago: University of Chicago Press, 2006) 10

Much of this work will undermine the fantasies of cultural exclusivity of both "Shakespeare" and "China," attending to the fact that even though every read-ing is a rewriting, more rewritings of a canonical text do not always translate into more radical rethinking of normative assumptions. It is with this convic-tion that I examine the transnational imaginary of China in Shakespearean performance *and* Shakespeare's place in Chinese cultural history from the first Opium War in 1839 to our times.

> Alexa Huang, *Chinese Shakespeares: Two Centuries of Cultural Exchange*
> (New York: Columbia University Press, 2009)

My basic hypothesis in this book is that both the institution of slavery and the culture of taste were fundamental to the shaping of modern identity, and that they did so not apart but as nonidentical twins, similar yet different.

> Simon Gikandi, *Slavery and the Culture of Taste*
> (Princeton: Princeton University Press, 2011) xii

Why do people stay attached to conventional good-life fantasies—say, of enduring reciprocity in couples, families, political systems, institutions, mar-kets, at work—when the evidence of their instability, fragility, and dear cost abounds? . . . Readers of my national sentimental trilogy—*The Anatomy of National Fantasy, The Female Complaint,* and *The Queen of American Goes to Washington City*—will recognize these questions as central to its investigation of U.S. aesthetics, erotics and politics over the last two centuries. . . . *Cruel*

Optimism expands the concerns of that work transnationally and temporally, extending them to the contemporary moment.

Lauren Berlant, *Cruel Optimism* (Durham, Duke University Press, 2011) 2–3

The problem is precisely that most accounts of the modern claim its European face and disavow these mixed forms, believing that the history of Europe or the West . . . can be written without reference to them. If, however, one can demonstrate that the thought of writers and intellectuals like Diderot and Burke is profoundly formed . . . by reflection upon slavery and conquest, then it ought to be possible to reconfigure the relationship between enlightenment, colonialism, and modernity in a more proximate and productive manner.

Sunil M. Agnani, *Hating Empire Properly: The Two Indies and the Limits of Enlightenment Anticolonialism* (New York: Fordham University Press, 2013) xxi

[T]his book tells a story of the historical accidents and reversals that led Spanish-Americans to imagine themselves not as sovereigns of new nations but as an unexpected and, increasingly, racialized group of peoples within the United States. . . . It traces the circulation of ideas and texts as these relate to the making of Latino intellectual life in the United States. It is a history. . . .

Raúl Coronado, *A World Not to Come: A History of Latino Writing and Print Culture*
(Cambridge: Harvard University Press, 2013) 17

Chapter Four

The Critical Unconscious

KUHN TELLS US that no paradigm can entirely master its field: all are troubled by doubts, provisos, and discontent. Whatever may be the value of this as a general proposition, it certainly has its merits as a way of understanding the last few decades in literary studies. The historicist/contextualist paradigm now dominates the discipline, and has done so for a generation—and yet like all dominant paradigms, it has not been entirely untroubled by a sense that something important may lie beyond its limits. Much good work senses and tests the existing boundaries, even as it fails to secure a breach. If one believes in the political—I am tempted to add "human"—importance of something like the project of criticism, then one wonders a great deal about these forms of dissent, some of which seem more sympathetic than others. The present dominance of the historicist/contextualist paradigm might lead one to predict, pessimistically, that the discipline is simply heading for more of the same—but is there a hidden trajectory? One way to answer this question is to look back on the more recent history of literary studies, trying to assess the extent to which various thinkers' attempts to test the boundaries of the scholarly paradigm might be readable as the first sketches of a fresh critical paradigm to come. Naturally, this is both speculative and performative, risking falling into either prophecy or manifesto—but it seems worth making the attempt in any case. When we look at the discipline's recent history, what can we find that might serve as the seed of a possible future for criticism?

In this chapter, we will take a rapid tour through some of the more interesting new tendencies that have sprung up within the discipline in recent years—tendencies that are by no means "literary critical" in their basic character, but that in the longer historical view seem readable as expressions of frustration with the narrowness of the current paradigm, and perhaps even as implicit attempts to make a break. For convenience, I group these under three headings: Pendulums, Intimations, and Expansions. Under the heading of "Pendulums," I bring together those whose sense of the narrowness of the dominant paradigm has led them to call for the return of the very terms that the historicist/contextualist paradigm traditionally has been most at pains to discredit. I take our period's various "new aestheticisms" and "new formalisms" as emblematic cases, trying to draw clear distinctions between nostalgic calls for a return to the old paradigm and genuine attempts to move forward onto new ground. Under the heading of "Intimations," I bring together those whose dissatisfactions with the dominant paradigm have led them to make proposals for new modes of reading ("surface reading," "reparative reading," and so on), as well as related developments in the study of affect. I suggest that proposals of this kind have implicitly registered the need for a disciplinary project of aesthetic—or at least *affective*—education, though as yet that project, such as it is, is being carried out in an unsystematic and preparadigmatic way. Finally, under the heading of "Expansions" I bring together the many proposals that we have seen over the last thirty years for dramatically expanded contextual frames: the key terms here are of the order "transnational," "global," "deep time," "world literature," "Anthropocene," and so on. These, I suggest, need to be read together in series as a long collective attempt to break out of the narrow confines of contextualism as usual. This breakout attempt might appear merely an effort to extend the reach of the existing paradigm, but if one is willing to understand its underlying motivation as a frustration with field specialization or even scholarly specialization per se, then it comes to seem as if it, too, ought to be read as one of the many means by which the discipline has registered, at quite a deep structural level, the loss of the generalist paradigm of criticism.

I think the history of these three tendencies is quite exciting, but I might as well admit from the outset that it is a somewhat repetitive one. For in this chapter, we will see the same pattern again and again: an incisive thinker encounters a limit in their local sphere that is in fact one of the boundaries of the dominant paradigm, though this goes unrecognized as such.

Frustrated by that limit, the thinker proceeds to critique certain elements of the dominant paradigm—a critique that turns out to be partial, since for historical reasons the paradigm itself is never quite brought fully into view. Being partial, the critique is then regathered fairly completely into the mainstream of scholarly work, though the core of the critique continues to gesture toward something beyond it. That is the pattern, and once one has seen it, or something very like it, recurring across a range of different discourses, one begins to feel that one is really looking at a much broader phenomenon than any account that deals merely with individual instances will be able to keep in view. Thus in what follows, I will be suggesting that many of the more interesting methodological thinkers of recent decades have in fact been working on the same problem, though this has not generally been recognized: the problem being the absence of a paradigm for criticism as such. What we are looking at, I think, is a richly preparadigmatic scene of local innovations, each frustrated by specific elements of the dominant paradigm, but as yet unable to achieve a synthesis that would give expression to all their frustrations in a unitary and thus determinative way. Putting things more positively, one could argue that the new tendencies we see springing into being all around us may turn out to have been the first stirrings of a collective attempt to think a way toward a genuinely alternative paradigm for criticism, if only they were able to recognize themselves as such.

I am not unaware that claims of this kind will strike many as merely tendentious—it may be said that I am taking some of the most influential thinkers in the contemporary scene, baldly asserting that they do not really understand what they are doing, and then reading their proposals as forebodings of a future that may never come to pass. I will have more to say about this at the end of the chapter, but for now let me simply insist that my claim is really not so absurd as all that. As we have seen, for the bulk of the twentieth century there were two paradigms; having lost one of them, it is only to be expected that existing work within the discipline would register the lack. The registering of that lack might well be implicit, rather than explicit, since the thinkers involved have been confronting an unprecedented situation: viewed historically, the lack of a true paradigm for criticism is quite a novel problem for the discipline—a problem that it has not faced since the 1920s. To these somewhat consoling comments, I only want to add that the problem facing the discipline is not an *entirely* new one, for in a broad sense it is much the same problem that the critical revolution of the 1920s managed to solve: the problem of creating a true paradigm for criticism—the problem of how to build an institution that would cultivate new, deeper forms of subjectivity and collectivity in a rigorous and repeatable way. It remains to be seen whether or not the discipline will manage to solve that problem for present purposes, and if so, whether it will manage to solve it in a better manner. I hope so.

As one moves through these various tendencies, tracing local debates, impasses, breakthroughs, and so on, it is easy enough to begin pitting them against each other in one's mind. Which of these new tendencies has proved better? Which of their proposals ought we to believe? And so on. These questions are not bad ones, but for the most part, they have not been mine. Instead, I have tried to assume as often as possible that the frustrations that gave rise to the tendency in question were to a significant extent real and justified, and also that the most interesting proposals made were all worthwhile in their essentials, at least in their own sphere. My guiding questions have therefore been of the order: how might one go about accepting all these new counter-tendencies simultaneously? What would it mean to think through all their best proposals in a single movement, despite how differently their decisive emphases seem to fall? Within that broader line of questioning, the central challenge has been to distinguish sharply between, first, nostalgic proposals for the revival of residual forms of mid-century criticism; second, proposals that implicitly regather potential sources of dissent back into the dominant paradigm; and third, proposals that seem to plant the seeds of what may or may not prove the emergent forms of a radical critical paradigm to come.

These methodological questions are ultimately political ones, and yet as readers will quickly perceive, I do not make the distinction between residual, dominant, and emergent primarily on the basis of the professed politics of the thinkers in question. To put bluntly what will in any case become apparent in the course of what follows, many of those who have been offering exciting methodological propositions also seem to me to be inhabiting political positions of a naively liberal kind, whereas for reasons we have already explored many of the discipline's most impressive figures on the left, whose politics are more sympathetic from my point of view, are also some of the more committed exponents of the dominant paradigm—the paradigm that, in my view, we so urgently need to find a way to move beyond. Here then the distinction between residual, dominant, and emergent cannot be drawn simply on the basis of professed politics, if indeed it ever can. As readers will see, I have instead tended to draw it on the basis of the kinds of positions being adopted in aesthetics, since I take it that the question of the aesthetic is one of the fundamental questions on which one's consequent position with respect to the status and value of the literary depends. Generally speaking, I have taken to be residual those whose proposals have, in effect, been for the return of an older, idealist mode; I have taken to be dominant those who have continued to call for a wholesale rejection of aesthetic discourse, though clearly there are also newly emergent scholarly forms that operate in this vein; and lastly, more speculatively, I have taken to be emergent those who have sought to lay the groundwork for a newly materialist conception of the aesthetic value of the literary, particularly those for whom, however distantly, some project of criticism proper seems on the horizon.

This leads me to a final proviso, though I hope an unnecessary one. As in previous chapters, my method will be to avoid mere lists of names wherever possible, and instead to direct attention toward specific figures as means by which to take the temperature of the broader tendencies in question. Given this, and given also that I am writing here of what is still in many ways the contemporary critical scene, it is perhaps worth repeating once again that my aim is neither to conduct a comprehensive taxonomy of recent work, nor to assemble some sort of honor roll of the best and brightest, whatever that would mean. Though obviously all the figures here are of considerable interest, I make no claims as to their being representative of the most exciting work in the discipline: indeed, I take it that much of the best work in our period is still being carried out in the mainstream of the dominant paradigm, just as one would expect. Nor am I claiming that these are the only recent tendencies that can fairly be thought of as running counter to the main current. Rather, I have selected these particular tendencies, and these particular figures within those tendencies, because they offer a convenient range of reference points with which to mark out the shape of what I take to be a certain important kind of dissent in our period: a series of disconnected points of tension or frustration with the current paradigm, which only connect up into a coherent picture at the moment at which one is able to hold a rough sketch of a newly emergent paradigm in view.

Part One: Pendulums

As we have seen, our current historicist/contextualist paradigm was launched in part by a sweeping critique of the category of the aesthetic. Thus it is not perhaps so surprising to find that the earliest signs of what one could, thinking in hope, call the first seeds of a new, more radical critical paradigm were calls for the rehabilitation of the aesthetic on other terms. The earliest forms of something that called itself a "new aestheticism" in this sense were launched in Britain in the early 1990s, but subsequently there were many others: by the mid-1990s there was a cluster of field-spanning work going on under the same name in the USA; there were also self-described "new aestheticisms" among specific historicist specialists such as early modernists, Victorianists, and Americanists; and there were, in addition, many other uses of the phrase that do not fit easily into any of these categories, such as Rei Terada's early proposal for a "new aestheticism" that would offer a kind of defense of deconstruction against its detractors.[1] Naturally some of these clusters of work were richer than others. To my mind, the early constellation in Britain remains the most interesting, none of the subsequent groups yet having outshone it in terms of the clarity with which it was able to survey, and then respond to, the surrounding disciplinary terrain. Some of the more important sites for this early British "new aestheticism" included a largely Cambridge-based attempt to revive an advanced Kantian aesthetics; a separate debate, as interesting for its confusions as for what it illuminated, that began in the pages of the New Left Review and centered around the idea of a return to Adorno; and—to my mind the most interesting—the work of Isobel Armstrong. The fact that all these clusters of work ended up adopting the same title might lead us to conclude that we are looking at a single turn or movement, but this would be a mistake: for the most part they were developed locally, often without the benefit of any very clear sense of what others were doing under the same name in other places, and though a common mood is certainly discernable, the actual proposals made differ in their implications. It therefore seems best to consider the "new aestheticisms" of the 1990s as a fairly heterogeneous series of largely independent local clusters that offered simultaneous, sometimes parallel responses to the anti-aesthetic tenor of the dominant paradigm.

Roughly around the turn of the millennium there was a consolidation of "new aestheticist" work accompanied by a shift in terminology: reading back through the 2000s one finds first that the local clusters of work are increasingly aware of one another, the landmark edited collections having been published and read, and second that the term "new aestheticism" attracts fewer and fewer adherents, to be replaced in effect by "new formalism," though in a broad sense quite similar arguments continued to be offered under both headings, and indeed many of the same figures continued to be claimed. Stepping back to survey the development of the whole tendency, then, it seems best to treat the names "new aestheticism" and "new formalism" as the two ends of a single timeline. I do so with some misgivings, not because some of today's "new formalists" seem quite innocent of any familiarity with the earlier work—that seems simply an error—but because by tracing the history in a single line I risk repeating one of the confusions I will be at pains to point out in what follows: the easy slide from "aesthetic" to "formal" that, as I see it, has done so much to conceal the real stakes of the debate from many of those involved in it, and has thereby become the cause of some of the specific confusions that underpin much prominent work performed in this vein today.

New Aestheticisms

But to begin with the "new aestheticisms." For the most part, the thinkers who united under the various new aestheticist banners of the 1990s were those who had noticed at least something of the scale of the transformation that had occurred within the discipline as a result of the widespread rejection of the category of the aesthetic through the 1980s, and who felt that something important was now missing as a result. Just what that missing "something" was varied from account to account. Some accounts principally emphasized how much had been lost when the discipline became unwilling to make disciplined judgments as to the aesthetic value of specific literary texts: often the argument was that, since aesthetic judgments of one kind or another were inevitable in any case, our new unwillingness to make them in an explicit way simply left us having to make them implicitly instead. This was unfortunate, it was felt, because it often meant quietly endorsing the most traditional of canons while rendering our principles of judgment unavailable for critique. Other accounts chiefly missed the aesthetic in its capacity as a means by which to distinguish the literary from the nonliterary: here it was argued that in the absence of a way to define literariness *per se,* we were left treating works of literature simply as yet further instances of the unreasonably broad category "texts in general," which made it impossible to acknowledge the specificity of literary texts. Still other accounts argued that, without a commitment to the aesthetic, the discipline had become stuck in a suspicious and diagnostic mode of reading that was enabling for ideology critique but crippling for any serious attempt to cultivate a positive relation to the aesthetic pleasures of the text (an argument that would echo again and again over the next two decades, with or without the initial emphasis on the loss of the aesthetic per se). There were times when these three arguments were made independently of one another, but for the most part the core new aestheticist work of this period made them in combination, with varying emphases. In any case, those who identified with the new aestheticism felt that we needed the aesthetic back, and the question was as to the terms on which we might now be able to have it.

As we have seen, there was certainly something quite accurate about the map of the discipline on which such arguments were plotted. It was indeed true to say that there had been a critique of the category of the aesthetic so sweeping that it had led many of the key figures in the discipline to reject the category outright. It was also true to observe that this critique of the aesthetic had been at the root of a large-scale shift in the basic orientation of the discipline. Moreover, this shift had indeed been of such a kind as to make the specific operations that the new aestheticists missed much more difficult to justify in principle, as well as more difficult to perform in practice: by the 1990s, the mainstream of the discipline no longer possessed a paradigmatic method for making explicit and disciplined aesthetic judgments, nor a paradigmatic method for specifying the boundaries of the literary, nor a paradigmatic method for cultivating a positive relationship to the pleasures of the text. By this stage, the historicist/contextualist critique of the aesthetic had made projects of that kind look regressive in principle, at least to many—and even those who were not yet quite convinced by the principle in its strictest form were tending to pursue other projects, since the questions thought most exciting were simply of other kinds. To that extent, one can say that the new aestheticism began with the benefit of an unusually clear sense of the surrounding disciplinary terrain.[2]

One must then go on to add that there were important levels at which the new aestheticist tendency, taken as a whole, evidently found it difficult to recognize the full shape of the situation to which it was responding. For of course it was not simply the category of the aesthetic that had been rejected—the category of the aesthetic together with generally accepted methods for making aesthetic judgments, for defining literariness, and for encountering textual pleasures—but a whole paradigm for criticism: a paradigm that, for all its many flaws, had once offered a unified way simultaneously to pursue each of these projects, together with others, as part of a single, relatively coherent intellectual practice. As we have seen, it was in fact a whole synthesis, a whole integrated method by which to approach problems of this order, that had been discredited. The best observers were able to discern something like this even without the benefit of hindsight; still in the thick of the events themselves, the tendency as a whole did not. It is this underestimation of the size of the target that explains, in part, the evident failure of the new aestheticist critique ultimately to find its mark. For the result was that the tendency as a whole was quite unclear not only about what it was attacking—which, from a certain angle, ought to have been the triumph of literary scholarship per se—but also about what it was seeking to defend: implicitly, the practice of literary criticism itself. Without recognizing that they were really involved in a defense of criticism per se, the thinkers involved were often unable fully to register the real force of the left critique that had discredited criticism in its mid-century modes. For this reason, and also simply because the tendency arrived as early as it did, the genuinely "new" elements of the "new aestheticism" are sometimes hard to distinguish from residual defenses of the old paradigm—defenses that crumbled quickly under the existing critique. They were then unable to drag the mass of the discipline any significant distance in their direction.

This is despite the fact that all the major proponents were at pains to distinguish their own proposals from, in the words of John. J Joughin and Simon Malpas, "a case for a return to the notion of art as a universally and apolitically humanist activity presided over by a benign council of critical patriarchs" (3).[3] Joughin and Malpas were much more perceptive than most about the history with which they were engaging, but I am afraid the exaggeration of the terms here is not atypical, and perhaps suggests how little was really being disavowed. For in fact what happened so often was that the insistence that one was sympathetic *both* to the category of the aesthetic *and* to the dominant historicist/contextualist critique of it led to a certain amount of confusion, which in turn led to an effective return, as if by habit, to an older set of terms. Thus, for example, when George Levine wrote the introduction to *Aesthetics and Ideology* (1994), a collection that many would later see as having planted the flag for certain liberal strand of new aestheticism in the United States—and a collection that would later go on to be claimed by the "New Formalists," as well—he of course began by offering the usual demurrals: he was not in the business of talking about "transcendental or universal value," he was not going deny that the aesthetic was "historically bound to ideology," and so on. He then moved to propose a new commitment to the aesthetic: one that would not fall prey to the existing antiaesthetic critique. Yet his positive account of the aesthetic was as follows:

> The aesthetic remains a rare if not unique place for *almost* free play, a place where the very real connections with the political and the ideological are *at least partly* short circuited. . . . The aesthetic is a realm where *something like* disinterest and impersonality are possible. . . . [T]he aesthetic provides a space where the *immediate* pressures of ethical and political decisions are *deferred*. (17; my italics)

"Almost," "at least partly," "something like," "deferred": in cases of this kind, it is quite difficult for even a sympathetic observer to say that new claims are being made for the aesthetic, for this sounds very much like a reassertion of the *old* claims, albeit in more modest terms. Once one had accepted the existing critique of idealist aesthetics, one needed to be given something quite new if one was to accept the aesthetic at all. Were arguments of this kind offering us a new, more acceptable model of the aesthetic, or were they simply restating the old idealisms in a chastened tone?

It is perhaps tempting to conclude the latter, but in regard to the new aestheticist tendency as a whole, that would be too quick and too harsh: it is more accurate, and certainly more generous, to say that the question is not finally answerable, at least when asked at this more general level. For dissent of this kind was spoken from the margins of the dominant paradigm by many quite different voices, and underlying conditions were not yet such that the incipient collective, taken as a whole, was able to make sharp distinctions between residual arguments and emergent ones. Yet having acknowledged the ambivalence of the formation on this central point, it is important also to observe that one of the immediate effects of the collective uncertainty was the flourishing of a range of reinstated idealisms, more or less continuous with rearguard defenses of the old paradigm: renewed critiques of the "politiciza-tion" of what ought to be an autonomous aesthetic sphere, renewed commit-ments to an autotelic model of the aesthetic—in the worst cases, simply a renewed faith in the transcendental power of the phrase "for its own sake." With a few crucial exceptions, to which we will come shortly, the liberal camp achieved this by calling for a return to Kant, and a smaller camp on the left echoed them by calling for a return to Kant via Adorno, on the principle that Kantian aesthetics was neither bourgeois nor liberal when proposed by Marxists. It was rare to come across a new aestheticist argument with a strong sense that it might be desirable or even possible to argue for the aesthetic in other than autonomous terms, and rarer still to come across arguments which recognized that the critical wing of the discipline had been founded on an aesthetics of that order to begin with. It is when reflecting on moments of this kind that it seems particularly regrettable that William's "saving clauses" had been forgotten: one imagines that it could have been quite clarifying— particularly for those on the left, who were instead turning to Adorno—if, at such a moment, the anti-aesthetic position to which the new aestheticists were responding could have been seen as a clearing operation designed to sweep the field clear of idealist aesthetics so as to make way for an eventual reconstruction of the category in materialist terms.

But the left were in the minority here, which is to say that any genuine assessment of the mainstream of new aestheticist work must be quite clear about its strongly liberal character. A moment ago, I noted that there were three related arguments that recurred again and again in new aestheticist work, but when one restricts oneself to discussing the liberal core of the tendency, those three arguments tend eventually to reduce to one: that the politicization of literary studies from the left had gone too far. Rereading the liberal new aestheticist work today, one hears this so often that it begins to sound like a refrain. Generally, it is intoned in a measured way, as a princi-pled statement of a traditional liberal doctrine, but occasionally the tone lapses and one can just make out a deeper chord of "It's political correctness gone mad!" Levine:

> While I am obviously not entirely enamored of the developments I have out-lined, my objections are to reductivism and simplification, not to the broad tendencies. As with most of the colleagues I respect, my "anti's" are impecca-ble: I am anti-foundationalist, anti-essentialist, anti-universalist, and I do not believe in the possibility of that view from nowhere that gets one beyond contingency. I welcome the new historicism, in lower case, as well as the rec-ognition that all literature needs to be understood in relation to the local and the time-bound; and I am as comfortable as one can be with the necessarily uncomfortable inevitability of diversity and undecidability, whose absence in criticism always leaves me a bit nervous. (2)

This is of some historical interest as a concise summary of one expected lib-eral position as it stood in the 1990s, right down to the expected range of affect. The central note is the importance of "critical thinking" in every-thing, particularly regarding large claims (thus "contingency," "local," "time-bound," "necessarily uncomfortable," "diversity," "undecidability," "nervous"); there is also a slight undertone of resentment at having the necessity of politics forced upon one from outside ("my 'anti's' are impec-cable"). Notable in its absence is any positive commitment to the political per se, which in fact quickly turns out to be the enemy. These are the lines immediately following:

> My uneasiness with the current critical scene is that whereas critics like Fredric Jameson, Edward Said, Stephen Greenblatt, and Eve Kosofsky Sedgwick (not to mention several of the contributors to this volume) have wonderfully enriched the possibilities of literary criticism, their sensitive and complex relation to texts and strong conviction that those texts have enormous cultural significance often, in their followers, reduce critical practice to exercises in political position-ing. In the current critical scene, literature is all too often demeaned, the aes-thetic experience denigrated or reduced to mystified ideology. (2–3)

Like the insistence in the previous paragraph that the objection is to "reductivism and simplification, not to the broad tendencies," the phrase "in their followers" here shirks the burden that the argument claims to carry elsewhere. Indeed, without wanting to be cruel, it is perhaps not unfair to point out that the equivocation as to the target of the critique breaks the grammar: is it really Jameson and company's "sensitivity" and "conviction" that "reduce critical practice to exercises in political positioning" in their followers? Surely what one wants to say is that Jameson and company's "sensitivity" and "conviction" *distinguish* them from their followers, the claim being that it is precisely the followers' *lack* of these two things that condemns them to a critical practice consisting of nothing more substantial than "political positioning." Framed in that way, it would be a modest claim, acceptable to anyone who believes that political convictions are things that happen to people who are missing a liberal appreciation of ambivalence and a proper deference to the text, and it would also allow one to critique politicization while avoiding having to argue against its big thinkers. But instead the grammar gets confused and says something else, because behind the writing there is the strong feeling that Jameson and company are the agents of the reduction after all. They thus stand accused without having to be confronted, and the performance of even-handedness fails to conceal the aggression on which it is based.

The real argument in new aestheticist work of this kind is not against wayward epigones, but against the anti-aesthetic tenor of the whole paradigm, and the claim made most often, and most forcefully, is the old liberal one that in allowing the bulwark of idealist aesthetics to be breached, we are abandoning the literary to the political, from which it ought to be saved. Levine here is unusually direct, but the general form of argument is typical. Winfried Fluck offered the same argument in more sophisticated form in his claim that the Marxist "politicization of aesthetics" had now gone so far that it could only result in an equal and opposite "aestheticization of politics." When one recalls the phrase from Benjamin being borrowed, one sees the political valence of the argument, amounting to the traditional centrist fantasy that extremes meet, and that Communism and Fascism are the same.[4] To take another example, Emory Elliott, in his introduction to another of the new aestheticism's landmark edited collections, *Aesthetics in a Multicultural Age* (2002), sought to distinguish his own position from that of conservative "culture warriors" who championed a "mainly white, male Euro-American canon" by stating that "[s]uch emotionally charged issues in which conflicts of identity and culture are inscribed do tend to produce extremism of the right and left and silence among those who seek to negotiate the unstable middle ground" (10). To distinguish oneself from conservatives, it seemed one needed also to distinguish oneself from the left, the performance of even-handedness once again being the thing. All this rough talk of politics had silenced the center, we were being told, and it was now time to allow those who had been silenced—those liberal experts in "negotiation" and "instability"—to stand up and be heard.

Some readers will think I am being overly harsh on this, and that may be: for the most part, this is an older form of liberalism, long since supplanted by updated modes. Yet muddled arguments from the center against a perceived over-politicization of literary studies really do deserve fairly stern critique wherever they appear, and I am afraid this is all the more true when they are made in an amiable form. For there is much at stake here, particularly for those of us on the left who also feel that we need something like the aesthetic, but are fundamentally opposed to the political register in which it is here being thought. When Levine writes of the "necessarily uncomfortable inevitability of diversity," it is perhaps easy for some to slide by, nodding— but *is* the prospect of "diversity" really "necessarily uncomfortable"? To whom? Why, in 1994, does diversity feel "inevitable" to someone in this subject-position—with all the dark foreboding that the word "inevitable" implies? One can perhaps bend over backward to excuse the phrase by saying that it is simply a case of a conventional liberal rhetoric of "critical thinking" (comfort-with-discomfort, and so forth) getting confused with a conventional liberal rhetoric of support for "diversity"—but really here, speaking plainly, the more disturbing tones of the underlying sensibility are starting to show through: a sensibility to which equality itself has something of the taste of a necessary evil. It is this underlying sensibility that the rhetorics of critical thinking and diversity, properly executed, are usually able to manage and conceal. I note that critiques offered at the level of sensibility are sometimes read as *ad hominem* attacks, and I certainly do not offer mine in that sense—Levine was larger than this as a scholar, and no doubt as a person, too—but if we are to understand the core of the new aestheticism as a phenomenon, then the sensibility in question, as it extends across the median range of new aestheticist work, needs to be seen for what it is. For what we are looking at is, in the main, an aging centrist formation in the process of discovering that the left has gone too far and arguing on that basis for a conservative backlash. In Chapter 2, I noted that the initial critique of the aesthetic offered by Williams had swept the field clear of aesthetic idealisms without finding a way to occupy the territory so cleared; here it is tempting to conclude the metaphor by observing that if a field so cleared is not soon occupied, the flowers native to capital will soon spring up once again. But perhaps that appears too cruel.

Not all the independent clusters of work that adopted "New Aestheticism" as a title were of this political cast, though some of the more explicitly leftist formations were situated outside literary studies. It is worth taking a brief detour to take a look at one of the more progressive strands, which clarifies by contrast. Both sides of the "Philistine Controversy" that began in the *New Left Review* and continued in *The Philistine Controversy* (2002) and in *The New Aestheticism* (2003) understood themselves in broadly Marxist terms, though the central new aestheticist proposal for a return to autonomy in a fairly traditional Kantian sense was, at a minimum, quite difficult to square with historical materialism at large. For our purposes it is perhaps most illuminating to focus on the other side of the debate—the self-declared "philistines"—since they were also proposing a return to the aesthetic, though in what they understood as more acceptably materialist terms. Dave Beech and John Roberts saw this other "new aestheticist" position as backsliding, and were not afraid to say so: one thinks, for instance, of their use of the subtle phrase "Liberal Delusions" as a section heading (35). Responding to what they saw as regression, they wrote quite powerfully of the importance of honoring to its full extent the existing left critique of the aesthetic:

> It is a political achievement that the grand humanist categories and canonic distinctions of dominant culture have been fractured according to the specificities and fault-lines of class, race, gender, and sexuality. It is a political and cultural achievement that art has been 'secularized' through the liberation of the 'meanings of the dominated' across a range of subject positions and social locations. And it is the diminishment of this achievement that we want to repudiate. (32)

Yet their position was by no means a simple reaffirmation of the existing critique of the aesthetic: for Beech and Roberts, the left's victory over the old idealist aesthetics was a "political achievement" that needed to be defended, but it was also a mistake that needed to be moved beyond. In the last analysis, the aesthetic needed to be, not rejected, but rethought. Thus they wrote regretfully of "a period in which the Left's attitude to aesthetics has not been of simple neglect but of aggressive suspicion and denunciation," and they rejected the move to transform any "discussion of aesthetics into a discussion of ideology" that they felt had been the knee-jerk response of the left since the "nineteen-seventies and early nineteen-eighties" (16).

In this the "philistines" were at one with the "new aestheticists" who were the object of their critique. For both sides of the philistine controversy, the question was as to how we might rethink the aesthetic without giving up on our commitment to the original anti-aesthetic critique; for both sides, the answer to this question lay in a recommitment to the doctrine of aesthetic autonomy; and both sides also concurred, more or less, in feeling that this return to a seemingly idealist language could be authorized by appeal to the authority of Adorno. The difference was that they read Adorno's idea of aesthetic autonomy in quite different ways. Beech and Roberts felt that the left could return to a doctrine of aesthetic autonomy as long as it realized that "the separation of the social from the aesthetic is not necessary for the maintenance of art's autonomy" (35). If you suspect this argument of emptying the concept of aesthetic autonomy of much of its meaning, you have my sympathies, but of course this is not the place to try to adjudicate these claims.[5] For our purposes, the chief importance of the "philistine controversy" is as an example of the kind of thinking that was, in principle, available to the left of the discipline at this moment. For even given all its faults, the controversy represented a very rare thing: an explicitly Marxist attempt to argue out a new and positive conception of the aesthetic without giving up any of the ground won by the left's existing anti-aesthetic critique. Sadly it was largely a debate in art history and in philosophy, especially in its initial moments; despite the presence of a number of insightful literary thinkers in Joughin and Malpas' subsequent volume *The New Aestheticism* (2003), this particular cluster of attempts to rethink aesthetic autonomy in less obviously Kantian terms was ultimately to make relatively few inroads into the field of literary studies. For the left of the discipline, it still stands as one marker of a road not taken. There are other markers pointing to that road, as we shall see.

New Formalisms

Returning for now to the liberal mainstream of the tendency, one misses Beech and Roberts' commitment to honoring the full force of the existing anti-aesthetic critique. For as the timeline continues, a certain haziness as to the terms of the initial anti-aesthetic position against which the argument is ostensibly being posed becomes increasingly common, as does a confusion between "aesthetics" and "form"—a confusion that eventually leads to the replacement of the former by the latter, and thus to the loss of the tendency's initial clarity regarding the contours of the disciplinary situation it was seeking to change. For as one reads forward toward today's "new formalisms," one repeatedly witnesses thinkers proclaiming a break while in fact either effectively calling for a return of the residual order or merely reiterating the terms of the dominant paradigm.

Here we come to the "Pendulums" of my heading, for a typical pattern here seems to be that one begins by recalling, as if it were simply a matter of common knowledge, that intellectual trends swing back and forth like a pendulum, and one then relies on this as an implicit justification for a call to return to an older set of terms. Thus Levine, at a very early point in the timeline:

> I believe that the most important thing this book can do, in forcing reconceptualization of the aesthetic, is push the pendulum back toward the formal elements that have for so long been denigrated as literary intellectuals complete their reaction to the excesses of the New criticism. . . . In effect, the book is a plea for a new kind of formalism. . . . (23)[6]

We will return to the "new . . . formalism" implied here. For now, my point is that centrists seem to gravitate to pendulums: the trope allows one to feel that in the long run every objectionable extremism will find its antithesis, thus revealing history as a series of oscillations around a common-sense middle ground. To a centrist backed into a corner, though, a pendulum is not quite so comforting: in the lines just quoted, it does seem that history is on our side, the pendulum having swung too far to one extreme, yet at the same time it seems as if history is against us, since we have to "force" the pendulum back into its natural state; this makes us feel small to the point of

being Lilliputian ("push the pendulum") and even abject, despairing, or vic-
timized ("plea").

As the years pass, and the "aesthetic" drops away to be replaced by "form,"
that pendulum returns again and again, though its tenor changes. Thus
Timothy Peltason in 1999: "no one is calling just now for a new formalism,
but the pendulum logic of the profession will likely lead to that, too." Or
Paul J. Alpers in 2007: "With the advent of the new historicism, the pendulum of criticism swung from form to context. There are many signs that
it is now swinging back. . . ." Or Stephen Cohen, also in 2007, offering a
fresh take on the trope: "[historical formalism ought to reinvigorate] New
Historicism as a source of theoretical innovation . . . by engaging it with the
period's formal complexity, and in so doing, to arrest the form-history pendulum by producing a historically and ideologically sensitive formalism."[7]
The latter in particular reveals something about the fantasy that the trope
underwrites: perhaps what one really wants to do is stop history in the
center, so that no further extremisms can be produced. In any case, Rachel
Sagner Buurma and Laura Heffernan caught the right trope when they
observed, in 2013, that "[t]hose who label these new methods formalist
understand their arrival as a swing of the disciplinary pendulum back to the
text after decades of hegemonic historicism and its supposedly strongest
expression, ideology critique."[8]

I point out this rhythmic recurrence not in order to criticize those indi-
viduals who happen to make use of the trope, but in order to make a broader
point, which is perhaps in any case already obvious to most observers: that
part of the appeal of the "new aestheticist" and "new formalist" positions,
such as it is, has been derived from an assumption that the discipline proceeds in a pendular fashion, meaning that one should expect the eventual
return of whatever term one feels is now being rejected most strongly. For
Levine, calling for both a "new aestheticism" and a "new kind of formalism"
at the start of the timeline, the trope seems natural but uncomfortable: the
ambivalent affect reveals the difficulty of his position, still in close proximity
to those who are able to make the left critique of the aesthetic in its strongest
early form. But by the end of the timeline the terms of the initial anti-
aesthetic critique have been either blunted or forgotten, and in any case the
controversial proposal for a return to the aesthetic has been abandoned, the
much more generally acceptable term "form" being adopted instead. It is at

this point that we begin to see the trope being used with confidence, by those who feel that the pendulum is now swinging their way.

Am I taking this trope too seriously? Is it worth pointing out, in response to it, that history never moves like a pendulum—that in the hundred years of its history the discipline has never yet moved like a pendulum—and then wondering what is at stake in this repeated recourse to the assumption that it does? The appearance of a pendulum as a metaphor for the movement of history is almost always a sign that the dialectic is being misread; I take it that its presence here is also an indication of a conceptual impasse: one wants to go forward, but one does not yet know how to do so, except by going back. For the call to a pendular return is typical of this whole line of work, and not just of its more nostalgic elements, the difference between the "new aestheticist" and the "new formalist" ends of the timeline residing mainly in their answers to the question of what, precisely, the discipline has lost, and what therefore will inevitably make its way back. For the early "new aestheticisms," this was the "aesthetic"; for today's "new formalisms," it is "attention to form." This shift of terms ought to tell us something about the "new formalism," its mode of argument and its motivations for arguing being otherwise so similar to those of its predecessor.

To determine what really motivated this slide to "form," the best place to start is Marjorie Levinson's survey of "new formalisms"—a survey that has now become a standard reference point for anyone discussing the tendency. Levinson distinguished between two different camps within the new formalism: one nostalgic and conservative, and the other innovative and progressive. She figured both as calls for the return of earlier modes. The first camp—that of "normative formalism"—was:

> campaign[ing] to bring back a sharp demarcation between history and art, discourse and literature, with form (regarded as the condition of aesthetic experience as traced to Kant—i.e. disinterested, autotelic, playful, pleasurable, consensus-generating and therefore both individually liberating and conducive to affective social cohesion) the prerogative of art. (122)

Levinson dismissed arguments of this kind as "backlash formalism," and, reading through the work, one can certainly see what she means: much of what has been done under the sign of the "new formalism" has indeed amounted to a nostalgic attempt to reinstate an idealist model of the aesthetic as the philosophical foundation of the discipline, as we saw in Levine.

I hasten to add that some of this work has been very fine indeed. Angela Leighton's *On Form* (2007) offers us a good test case here in being both typical of this strand in its commitments and exceptional in the brilliance of its execution. The book begins by tracking the various uses of the word "form," and proceeds to rich and nuanced readings of individual figures. The mode is recognizably that of a certain strand of liberalism—one wants to call it a local Cambridge liberalism, but perhaps that is going too far—the intense reasonableness of which makes it very effective when puncturing the inflated claims of charismatic and unreasonable figures such as Wilde and Pound. Here all extreme claims find themselves tempered, Leighton's fine irony pulling them back to a common-sense middle ground. The effect of this mode is to make her look very reasonable even when she is in fact making the most regressive claims. The book's individual readings are exceptionally acute and beautiful; she has a wonderful ear for tone, and is certainly a much clearer (and funnier) writer than Isobel Armstrong, whose praises I am about to sing, and yet the result, in the end, is a collapse back into an older position: she closes with a retreat into an aesthetic mysticism of all too familiar a kind, from which the only positive claims that can be made are gnomic ones: "the wise nothings of poetry," and so forth (265). The final chapter is entitled "Nothing." Certainly sage and arcane things can be said on the theme of nothing, and Leighton's meditation is rich and interesting—in many ways it represents this line of thought in its strongest contemporary form. Yet at the same time it is hard not to feel that, in this circle back to idealist aesthetics, something of a dead end has been reached.

Levinson's diagnosis of the character of the second camp was no less accurate. Following Susan Wolfson, she named it—flatteringly—"activist formalism." She saw this as the camp of those who sought:

> to restore to today's reductive reinscription of historical reading its original focus on form (traced by those critics to sources foundational for materialist critique—e.g. Hegel, Marx, Freud, Adorno, Althusser, Jameson). (122)

This she hailed as a return to the "formalist" roots of real historicism. Levinson here is trying to draw a clear distinction between the residual and the emergent, which I take to be a very important task. She performs that task in the historicist/contextualist spirit: she wants to reject any talk of a return to idealist aesthetics so as to prevent backsliding into mid-century modes, and she wants instead to endorse calls for better "historical reading." We should note in passing the period assumption that "historical reading," done correctly, is politically salutary as such.[9] Her categorization of the two camps within the "new formalist" tendency seems to me quite accurate in its essentials, and she is of course right in her rejection of positions that effectively call for the return of aesthetic idealism. I only want to add that when one reads this in the context of the longer history we have been tracing, one sees that the distinction being drawn is between those calling for a return to the aesthetic idealisms of the mid-century, and those calling for a recommitment to the basic priorities of the historicist/contextualist paradigm in its best or "original" mode.[10] If she is right, then the choice the "new formalisms" offer us is a choice between a return to the residual and a return to the best existing forms of the dominant. The emergent is nowhere to be found.

To accept this would not be to deny the richness and perceptiveness of the best "new formalist" work—it would merely be to restrict the "new" of the title to a much more modest compass. Still, it would be a fairly dispiriting conclusion. In our efforts to find the truly emergent here, I think perhaps it is better to turn Levinson's diagnosis around, as it were, in order to find the positive elements even of the work she sees as regressive, without of course losing the force of her existing critique of idealist aesthetics, which I take to be quite right. For in our terms it begins to seem as if what Levinson is really attempting is to cut away the new aestheticisms from the new formalisms, the better to celebrate the historicist potential of the latter. But this is problematic, since as we just noted the earlier new aestheticisms, for all their faults, had at least the virtue of being based on a substantially correct diagnosis of the state of the field: the "aesthetic" *had* been rejected very widely, and this had indeed led to consequences of just the kind that the new aestheticists identified. It is at this level that one can say that the tendency as a whole began its journey with quite an accurate map of the surrounding disciplinary terrain. Yet as the difficult term "aesthetic" was committed to less and less frequently, to be replaced more and more often (though never entirely) by the much more widely acceptable term "form," this map became increasingly blurred. Once one has seen this, it starts to look unwise to endorse the later end of the timeline at the expense of the earlier work.

We see this more clearly when we examine the claims that the "new formalist" end of the timeline has tended to make about its place in the history of the discipline. In the kind of "new formalist" work that Levinson endorses, the disciplinary-historical argument is generally as follows: "formalism" has been the discipline's great enemy over the last two-to-four decades; this rejection of "formalism" has been good in that it has allowed us to become more attentive to history, but bad in that it has led us to be culpably inattentive to form; we therefore need to bring form back, so as to be attentive to both history *and* form, at the same time. Yet what does "formalism" here really mean? Generally speaking, the new formalists Levinson endorses have used the term "formalism" to indicate something like "attentiveness to form." To define the term in this way is to cast a very wide net, which can be a virtue. At the same time, it is not unfair to observe that this is the shallowest of all extant meanings of the term. This hollowing out of the central term has presented difficulties for those attempting to use it as a tool for thought. For one can accept the basic new formalist claim that "formalism" has been the great enemy of historicism only if one understands "formalism" in one of the richer senses it has usually carried in better work over the last four decades: as indicating a commitment to something in the range of self-authorizing, self-sufficient, autonomous, or autotelic form—which is to say, a commitment to idealist aesthetics, of one kind or another. Whereas if one uses the term in such a way as to indicate merely "attention to form," then one has secured a new breadth of meaning at the cost of giving up one's right to use it as the name of the great enemy. To echo for a moment a question that many others have already asked, if "formalism" in the sense of "attentiveness to form" really is what the discipline has been rejecting for the last three or four decades, why do we consistently find all the major figures of the last three decades pay so much attention to form?

In fact, as so many have observed, the historicist/contextualist paradigm has never been hostile to form per se: the chief New Historicists who are so often the targets of new formalist critique certainly were not, and to see this even more clearly one only has to look at the Marxist tradition from which the paradigm ultimately springs—a tradition in which the primary task has very often been the diagnosis of the social significance of form, Jameson being the inevitable example. As Levinson rightly notes, "new formalist" work is often forced to admit this quite quickly, excusing the most prominent New Historicists of all charges, holding up Jameson as an example of best practice, and so on, which often leaves us with the claim that the argument is merely with the epigones—the claim we saw George Levine making just now.[11] If so, well and good; but then the argument is simply that we ought to do the existing historicism as well as the best existing historicists, and the "new" in the kind of "new formalism" Levinson endorses starts to look a little wan. Once again the argument ought to be with the existing paradigm at its best. But when we take the argument in that sense we find that it is quite problematic, since the central term means one thing in claims about the relationship between new formalism and the history of the discipline, and quite another when "new" methodologies are being proposed.

At best, this fudging of the definition of the key term "formalism" is an unwitting confusion that enables interesting work to be performed. Yet one notes with some discomfort the fact that it has happened to prove very convenient for the purposes of publicity: indeed, a skeptical observer might say that the term "new formalism" has allowed some of those involved to attract a crowd by posing in the mantle of the great enemy, only to reveal, once we are inside the tent, that what they are in fact proposing is simply historicism as usual, plus form. From the perspective of the mainstream of the discipline, strongly historicist/contextualist in orientation as well as more or less on board with the discipline's perennial emphasis on reading the significance of form, one can imagine few things cozier. Setting this alongside the odd centrality of the assumption that disciplinary history swings like a pendulum, it is hard not to begin to wonder whether there has sometimes been a greater than usual quotient of careerism here. If "formalism" has been the great enemy for quite a while, and you believe that disciplinary trends swing to and fro like a pendulum, would it not be wise to declare oneself a "formalist" so as to get along for the ride? Not to propose "formalism" really, of course, in the old aesthetic way—that would be suicide—rather, simply to propose "attention to form" in the best historicist/contextualist fashion. Seeing the matter in this murky light puts our skeptical observer at risk of mistaking the "new formalism" for a formation built around neither liberalism nor leftism, but careerism, plain and simple.

But of course the best new formalist work is much better than this. If the slide from "aesthetic" to "formal" has at many points meant the loss of the

clear-eyed sense of disciplinary history that guided the early "new aestheticisms," there have been some compensating advantages. The attentiveness to
matters formal is generally quite real, and stands in contrast to much, though
not all, existing historicist/contextualist work; when one assesses it as a shift
of emphasis within, rather than against, historicist/contextualist scholarship
as usual, this end of the timeline has its strengths. In any case—and this is
really much more important from the point of view of the longer history—
the strong urge to move at all is the result of a genuine insight into the limits
of the discipline under present conditions. This is to say that many of those
who have found themselves convinced, at least in part, by new aestheticist or
new formalist arguments have been moved by quite an accurate sense that the
discipline, as currently configured, is failing to meet an important set of
demands that it ought to be meeting—and failing for lack of something that
it once had. Everything then rides on our sense of what, exactly, that missing
something is. The usual diagnosis offered in "new formalist" work—that the
loss of an "attention to form" is the heart of the matter, and that "new historicism" was the culprit—seems to me quite wrong, but the basic intuition of
the tendency as a whole, from the new aestheticisms of the early 90s through
to today's new formalisms, strikes me as a good one. That basic intuition, I
take to run as follows: first, that the discipline lost something important in
the turn to its current mode in the late 1970s and early 1980s; second, that
this missing something is related in some way to the aesthetic, or perhaps to
the formal; and third that in order to address this we need to achieve a break
with something like "historicism."[12] The question then is as to how to do
justice to the strength of that intuition, without leading off into the vagueness of the usual mistakes. If the first line Levinson identified—that of "normative formalism," trying to reinvigorate an idealist aesthetics—might be
taken to point the discipline toward a dead end in this regard, the second
line—that of "activist formalism," trying to use form as a way to reinvigorate
the dominant historicist/contextualist methods—seems something of a dead
end, too, at least if we are truly looking to break with the dominant. Having
reached a twin impasse of this kind, with both of our "pendular" movements
merely leading us in circles, how are we to move forward onto new ground?

Here I think it is helpful to look again at some of the early "new aestheticist" work, written as it was with a clearer sense of the larger disciplinary situation. The blockage here seems to be the failure to develop a

model of the aesthetic that would be compatible with a full commitment to our existing critique of the idealist mainstream of aesthetic thought. The fact that this blockage appears with such clarity here is a testament to the perceptiveness of the underlying analysis, for as we have seen, this is in fact a version of one of the basic intellectual limits of the historicist/contextualist paradigm itself. Confronting this fundamental boundary, much "new aestheticist" work simply rebounded into a nostalgia for older modes— and yet other work, more clear-sighted, was able truly to sense the nature of the boundary, and even to chart it, test it, and then put it under a certain amount of strain. I would like then to close this section by briefly exploring the work of a figure whose thought is especially rich in this regard: the British feminist thinker Isobel Armstrong. I take her as an example of what the "new aestheticism" was capable of, in its better instances, as a collective attempt to chart a way past one of the defining impasses of historicist/contextualist thought.

Isobel Armstrong

In a series of essays written throughout the 1990s, some of which were later collected in *The Radical Aesthetic* (2000), Armstrong attempted to track the "convergence of a conservative and a left anti-aesthetic," thereby showing that "the 'left' aesthetics of cultural materialism was oddly twinned with Thatcherism" (14).[13] She saw quite accurately that this "left anti-aesthetic" was being derived variously from the work of Eagleton, Derrida, de Man, and Bourdieu, and she critiqued each of them in turn via a form of argument that runs closely parallel to the argument I made in Chapter 2 in relation to the earlier work of Williams. Here she introduces the argument in relation to Eagleton's *The Ideology of the Aesthetic* (1990):

> A major work of suspicious hermeneutics, this book aligns itself with cultural materialism but widens the scope of critique. Nothing less than the impossibility of the category of the aesthetic is its theme. [For Eagleton, the category of the aesthetic] and Kant's work, in particular, serve a succession of different oppressive systems[:] bourgeois hegemony, commodity culture, and, ultimately, Fascism. (16)

This was well observed: as we have seen, Eagleton's book was indeed an "expansion" of the existing cultural materialist critique of the aesthetic—specifically, it was Williams' critique of the aesthetic, expanded beyond the limits previously set by its two saving clauses. Armstrong accepted the general form of this critique, but sought to bring the argument forward into new territory by calling for the construction of new models of the aesthetic—new models that would meet the objections that the existing left critique of the aesthetic had raised.

> Eagleton's study offered a salutary, virtuosic analysis of the intrinsic political and ideological problems of the aesthetic in the history of our culture. But the book was not seriously interested in envisioning alternatives, or in imagining what a changed understanding of the aesthetic would look like. Chapter 1 of my book, 'The Aesthetic and the Polis: Marxist Deconstruction', is a response to Eagleton's argument. It seeks, with deliberate eclecticism, to develop other ways of describing the aesthetic, both cognitively and affectively. (16)

Where Eagleton had "effectively concede[d] the concept of the aesthetic to the right," Armstrong would instead seek out a way to think a truly "radical aesthetic": one that would neither give ground on the existing critique of idealist aesthetics nor cede the territory that the right traditionally had used the category of the aesthetic to claim (45). It was a maneuver she was happy to repeat in response to the claims of other central anti-aesthetic thinkers:

> [T]he elements of the aesthetic deconstructed by both Derrida and de Man are the components of an archaic, individualist theory of art we associate historically with the nineteenth century. But this obsolete, subject-based bourgeois account of the aesthetic is universalized as *the* aesthetic, and thus both writers sometimes look as if they are doing more than they actually are. . . . [Thus] [t]he possibility for an alternative aesthetic latent in nineteenth-century texts, which can arrived at by going around Derrida and de Man rather than confronting them, occupies the next stage of this discussion. (54–55)

As with Eagleton, so with Derrida, de Man, and later Bourdieu: in each case Armstrong's move was, in effect, to show that the critique of the aesthetic being offered was not really a critique of the category of the aesthetic *tout court,* but in fact a critique of a specifically idealist (often neo-Kantian) aesthetics; she then accepted the critique in that more limited form, and proceeded to try to push the argument forward into new territory by rethinking the aesthetic in other terms.

All of this strikes me as extremely insightful, showing how accurate a sense Armstrong had of the surrounding terrain, even without our benefit of hindsight. Her clarity as to the disposition of forces in the field had as its corollary a more focused clarity with respect to specific matters, too: thus, for instance, Armstrong was able to see Eagleton's book as an expanded statement of the existing anti-aesthetic position at a time when others were misreading the book as a call for the *revival* of the aesthetic and were therefore fêting it as a watershed between the left's existing anti-aesthetic position and a new pro-aesthetic turn: as one of the "opening shots of what has become the new aestheticism," in Beech and Roberts' terms (18).[14] Armstrong was not fooled by that—and while writing in the mode of praise I cannot help but add that when reading her one sometimes feels one has been delivered from bad company by the good grace of her incisiveness on questions of gender, which repeatedly throws the implicit masculinism of much existing pro- or anti-aesthetic discourse into stark relief. Among those proposing "new aestheticisms" she remains exemplary for the clarity with which she saw the need to make a sharp distinction between nostalgic attachments to residual idealisms, on the one hand, and genuine calls for a new materialist account of the aesthetic, on the other. In short, she is an unusually perceptive guide, particularly on the crucial question of what happened to the aesthetic within the discipline, and what the left might want to do about it.

The question then becomes as to how far her positive rethinking of the aesthetic was able to proceed. What was the alternative model of the aesthetic that she proposed, and how did she go about developing it? The general shape of her argument here will, I hope, strike the reader as familiar, for what Armstrong proposes again and again is the breaking down of the boundaries with which the idealist mainstream of aesthetic thought seeks to cordon the category off from the rest of practical life. "An aesthetic needs to be grounded in experience that happens to everybody" (58). "I have suggested that the artwork be [viewed as] embedded in the ordinary processes of being alive . . . rather than as a privileged kind of creativity cut off from experiences that everyone goes through" (79–80). And so on. For Armstrong, putting the aesthetic back into contact with the processes of life in this way meant marshalling a wide range of disparate figures and sending them out to tear down specific Kantian or post-Kantian boundaries: Vygotsky and Winnicott to connect the aesthetic with the act of play in its ordinary sense, rather than in its more rarefied Kantian sense; Freud, Levinas, Ricoeur, Silvan Tomkins, André Green, Wilfred Bion, and Vygotsy again, as well as others, to try to challenge the cordoning-off of the cognitive from the affective, and instead to unite them as parts of the same living process; Gillian Rose to undo the either/or binarisms of poststructuralist thinking and to allow us instead to inhabit the "broken middle"; and John Dewey for the claim that (grasping the bull now by the horns) "ordinary experience is in continuity with aesthetic production"—to mention just a few of her figures (163). Reading down the list of names, one immediately sees how broad her range of reference is: she has assembled quite an army. The task she proposes to give that army—the task of building a new, expanded model of the aesthetic by tearing down the boundaries that have traditionally been taken to secure the aesthetic realm from ordinary life—seems to me a crucial one. As we have seen, it is also a task that has a claim to be serving the central historical work of the discipline itself.

And yet, if the roster of thinkers Armstrong manages to marshal together is impressive in its heterogeneity, it is also, for the same reason, at risk of being somewhat scattershot, making it possible to suspect that there may be something less than coherent about the position won. When your guide begins to enthuse about the sheer variety of different paths available, it may be a sign that you are lost. Her tone is invariably confident—indeed, at times it borders on the Olympian—but we ought not to let this fool us: her confidence, as well as the buckshot method she sought to own as a "deliberate eclecticism," are really, I think, signs of her embattlement, and of how relatively friendless her project leaves her at her moment in the discipline's history: she is casting about for alternatives, and if she seems to find an embarrassment of riches, this may be because nothing she finds is really what she seeks. Having battled through the thickets of her prose and come to grips with each of her suggestive arguments on specific points, one starts to want to ask her some broader questions about the possibility of a synthesis. How, precisely, were we to connect this framing of the aesthetic as a form of play to the commitment to writing from the "broken middle"? Assuming we accepted her repeated insistence that the cognitive ought not to be thought of as insulated from matters of affect, how precisely was this to change our theory of the aesthetic as play, itself newly combined with the question of the "broken middle"? It is difficult to say. Each element of the theory is appealing on its own, and cries out for more development—but what language were we to use to think the different elements of the project simultaneously? Armstrong's unusually keen sense of the geography of the discipline allowed her to identify the need for a rethinking of the aesthetic in a much more precise way than many others were able to, and she was therefore able to gesture toward the general terms under which that rethinking would have to be carried out. But once we reach that point—the point at which the largely unknown territory of a materialist aesthetics begins—she begins to take us up each path a short way, only to turn back and try another, and then another, and another. One then begins to wonder if we have arrived at another impasse after all.

Viewed as part of the longer history we have been tracing, one of the ironies of Armstrong's position is that she looked everywhere for a materialist aesthetics without ever being able to bring into focus the incipiently materialist aesthetics that lay so close to hand: that of the early critical paradigm, right there at the foundation of her own discipline. This was despite her very precise *obiter dicta* on the history of close reading—some of the more insightful I have seen.[15] Of Richards, she was able to say that he "believed that he had found a technique for achieving absolutely undistorted communication." This is Richards only in the sense that a negative can be called a photographic print, for in fact his emphasis is almost invariably on the nigh-insuperable *difficulties* of communication:

> The only proper attitude is to look upon a successful interpretation, a correct understanding, as a triumph against the odds. We must cease to regard a misinterpretation as a mere unlucky accident. We must treat it as the normal and probable event. (*Principles,* 315)

I make this point not in order to chide Armstrong for her misreading of a figure who was, after all, not her central concern, but in order to emphasize once again how muddled the story of the origins of criticism had become by this point in the discipline's history: the situation was now such that a subtle thinker, and a thinker who in other respects was unusually perceptive about the history of the discipline, found it possible to make claims of this quite erroneous kind about a founding figure, and they were allowed to stand. By this stage in the discipline's history, the question of the aesthetic roots of criticism was simply not being given serious attention in any widespread way. In the absence of a developed sense of the resources that lay at her feet, Armstrong turned instead to Dewey, who offered a different, nondisciplinary route to something similar: an anti-Kantian aesthetics that insisted that "ordinary experience is in continuity with aesthetic production." In this, she was moving in parallel with the liberal mainstream of the "new aestheticist" tendency: Winfried Fluck, for instance, was proposing a turn to Dewey of just this kind. The effect was to miss the birth of criticism entirely.

To be clear, I have no intention of claiming, even by implication, that the early critical paradigm somehow held the solutions to all the problems in aesthetics Armstrong had posed for herself: obviously not. Richards, for his part, had proposed solutions that were, in their specifics, either too liberal or too dated to be of use to her; the other early thinkers of criticism had still less to offer in this key respect. My point is a different one: that the historicist/contextualist discipline around Armstrong was unable to provide her with the tools she needed to recognize that modern disciplinary criticism itself had been founded on the basis of a serious attempt to address the very class of problems that she now sought to solve—and an attempt, moreover, that had opened up new territory in just the direction she now felt she had to move. This mattered chiefly because it prevented her from seeing clearly what an attempt to address the problem of a non- or anti-idealist aesthetics might look when put into practice: what it might mean to address the problem of the aesthetic as a problem of cultural or political intervention, and not merely as a problem for theory. Stepping back for a moment, one might observe that the example of the early critical paradigm shows how much can be done both at an intellectual and at an institutional level when an instrumental or incipiently materialist aesthetics is set to work as a series of practical educational proposals. In the 1920s, this combination allowed the birth of a rigorous discipline of aesthetic education—one flawed in such a way as to allow its quick co-opting by more conservative forces, and yet, even so, one that standsas one of the only extant cases of a rigorous and widespread institutionalized method of aesthetic education surviving under Anglo-American capital for a number of generations at a stretch.

One then wonders what it might have led to if, at this point in the discipline's history, a thinker of Armstrong's perceptiveness and conviction had managed to synthesize the elements of a materialist aesthetics that were to hand, and had then managed to use that aesthetics as the philosophical basis on which to develop a new set of pedagogical and critical tools for active aesthetic intervention in the culture at large. At an institutional level, perhaps it would have led to very little—after all, a whole tide of material factors were against her. In this regard, the contrast between her moment and the moment of the birth of modern criticism in the 1920s is fairly stark. Yet the purely intellectual gains could have been significant, even in the absence of a genuine institutional advance. This counter-factual may seem merely fanciful, but Armstrong was already in sight of the territory—she closes one of her finest essays with the questions: "What would today's aesthetic education look like? And what kind of society would it be that valued aesthetic education among its projects?" (80). The implied call for whole new methods, even whole new institutions, strikes me as an affecting one. This was the class of questions to which this line of thinking led her, and they are critical questions in the full sense of the word. Indeed, it is to questions of this kind that the line of thinking that began with the "new aestheticisms" ought to have led us, rather than to a nostalgia for idealist aesthetics, or to the mysticism of "nothing," or to the cozy impasse of historicism plus form. Given how little help the discipline around her offered, the fact that Armstrong was able to think her way to a position from which to pose questions of this kind in a serious manner is a significant achievement. The task of answering them remains.

Part Two: Intimations

We can now move to the second of the three broad tendencies we are tracking. One of the distinctive features of the historicist/contextualist paradigm—and one that has in effect been remarked on by many, at least by implication—is its methodological commitment to interpretative practices of a diagnostic rather than, say, appreciative or therapeutic kind: a "hermeneutics of suspicion," if you like.[16] In recent decades, though, a number of sensitive and intelligent methodological arguments have been made against interpretative practices of this order, perhaps the most influential of which have been Eve Sedgwick's proposal to replace "paranoid reading" with "reparative reading" and Stephen Best's and Sharon Marcus's later proposal to replace "symptomatic reading" with "surface reading." As the terms suggest, these arguments have been framed against specific modes of reading, but it strikes me that in both cases what has really been pointed to is something more general—and something that we cannot simply reject or move on from, since it is a necessary element of any project of interpretative cultural analysis. I think perhaps a better term for this larger thing—better because both more general and more neutral—would be something like "diagnostic reading": a reading practice that uses the text as a means by which diagnose the state of the wider culture. Or if you prefer to be even broader, "scholarly reading": a reading practice that sees the text chiefly as an occasion for cultural analysis. To use either of these latter phrases is to point to a much wider range of reading practices; moreover, it is to point to reading practices that are necessary, not simply to any scholarship, but to any politics worth the name. If one then wants to critique those kinds of reading practices—or at least to draw a distinction between those practices and others, in the interests of opening up a space for new orientations—then one must broaden the critique so as to include even many of the alternative reading practices that have been proposed: Best and Marcus' "surface reading" is clearly oriented toward producing further and better cultural analyses, for instance.[17] Having seen this, one begins to fear that, on closer examination, many recent critiques of our discipline's dominant reading practices will simply turn out to be continuations of the usual historicist/contextualist project under another name.

And yet in their best moments, some of these critiques of our paradigmatic reading practices have moved in a genuinely new direction—sometimes even pointing, in effect if never explicitly by intention, away from the underlying project of scholarly cultural analysis itself. In this section, we will turn our attention particularly to those arguments that have emphasized the political importance of entering into a more positive affective relationship to the text than the existing paradigm, in its strictest forms, would appear to allow. We saw this emphasis a moment ago in the new aestheticisms and new formalisms, though there the questions were chiefly philosophical in nature, the search being for a rigorous way to rethink the aesthetic value of the literary as a source of value. In the arguments we will glance at here, something like the same emphasis recurs, though at the different level of hermeneutics: here, the search has been for new methodologies of reading that would allow for, or even cultivate, a more positive relationship to the text. I have chosen to group tendencies of this kind under the heading of "Intimations" because the word might plausibly be taken to capture something both about the *object* of that search—a rigorous method for achieving a positive intimacy with the literary text, where that achieved intimacy is treated as a central site of intellectual value—and also about the *incompleteness* of the search—what have so far been discovered are, in my view, merely hints at such a method; the search continues. I also intend the buried word "Intimacies" here as an indication of the particular field in which this thinking has been carried out most sensitively in our period: queer theory, the same field in which broader questions about the character of our affective intimacies in general has been thought through in the most interesting and extended way. It may be that I should apologize for the wordplay in the heading, which is perhaps unsuccessful. In any case, glancing briefly at the work of three key figures will be enough at least to sketch a broad pattern of thought here. We will begin with Eve Sedgwick and D. A. Miller, and then move to discuss the somewhat different work of Lauren Berlant.

Eve Sedgwick

Eve Sedgwick and D. A. Miller have been two of the more prominent figures in queer theory in our period, and as many have noted, in a broad sense their thinking developed in parallel. In their early work, both offered exceptionally rich Foucauldian readings in precisely the paradigmatic mode: the key examples are Sedgwick's *Between Men: English Literature and Male Homosocial Desire* (1985) and *Epistemology of the Closet* (1990), and Miller's *The Novel and the Police* (1988). As they became more senior figures in the discipline, though, both began to turn away from what Sedgwick described as "paranoid reading" and toward reading practices that were more intimate, personal, and affective, in search of (among other things) a rigorous way to work through a positive relationship with the pleasures of the text. Sedgwick's claims for a "reparative reading" practice were exemplary here, as was

Miller's brief and incandescent *Jane Austen, or the Secret of Style* (2003). It would be wrong to say that Sedgwick's "reparative reading" was the theory that Miller's *Jane Austen* put into practice—they were working much more independently than this would imply. Yet it would not be so wrong as to be entirely misleading, for they were very much part of the same larger conversation, and they were clearly pursuing the same class of methodological problems at just the same time, and in a similar spirit.

About "reparative reading" itself, there is a lot to be said. Many people have seized on the phrase on the assumption that it offers us a new reading method, but in fact if you go back to the original essay—memorably entitled "Paranoid Reading And Reparative Reading, Or, You're So Paranoid, You Probably Think This Introduction Is About You"—you find Sedgwick offering it not primarily as a positive methodological proposal, but simply as a kind of generous re-description of the work she saw going on around her—specifically, the work in the edited collection to which her essay was the introduction.[18] Examining what she took to be some of the better queer theory of her moment, she detected a number of characteristic emphases that, she felt, could be taken together to constitute something like a new, more positive reading practice. Among them were emphases that by now may have acquired a familiar ring: "affect and cognition are not every distant processes"; "pleasure, grief, excitement, boredom, satisfaction are the substance of politics rather than their antithesis"; and most tellingly, perhaps, "it's well to attend intimately to literary texts, not because their transformative energies either transcend or disguise the coarser stuff of ordinary being, but because those energies are the stuff of ordinary being" (1–2). As we have seen, these were very much the emphases being drawn at the same time by the best of the "new aestheticisms," particularly those on the other side of the Atlantic—indeed, any of these sentences could have been the centerpiece of an essay by Isobel Armstrong, though she was writing in what might seem quite a different intellectual context. The dominant paradigm was provoking multiple, largely independent clusters of intellectual dissatisfaction, and those clusters were making their critiques in similar terms.

Like Armstrong, Sedgwick wanted to:

> open a space for moving from the rather fixated question "Is a particular piece of knowledge true, and how can we know?" to the further questions,

"What does knowledge *do*—the pursuit of it, the having and exposing of it, the receiving-again of knowledge of what one already knows? *How,* in short, is knowledge performative, and how best does one move among its causes and effects?" (4)

One can still hear Foucault speaking quite loudly here, and indeed Sedgwick immediately went on to remark that this might seem an "unremarkable epiphany: that knowledge *does* rather than simply *is,* it is by now very routine to discover" (4). And yet her insight was not really the old one, that knowledge and power were inextricable—it was, on the contrary, a new insight into the curious powerlessness of knowledge-production itself. It may be, she was saying, that knowledge is *not* performative after all, at least not where it counts. She drew attention to the "extraordinary stress" that contemporary literary studies seemed to place on "the efficacy of knowledge per se—knowledge in the form of exposure" (17). This faith in exposure seemed to her to be misguided, for exposing the truth did not necessarily lead to any positive change. Yet literary studies refused to recognize this, and instead kept recommitting to projects that promised to use the literary as an occasion for exposing the dark truths of culture, as if doing so was bound to make a difference. It was her sense of the futility of this project of exposure, together with her sense that literary studies' default mode was now to search everywhere for hidden threats, seeking the negative affects that were, it was sure, concealed beneath the positive ones, that led Sedgwick to diagnose the whole scene as "paranoid."

Understandably, she then wondered how this had come to be. How was it that queer theory, and with it literary studies as a whole, had become trapped in a pattern of merely "paranoid reading"? To the local version of the question—restricted to queer theory alone—she felt she had the answer:

Paranoia . . . became by the mid-1980s a privileged *object* of anti-homophobic theory. How did it spread so quickly from that status to being its uniquely sanctioned *methodology?* I have been looking back into my own writing of the 1980s as well as that of some other critics, trying to retrace that transition—one that seems worthy of remark now but seemed at the time, I think, the most natural move in the world. Part of the answer lies in a property of paranoia itself: simply put, paranoia tends to be contagious. . . . Given that paranoia seems to have a peculiarly intimate relation to the phobic dynamics around homosexuality, then, it may have been structurally inevitable that the reading practices that became most available and fruitful in antihomophobic work would often in turn have been paranoid ones. (6–7)

The local answer, then, was that due to its concern with the psychological dynamics of homophobia, the field had naturally lighted on paranoia as a central object of study; this object of study was "contagious" by its nature, and therefore came to infect the field's methodology. I am not here going to try properly to assess the persuasiveness of this intuition—in passing, let me simply observe that in order to be convinced by it, one has to have a great deal of confidence in psychoanalysis as a tool for analyzing medium-scale institutional transformations. For our purposes it is more important to note that, when confronted with the more general question of why this kind of methodology had come to dominate, not just queer theory, but literary studies as a whole, Sedgwick was open about drawing a blank:

> There must have been historical as well as structural reasons for this development . . . since it is less easy to account on structural terms for the frequent privileging of paranoid methodologies in recent non-queer critical projects such as feminist theory, psychoanalytic theory, deconstruction, Marxist criticism, or the New Historicism. (7)

Here Sedgwick's method of analysis in this essay reaches its limits: diagnosing the cultural malady as "paranoia" enabled her to analyze it as a synchronic structure by analogy with psychological processes, but it left her unable to trace the causes of that malady in any more general way. I say this with her, not against her: she is herself quite clear about the impossibility of understanding the turn to "paranoid reading" simply by analyzing the psychological structure of the paranoiac position. Sedgwick knew that there "must have been" larger historical forces at play, but what they were, exactly, she did not feel in a position to say.

Yet at other moments, she was able at least to gesture toward the elements of a more genuinely historical account. Once again moving in (presumably unwitting) synchrony with Armstrong, Sedgwick sensed that the kinds of "exposure" that had seemed worthwhile under the Keynesian regimes no

longer had real political purchase in her own period—the period that we
have now learned to call "neoliberal," which appears in Armstrong under the
name "Thatcherism," and in Sedgwick under the names "Reaganism" and
"the tax revolt." Here she offers a critique of the Foucauldian assumptions
underpinning Miller's *The Novel and the Police* (1988) as well as, by implication, her own earlier work—a critique that quickly widens out to encompass
the "New Historicism" taken in very broad sense, as a synecdoche for the
work of the whole period:

> Writing in 1988—that is, after two full terms of Reaganism in the United
> States—D. A. Miller proposes to follow Foucault in demystifying "the inten-
> sive and continuous 'pastoral' care that liberal society proposed to take of each
> and every one of its charges." As if! I'm a lot less worried about being pathol-
> ogized by my shrink than about my vanishing mental health coverage—and
> that's given the great good luck of having health insurance at all. Since the
> beginning of the tax revolt, the government of the United States—and,
> increasingly, those of other so-called liberal democracies—has been positively
> rushing to divest itself of answerability for care to its charges (cf. "entitlement
> programs")—with no other institutions proposing to fill the gap. This devel-
> opment is the last thing anyone could have expected from reading New His-
> toricist prose, which constitutes a full genealogy of the secular welfare state
> that peaked in the 1960s and 1970s, along with a watertight proof of why
> things must become more and more like that forever. . . . (19–20)

Sedgwick offers this as an argument about the mismatch between
Foucauldian/New Historicist projects of exposure and the actual historical
situation they (sometimes seem to) claim to want to change, rather than an
answer to the larger question of historical causation—the question as to *why*
the discipline turned to "paranoid reading" when it did. She did not claim
to be able to answer that question—yet one sees here that she already had
the basic elements of an answer to it within her grasp. As I have suggested,
it is true that the breakdown of the Keynesian regimes and the subsequent
turn to neoliberalism had ensured that the political claims of the dominant
historicist/contextualist paradigm were out of step with historical realities—
but that is not the whole truth, for it is to a large extent the historicist/con-
textualist paradigm's political futility that allowed it to prosper, the turn to
neoliberalism being, in that sense, part of its historical cause.

Having appreciated with remarkable sensitivity the real texture of the situation around her, Sedgwick attempted to feel her way toward a deeper kind of practice: an alternative practice of reading that would be more genuinely engaged with the actual historical conditions it sought to change. Here we come to the phrase "reparative reading," which was offered both as a description and a prescription. In the former capacity, it was a way of making explicit practices that, she felt, were already implicit in much existing work within literary studies, and particularly within queer theory. If one viewed the discipline negatively, she argued, one might simply see "paranoid reading" everywhere:

> Subversive and demystifying parody, suspicious archaeologies of the present, the detection of hidden patterns of violence and their exposure: as I have been arguing, these infinitely doable and teachable protocols of unveiling have become the common currency of cultural and historicist studies. (21)

And yet Sedgwick encouraged us instead to view the situation more positively, by emphasizing that the turn to the "present paranoid consensus" had not really "entirely displac[ed]" more positive ways of reading. Rather, it had "simply . . . required a certain disarticulation, disavowal, and misrecognition of other ways of knowing—ways less oriented around suspicion—that are actually being practiced, often by the same theorists and as part of the same projects" (22). She therefore intended the phrase "reparative reading" as a way to redescribe the achievements of existing work, so as to "[do] justice to the powerful reparative practices that, I am convinced, infuse self-avowedly critical projects" (8). This is a sensitive and generous way to read the critical scene, and there is certainly a lot to be said for going back to reflect on the richness and heterogeneity of actual practice, which the demand for methodological rigor so often conceals.

Yet the prescriptive ambitions motivating the phrase "reparative reading" were more circumscribed:

> My prescription . . . here is very modest: that our work grows more interesting, more responsive, more truthful, and more useful as we try to account for its motives in a less stylized fashion than we have been. Perhaps the unpacking, above, of several different elements of paranoid thought can suggest

several specific, divergent dimensions in which alternative approaches may also be available—may indeed be in practice in these pages. (23)

As a positive claim appearing at the end of an extremely provocative essay, this is indeed notable for its modesty. Perhaps it is the more persuasive for it. Taking the descriptive and prescriptive elements together, "reparative reading" appears to amount to the observation that in our best moments we already do many useful, nonparanoid things, but that our explicit commitment to a paranoid methodology masks and deforms this; this observation then justifies the argument that we ought to step back from our explicit methodological commitments, the better to see the rich range of alternative practices already in play. Putting it this way allows us to see both the span and the limits of the claim being made, for one can acknowledge the real force of this observation, and still be left wanting more from the argument. In particular, once one has agreed to cut down the old "paranoid" methodology, one wants to know whether it might be possible to do more than simply return to the fertile mulch of premethodological practice: one wants to know how to set about growing a new, more positive methodology at least as strong and various as the last.

I am not alone in wanting to see a more immodest Sedgwick here. In his 2004 essay "Uncritical Reading," Michael Warner observed precisely this, and drew out the implications:

> But is reparative reading a structured program of reading or explication? For the most part Sedgwick describes it as local, detailed, and unsystematized. . . . Sedgwick's reparative reading seems to be defined less by any project of its own than by its recoil from a manically programmatic intensification of the critical. It is not so much a method as (principled?) avoidance of method. (17–18)[19]

The question mark on "principled" is perhaps a little tough, but otherwise this seems quite right to me. What I want to add is simply that this is precisely what one expects to see when an incisive thinker pursues an interesting line of thought into a new territory *for which she has no paradigm.* The limits of the existing mode are being sensed and rejected, but no new paradigm is in view; instead, the thinker retreats from making explicit methodological claims and falls back instead on the more basic, more heterogeneous, but also more inchoate level of practice. It is in just that kind of broader disciplinary situation that one is tempted to claim one's lack of methodology as a virtue, as Sedgwick does here. In the later work of both Sedgwick and, as we shall soon see, Miller we find a strong sense of the limitations of the existing methodology, together with a call, express or implied, for something new—yet in the end no new methodology arrives, and what we get instead is charisma, local brilliance, contingency, idiosyncrasy, chance. If one wants to reinstate Warner's question mark on "principled" here, one can observe that at certain moments, moves of this kind threaten to throw us back into the anti-institutionalism, the suspicion of any form of positive collectivity, even the bad libertarianism, anarcho-liberalism, or simple neoliberalism that many have detected in Foucault.

But this is harsh, and Sedgwick's later work really does point richly to something far beyond this: her sense of the state of the discipline was unusually incisive, and though she did not put it in quite these terms, it is not to press too far beyond her own language to say that one of her guiding intuitions here was that further and better analyses of oppressive forces were of very limited use in the absence of a paradigmatic means by which to bring the results of that analysis to bear on the actual practices of social life. I take it that this is just the kind of intuition that literary studies in its present state most needs. Thus when I say that for those in search of a new, more positive hermeneutic method, beyond the boundaries of the historicist/contextualist paradigm, her later work remains of gestural value, I do not mean it as faint praise. "Reparative reading" may not be a new method in itself, still less the birth of a new paradigm—and yet if one is willing to take it in the "modest" spirit in which Sedgwick first proposed it, then it really does seem a very perceptive way of pointing in the direction in which a new, more genuinely critical method might eventually be found.

D. A. Miller

Oriented by this, we can turn to D. A. Miller in the hope of taking a step or two further forward. Here I think we will see just the same pattern recurring at another level. The reader will recall the long list of quotes with which we ended the last chapter: quotes that I intended as a rapid sketch of something at least suggestive of the historicist/contextualist paradigm. There, I included a fragment of Miller's *The Novel and the Police* (1988)— a fragment that I take to be Miller's single most concise summary of his book's central argument. For the reader's convenience, I reproduce it here:

> As I hope to show, the point of the [Victorian novel] . . . is to confirm the novel-reader in his identity as "liberal subject". . . . I further assume that the traditional novel . . . remains a vital consideration in our culture. . . . The "death of the novel" . . . has really meant the explosion everywhere of the novelistic. . . . To speak of the relation of the Victorian novel to the age of which it was . . . the mass culture, is thus to recognize a central episode in the genealogy of our present. [x][20]

This is an exemplary case of the historicist/contextualist paradigm in action. And yet, as Sedgwick asks, "who reads *The Novel and the Police* to find out whether its main argument is true?" (14). The book's real readers, she tells us, are "impelled through a grimly monolithic structure of strongly paranoid theory by successive engagement with quite varied, often apparently keenly pleasure-oriented, smaller-scale writerly and intellectual solicitations" (22). For Sedgwick, it is the latter that really make up the heart of the book; to recover them is to do part of the work of redescribing paranoid reading as reparative.

I think this is dead right, and to dramatize the truth of it, let me now reproduce the central argument of *The Novel and The Police* once again, restoring all the phrases that I had to redact in order to get at it. What I take to be Miller's central claim in the book actually runs as follows:

> As I hope to show, the point of the exercise, *relentlessly and often literally brought home as much in the novel's characteristic forms and conditions of reception as in its themes,* is to confirm the novel-reader in his identity as "liberal subject," *a term with which I allude not just to the subject whose private life, mental or domestic, is felt to produce constant inarguable evidence of his constitutive "freedom," but also to, broadly speaking, the political regime that sets store by this subject. Such confirmation is thoroughly imaginary, to be sure, but so too, I will eventually be suggesting, is the identity of the liberal subject, who seems to recognize himself most fully only when he forgets or disavows his functional implication in a system of carceral restraints or disciplinary injunctions.* I further

assume that the traditional novel—*the novel that many people define their modernity by no longer reading*—remains a vital consideration in our culture: *not in the pious and misleading sense that, for instance, "Masterpiece Theatre" has dramatized all but one of the novels I mainly discuss, but because the office that the traditional novel once performed has not disappeared along with it.* The "death of the novel" *(of that novel, at any rate)* has really meant the explosion everywhere of the novelistic, *no longer bound in three-deckers, but freely scattered across a far greater range of cultural experience.* To speak of the relation of the Victorian novel to the age of which it was, *faute de mieux,* the mass culture, is thus to recognize a central episode in the genealogy of our present. (x)

Evidently, the ellipses in the first version elided a great deal: not just additional complexities of argument, but also digressions, epigrams, metaphors, provisos, sudden leaps, second thoughts, suggestive instances, explanations that seem superfluous—even *pointedly* superfluous—snarls, tones, tics of style. The book's main argument is hard to quote concisely, because the marks of charisma keep jumping in. Marks of charisma—or else, if you prefer, the marks of a restless intellectual dissatisfaction. The core of Miller's early work is exemplary of the paradigm, but it chafes frustratedly against the paradigm's limits all the time: already in this early work, the author seems to feel that his uncompromising, strongly Foucauldian historicist/contextualist argument is somehow unsatisfying or insufficient. Armed with Sedgwick's program notes, one can approach Miller's early work a little differently: though it seems as if the book *ought* to want to keep the spotlight on its historicist/contextualist project, in fact one can already hear a rustling in the wings.

How different, and yet how similar, the opening lines of *Jane Austen,* when the extra charisma seems to leap forward and take over the show. The whole show, I mean, at every level: actor, script, and fictional action.

All of us who read Jane Austen early—say, at eleven or twelve, the age when she began writing—were lost to the siren lure of her voice. "How nicely you talk; I love to hear you. You understand everything." Yet whereas Emma's talk merely held Harriet with the charm of a *person,* what Austen's writing channeled for us was the considerably more exciting appeal of no longer being one. Here was a truly out-of-body voice, so stirringly free of what it abhorred as "particularity" or "singularity" that it seemed to come from no enunciator at all. It scanted person even in the linguistic sense, rarely acknowledging, by saying *I,* its originations in an authoring self, or, by saying *you,* its reception by any other. We rapt, admiring readers might feel we were only eavesdropping on delightful productions intended for nobody in particular. (1)

The critical voice speaking here is quite remarkable for the finesse with which it mimics the rhetorical effect it is describing. The finesse lies in an odd place, in that Miller here reproduces Austen's effect in an exaggerated manner, thereby training us to experience it in its more subtle original form. This I would like to call pedagogical. Austen's voice, we are told, is "out-of-body," lacking and abhorring particularity, and in the argument that follows the impersonality of that voice turns out to be a cover for the shame of her person ("What lies at the close heart of Austen Style is . . . a failed, or refused, but in any case shameful relation to the conjugal imperative" 28). Crucially, the critical voice that tells us this—Miller's voice—*also* seems to be trying to speak impersonally, but is making such a fuss of it that it keeps failing.

As so often in Austen, the complexities of the tone are paraded in the first line. Even just the first *part* of the first line: "All of us who read Jane Austen early—say, at eleven or twelve." The "All of us who read" here—rather than, say, "*I* read . . ."—seems an attempt to rise beyond the merely personal, but it is an attempt that fails very quickly—"say" is too conspicuously conventional a marker of a pretended casualness to prevent "eleven or twelve" from revealing itself as a merely particular, autobiographical detail. Evidently this is *not* an out-of-body voice—rather, this is Miller talking; Miller loudly performing the failure of an attempt to hide his personality. Another exaggerated example, two pages later: "But the same discovery that, sometimes even despite herself, made the girl a good girl, made the boy all wrong" (3). The practiced ineptitude of this—it is only too obvious that "the boy," ashamed, is Miller pretending to cover himself—trains us to see that whenever a voice of this kind seems to speak impersonally, it is making an effort to hide, or manage, or compensate for its very personal shame. When Austen performs this rhetorical maneuver, it fools us; Miller sees through it and then bungles it in slow motion for our benefit. It is by exposing himself that he exposes the work of the text.[21]

I find this performance tremendously convincing, not simply in its local insights, but in its recovery against all odds of what seems a genuinely critical impulse. For in its best moments *Jane Austen* abandons not just "paranoid reading" or a "hermeneutics of suspicion" but even what we might call simply "scholarly reading" itself. Now, clearly not all the moments in the book are of this kind. There are times when Miller manages the risk of exposure by performing cognitive precision of a familiar theoretical order, which is safe enough; and crucially, as we learn by the end of *Jane Austen,* Miller also manages it by framing his insights as, finally, insights into Austen in her context. This is to say that by the end of the book, there is a kind of collapse out of this deeply personal mode, and into something nominally more objective, more legible to historicist/contextualist norms. And yet if we focus on the most striking (because now so unfamiliar) elements of *Jane Austen,* disembedding them from the habitual contextualism in which we sometimes find them, we find that in its strongest, most resistant (or elated) moments, the book stakes its claim on our intellectual attention primarily by referring us to the depth, articulation, and affective intimacy of the critic's own subjective inwardness with the text, the necessarily idiosyncratic relationship between text and reader being secured by means of our common capabilities in such a way as to make itself available to others as a potentially representative one. Brought to bear in this way, Miller's own intimate insights into Austen acquire the force of more general insights, not simply into Austen, but into life.

I do hope the reader hears the echo of Leavis in my language here— specifically, the echo of Leavis' Arnold—because if you do hear it, it might be jarring enough to make you long, as I do, for a discipline that would set itself the task of trying to compose a better language to fall back upon in such instances. As Sedgwick put it:

> the vocabulary for articulating any reader's reparative motive toward a text or a culture has long been so sappy, so aestheticizing, defensive, anti-intellectual, or reactionary that it's no wonder few critics are willing to describe their acquaintance with such motives. The prohibitive problem, however, has been in the limitations of present theoretical vocabularies rather than in the reparative motive itself. (35)

Sedgwick's theoretical contrast between the "paranoid" and the "reparative" offers us a language through which at least to articulate our inability to talk of criticism proper—and yet for all its suggestiveness, Sedgwick's own proposal for "reparative reading" ultimately amounted to a refusal of method. Can we say the same of Miller here? Ought we to view this as a heroic refusal of the normal historicist/contextualist mode that nevertheless cannot find its way to anything more systematic or repeatable than a brilliantly charismatic belletrism—an impressionism, without real method, that retreats in the end to the usual contextualist claims?

No, for in fact Miller *does* have a rigorous disciplinary method here: nothing so novel as "reparative reading"—or "surface reading," say—but simply our old friend "close reading." (And indeed Miller begins the last chapter of *Jane Austen* by reflecting directly on the history and current status of close reading as a practice—reflections to which we shall return in a moment.) In his search for a new, more positive, more personal method of reading—a search that is, really, in a buried way, a search for a new paradigm for criticism proper—Miller finds precisely the central tool of the old critical paradigm, and pursues it so far that becomes something quite unfamiliar today. Disencumbering himself of many of the usual scholarly shibboleths, he mines down into the roots of close reading, thereby rediscovering it as a means by which to pursue a belletristic or aestheticist impulse in a rigorous and exacting way.

Was Miller then offering us a new paradigm for criticism—in effect, the old paradigm returning in a new mode? Was it repeatable by others, and on other terms? I do not think so. For the performance here is quite evidently not of such a kind as to be generally repeatable without massive adjustment, not only of the performance itself, but of the wider disciplinary context in which such efforts would have to take their place. For Miller's later work, like Sedgwick's, was recognizably marked and received as the work of thinkers at a very specific institutional site. In the first place, they were obviously senior, and thus insulated from pressing institutional demands like "field specificity" and "contribution to knowledge"—concerns that were nonnegotiable lower down the scale, and remain nonnegotiable today. It is not hard to imagine the difficulties a PhD student would encounter if trying to find a job on the basis of work of this kind, even were they to carry it out quite brilliantly—let alone if they were to carry it out at a level more realistically to be expected from junior critics at large. A junior scholar in literary studies who elects to write chiefly about the virtues of nondualist Buddhist thought, conceived pedagogically, as Sedgwick did; a newly-minted PhD with a dissertation that simply engages with the text in a personal way, claiming the representativeness and intellectual value of insights so discovered, in the absence of any further proof secured by means of rigorous historical or contextual analysis—I do not say it is impossible that such a person could be taken seriously by the discipline, but I do not think anyone who knows the field would deny that they would encounter difficulties on a scale not faced by those pursuing projects of the more usual kind.

But it is not just the seniority of the figures concerned that marks Miller's achievement as highly particular, rather than paradigmatic. Clearly *Jane Austen's* best moments provide us with a kind of writing about literature very different to that demanded by scholarly norms—I want to call it more "personal," but this is complicated, since it is precisely the possibility of a purely personal stake in the text that seems at issue. The fact that this *is* the issue is a clue to another way in which the book relied, for its effect, on its relationship to a very specific institutional context. The central drama of the book lies in its bravura performance of critical reading in a context where such things are unexpected, not to say dangerous; it offers us the spectacle of a rich and persuasive thinker walking the tightrope of an intimacy with the text, without (or at least, seemingly without) the safeguards of a scholarly net. This to say that the book is convincing precisely as a spectacle of daring the face of vulnerability, and much of this vulnerability derives from the book's necessarily fraught relationship with existing historicist/contextualist norms. As we have seen, today the discipline at large possesses no systematic way to articulate to itself the means by which a personal and affective intimacy with the text can be made a primary site of intellectual value—not through contextualizing or theorization, but through the force of its own inwardness—not, that is to say, by staking its claims to intellectual rigor on its perceptiveness or utility as cultural analysis, but by staking them instead on the power and subtlety of its attempt to cultivate our common capabilities. In such a context, any work that would stake its claims on a "merely" personal intimacy with the text must run the risk of being revealed as mere impressionism or belletrism, such as cannot be taken seriously by the strictest scholarly standards. Miller manages that risk by both thematizing and performing it. At the most obviously vulnerable moments, he finesses his vulnerability by performing charisma—by staging repeatedly the transformation of his vulnerable and particular personality into critical authority, if you like—or, if you prefer, by performing with breathtaking precision an unfortunate failure of Style. My point is that both Miller's style and his choice of subject—he is investigating the range of rhetorical techniques by which people manage the shame of self-exposure—are overdetermined, being in part symptomatic of the risks that must be run by any attempt to return to a more personal and affective mode in a context that cannot as a rule take such things with the highest seriousness, except as special cases. If one is trying to make a claim for the importance of a genuinely critical relationship to the literary, in a context where this is seen as either regressive or undisciplinary, then one might well have to do so by writing a whole book that both analyses and deploys precisely the kinds of rhetorical strategies that people use to manage the shame of the particularity of their person; the shame of self-exposure. In the discipline as it stood at that point, could one have pulled off a performance of this kind with such élan, if the performance had been about something else?

Seeing this allows us some insight into why this return to something like criticism in a personal and affective sense is occurring in queer theory, of all places. Here it strikes me that Sedgwick's intuition that queer theory was more liable to paranoia than other fields has the potential to mislead us, for the striking fact that needs to be explained is just the opposite: why was it that queer theory was so quick to see the need to move on? I am not going to try to answer that question in a serious way here, except to note that in queer theory, in the period leading up to this kind of work, there had been a deep collective thinking-though of questions of performance, personality, shame, self-exposure—moreover, there had been a concerted effort to recover for serious intellectual life the possibilities of modes of personal relation that went beyond simply the production of theory or knowledge in the expected scholarly mode. Here it is surely relevant that both Sedgwick and Miller were emblematic precisely for their performance of charisma, chutzpah, verve, personality, camp. Inevitably, given the period, work of this kind had usually taken the form of cultural analysis: further and better historicizations and theorizations of sexuality and gender; the recovery of lost queer histories, figures, lines of thought; new accounts of the role of affect in the culture at large—all of which was rich in implications for the analysis of sociality and subjectivity more broadly. And yet there had also been other, more direct attempts actively to cultivate and embody different modes of personality, subjectivity, and collectivity, and here we approach something like criticism in the fuller sense.

At this point, as we note the presence in queer theory of a real, felt pressure to cultivate different modes of common being, it seems possible to detect the traces of the more fundamental historical situation in and by which that body of theory was formed, and to which it was an attempt to form an adequate response. For what we see here are the signs of the fact that of all the fields, sub-fields, and emphases within literary study that claimed a political mandate, it was queer theory, almost uniquely, that still had its roots in live and mobile social forces—collective forces that were actually making advances, albeit advances of a very problematic kind, in the wider world. I pass over vast complexities in saying this quickly, but it needs to be said, even at the cost of over-simplification. Putting things very rapidly, real collective action on class had stalled with the global turn to neoliberalism; collective action on gender and race had advanced a little further before being rerouted and turned back, much of the forward movement having been halted by the stalling of the underlying critique of class. But having gathered steam a little later, the collective struggle for a broader, more humane regime of sexuality was still making some kind of progress in the 1990s and 2000s, even if, as many have noted, that progress was inevitably of a very awkward and sometimes thoroughly pyrrhic kind. I put on hold for the moment the crucial question of the extent to which critiques based on gender, race and sexuality are, or are not, at odds with the determinative forces of capital, and at what particular conjunctures; pursuing it would take us too far out of our way here. My point is simply that it really does make a difference to the character of the work produced by an intellectual formation when those involved feel strongly their responsibility to the needs of fairly well-defined larger formation beyond the academy—a larger formation defined not simply by its "identity" but by its character as a living movement—which is to say, really, a formation defined by its always limited but nevertheless real ability to define itself by determining, collectively, the trajectory of its own development.

Miller's own comments on his relationship to the history of "close reading" offer an effective summary of my observations here. The final chapter of *Jane Austen* begins as follows. This is long, since I am now reluctant to straighten out the snarls.

> Picture, if you can, a past moment of literary criticism when, institutionally empowered and rewarded, close reading was the critic's chief tool of professional advancement; his command of a *text,* his capacity to tease from it a previously invisible *nuance,* or illuminate it under a fresh *insight,* would as good as light the pipe in his mouth and sew elbow patches on his jacket, so unfailingly did he thus distinguish himself as the compleat, the full professor of English Literature. Now picture, if you need to, a future moment of literary criticism in which the same practice has fallen into total dereliction, and the *esprit de finesse* has ceded all its previous authority and prestige to the *esprit de géométrie,* more familiarly known as "theory." Even more efficiently than it once promoted its practitioner through the ranks of the professoriat, close reading now transforms him into an emeritus, antiquated and rambling. . . . I don't mean to suggest by either exercise that, whether or not we ever lived in such a past, we should contemplate returning to it, or that, if such a future is indeed at hand, we should do our best to resist it. On the contrary, it is close reading in its humbled, futile, "minoritized" state that would win my preference in any contest. For only when close reading has lost its respectability, has ceased to be the slave of mere convenience, can it come out as a thing that, even under the high-minded (but now somewhat kitschy-sounding) rationales of its former mission, it had always been: an almost infantile desire to be *close,* period, as close as one can get, without literal plagiarism. (57–58)

One could quibble here about Miller's sense of his moment in the history of the discipline—today, with the benefit of hindsight, it is easy enough to see that "theory" was not at this moment on its way to becoming a dominant paradigm, as he seems to think—but this misreading of the turn to the current paradigm as a turn to theory should be familiar enough by now. What I want to note instead is that Miller here champions close reading, and I think by implication criticism itself, but precisely not as a paradigmatic method. He refuses to countenance returning to an (in any case illusory) mid-century when it was "institutionally empowered and rewarded," the "chief tool of professional advancement," and so on; indeed he envisions a future—even a present—in which it has almost totally collapsed into "theory," and refuses to say that this would be bad. Instead, he insists that he likes close reading most in its abject state. So when one points out, as I have tried to do here, that Miller is effectively fighting for criticism per se in this book, one must immediately go on to add that he does not appear to see any possibility of that fight succeeding.

Here perhaps you begin to see the parallel that I am trying to draw between the two thinkers, because it is precisely in situations of that kind, when there seems no prospect of winning, that it so very tempting to make a virtue out of not wanting to win. In Miller here it is a political virtue: close reading, as he likes it, is "humbled, futile, 'minoritized'"; it "has lost its respectability"; only thus can it "come out." Unlike Sedgwick, Miller does have a positive commitment to a method, yet at the same time he wants to claim as a positive good the absence of a broader paradigm that would make that method available for general use. If you are sympathetic to some of the spirit of this, I am with you, but when one takes a close look at the political sensibility that underpins it, it begins to look to me like one that we ought to reject. How to put this? Of course it is sometimes necessary to champion the virtues of the losing position, and the fact that Miller can do so with such confidence here testifies to the collective achievements of the larger cultural formation of which he is a part. Yet remarking the fact of one's being humbled as a virtue is useful only up to point—putting a large argument in a very short form, it is simply very hard to see how a politics based on virtues of this kind can ever make plans to win.

So in both thinkers we see the same pattern: Sedgwick and Miller both point us toward a more positive, more personal, ultimately more critical relationship to the text; yet in both cases this leads, not to a new method or a new paradigm, such as would allow this new kind of project to be carried out in an institutionally recognized way, but instead to an acceptance and even a celebration of the lack of any such method, the lack of any such paradigm. Set in its broader historical context, this pattern of response strikes me as doubly symptomatic. Locally, it speaks to the lack of any prospect of a true paradigm for criticism—the lack of any hope of putting together a paradigmatic way to use the literary directly to intervene in the social order. Globally, it speaks to the lack of any prospect of decisive political progress: despite the real gains made on the front of sexuality, "minoritized" still seems to be the best that we can hope for here. Both these symptoms strike me as typical of the period—a period in which it was in fact quite realistic to hold little hope for serious progress on the left.

Lauren Berlant

Let us then turn very briefly to the final figure we will address in this section. In recent years, "affect theory" has become more and more visible as an exciting part of the discipline's work. The defining emphasis here is a familiar one, since we have already seen it in both Armstrong and Sedgwick: an insistence on the inextricability of cognition and affect, and a concomitant call for a more careful study of the neglected latter term. In the face of strong existing emphases on cognition, many have found this alternative emphasis convincing, and it is perhaps not unfair to say that much of the energy in and around queer theory circles has now migrated into the study of affect, with both positive and negative results. On the negative side—writing for a moment as someone not from the United States—I shall risk remarking that when reading the work of leading affect theorists, there are moments when one cannot but feel that a peculiarly U.S. form of sentimentality is being pressed on one from the outside, a sensation familiar from daily life anywhere in the empire—and this is despite the seemingly radical intentions of many of those involved. That this was not true in the same way of much of the earlier queer work performed in the United States suggests that there may be something about the study of affect, as presently constituted, that calls nominally internationalist U.S. thinkers back home to merely local (but then projected) ranges of feeling in a problematic and often unacknowledged way. I point this out here since I rarely see it noted, though I am afraid I do so only to set it aside—pursuing this question in a serious manner would take us too far out of our way. In any case, I take it that to many non-U.S. readers I will merely be pointing out the obvious.

The more salient gains and losses of the general move toward affect are perhaps best seen by directing our attention toward a specific figure, and I will therefore close this section by turning briefly to Lauren Berlant, treating her as a means by which to take the temperature of the broader body of work. Berlant's "national sentimental trilogy"—*The Anatomy of National Fantasy* (1991), *The Queen of American Goes to Washington City* (1997) and *The Female Complaint* (2008)—has formed something like a backbone to much recent work in affect theory. Reading this through to *Cruel Optimism* (2011)—as of the time of writing, her most recent major work—one is struck by the strength and explicitness of her commitment to the historicist/contextualist project. Again and again she tells us that "affect theory is another phase in the history of ideology theory"—quoting here from the introduction to *Cruel Optimism*—and she traces with great precision the moments at which her own work is a continuation and development out of the work of the most central of historicist/contextualist figures, particularly Raymond Williams and Fredric Jameson, who appear in this capacity with great regularity (53). At the same time, she makes many of the nominally alternative gestures now expected of up-do-date work, repeatedly aligning herself with the tendencies we have just examined—thus, for instance, she emphasizes that "*Cruel Optimism* is a more formalist work" than other recent works in queer and affect theory with which it might otherwise be confused, and she notes also that her book "tries to avoid the closures of symptomatic reading," by which she seems to mean mainly that she avoids economic determinisms of a "vulgar Marxist" kind (13, 15). None of this, however, shifts her determinedly scholarly orientation: emphatically, the goal is still cultural analysis. She often uses the terms "aesthetic" and "formal" in an analytical rather than debunking or demystifying spirit, but they are virtually always treated as diagnostic registering apparatus in a Jamesonian mode: thus "I am claiming that the aesthetic or formal rendition of affective experience provides evidence of historical processes"; "these new aesthetic forms, I argue, emerge during the 1990s to register a shift in how older state-liberal-capitalist fantasies shape adjustments to . . ."—and so on (7, 16).

The challenge for the historian is then to determine whether one ought to read her—and with her, perhaps, the "turn" to affect as a whole—as a collapse and containment of earlier attempts at a break with historicist/contextualist norms, a gathering of the new pseudo- or proto-critical lexicons back into the scholarly fold—or whether, on the other hand, one ought to read her as we have been reading other such figures, looking beneath her explicit commitments to the dominant so as to detect the implied impulses toward a break that they manage and conceal. This is a genuine conundrum, and much is at stake in it, since "affect theory" has reached a position of some importance in the work of the discipline, and the question of whether it constitutes a containment or an expansion of the existing counter-tendencies therefore matters a great deal as a sign of more general trajectories. The fact that it is still very much a live formation makes it somewhat tempting to wait a little and see how things turn out before making a call. Yet that would be an abdication. I think perhaps it is best to take the second option, reading Berlant against the grain a little so as to glance just briefly at a couple of the moments at which her work seems to call out for a project of criticism. I do so partly on the basis of the principle that, in mobile situations of this kind, when the direction of events is still being determined, description is sometimes less useful than prescription. In any case, I take Berlant's work to be exemplary of some of the best that contemporary affect theory has to offer, and it strikes me that a genuine project of criticism of the kind for which I have been calling could make good use of it, whether or not affect theory itself is in fact heading toward a break with the dominant analytical mode.

To see this, one needs to note the strong congruence between Berlant's project of cultural analysis and what we earlier, in Chapter 1, called the "diagnostic" element of the early critical paradigm. There are a number of examples one can point to here, and for convenience I will once again use Richards as the emblem, though at the risk of making it seem as if he contains everything, which once again he emphatically does not. To begin with, we can observe that "affect" in Berlant names what Richards would have considered a partial span within the broad range of sensibilities, habits of evaluation, patterns of impulse, techniques of adaptation, and so on, that are best thought of as "aesthetic." Berlant's own use of the term "aesthetic" tends to place it in the smaller vicinity of specifically artistic practices, but it does wander out into this wider territory from time to time. If one is willing to press her use of the word a little further in that direction—a move already being made by other affect theorists, Sianne Ngai being perhaps the most prominent example—then one can observe that the core of Berlant's work is designed to track with great precision the specifically aesthetic means by which subjectivities and collectivities manage to undergo and respond to the world.[22] When she writes that attention to affect allows us to uncover "a kind of proprioceptive history," one cannot but hear Richards' attention to neural responses, to the social history of the kinaesthetic imagination, to the intuitional utility of micro-movements of the spine (20). Or, turning things around, I take it that anyone who has read Berlant will find familiar Richards' emphasis on "this aspect of experience as filled with incipient promptings, lightly stimulated tendencies to acts of one kind or another, faint preliminary preparations for doing this or that . . ."; the reader of the present book may also recall that in Chapter 1, we spoke of the diagnostic Richards who envisioned conducting "fieldwork in comparative ideology" toward a "natural history of human opinions and feelings" that would track, not simply avowed beliefs, but also "imaginal and incipient activities or tendencies to action."[23] Or again, when Berlant replaces Jameson's "waning of affect" with the "waning of genre," she provides us with an understanding of genre that Richards easily could have endorsed: "Genres provide an affective expectation of the experience of watching something unfold, whether that thing is in life or in art" (6). This is, if you like, a psychological account of an aesthetic category; moreover, it is an account that strongly asserts the continuity between artistic experiences and experience more generally conceived. Or once again, Berlant tells us that tracking affect "releases to view a poetics, a theory-in-practice of how a world works" (16). This, one might say, is quite a precise description of the aesthetic in the sense understood by the early critical paradigm from Richards through Leavis: the structured/creative ("poetics") and heuristic ("theory-in practice") activity by which subjects encounter and remake elements of their experience as sources of value, using the common experiential resources of the culture at large.

My point is simply that if one reads the scene in this light, then it once again begins to seem plausible to say that the discipline is currently in a preparadigmatic phase, in which the groundwork for something like a genuinely interventionist project of criticism is being laid. For once one has developed the ability to track all these things so closely as they circulate through the culture, surely the next step is to try to develop rigorous means by which to cultivate them? Affect theory as emblematized by Berlant seems a case-in-point here, for the project, while clearly historicist/contextualist in its basic orientation toward cultural analysis, seems to have been homing in on something that strongly recalls the old aesthetic concerns. Now, I am of course aware that my claim that the natural next step is a break toward criticism proper will strike many as absurd: we affect theorists, we literary scholars, intervene by *analyzing,* not by . . . well . . . intervening. And indeed, it is true to say that so far this new trajectory is still more or less bound within historicist/contextualist limits. For all her emphasis on affect, and on how inseparable it is from cognition, to read Berlant is to engage the latter without necessarily doing much to cultivate the former. Speaking more broadly, the "turn" to affect in our period has made it possible to diagnose affect as it circulates through the social body, but if we were to try to develop new and rigorous means by which to *cultivate* affective or aesthetic capabilities, in their various depths and ranges, then this would raise a very different set of questions, and require quite another mode. So it may be fair to say that there is as yet no real, concrete evidence of a turn in this direction.

And yet there are intimations. In a piece written in 2004 for the journal *Critical Inquiry,* Berlant records her membership in a small scholarly/artistic/activist group called "Feel Tank Chicago," part of a larger (but still evidently very small) "system" of "cells" in a number of other cities in the Unitied States: "cells" with names like "Transnational Feminism," "Sex and Freedom," "Organizing Gendered and Racialized Communities through the Axis of Class," and—perhaps most significantly for our purposes—"Public Feelings."

> We have hosted, for example, an International Day of the Politically Depressed. What does it mean to think of negativity not as an effect of bad power but as a way of being critical without consciousness, as we currently understand its cultivated form? How is it possible to think about cultivated subjectivity in the aesthetic sense without implying uplift, progress, or errancy? Situated in our own contradictions, we are also restless, angry, mournful, and strangely optimistic activists of the U.S. political sphere. I close with the slogan that will be on our first cache of T-shirts and stickers: Depressed? . . . It Might Be Political. (450–451)[24]

The emphasis on the positive potential of depression here comes on so strongly as U.S. American, of a certain stripe, that I have trouble breathing for the press of it, but again, we are putting that aside. The genuine interest of this kind of thinking lies in its felt need to create a new language with which to think through the kind of concerns that were once, in an older, discredited mode, referred to as "cultivated subjectivity in the aesthetic sense." It has not yet found that language, but it is clear about the need for it, and it is also clear in its rejection of the old language, which, it feels, would simply lead us back to the old ideologies. The specific terms used to point to those ideologies here are symptomatic of the moment: it was 2004,

and the work of many of the figures in this circuit returns again and again to
the horrors of U.S. neo-conservatism—in such a context, "uplift" and "progress" seemed available only as the terms of the enemy. It is worth keeping
that context in mind when we try to evaluate the new language that this
tendency *did* manage to form—the language of affect theory itself—a language which, as we have noted, is marked precisely by its refusal of any active
attempt to cultivate new ranges of affect, and its retreat back to the mere
analysis of affect.

And yet, even in such a context, the group evidently felt the need to try
to think a way toward some kind of worthwhile interventionist action. It is
only too easy to dismiss the printing of "Depressed? . . . It Might Be Political" slogans on T-Shirts as simply another failed attempt at activist performance art; it is harder, but I think better, to make the effort to see the
intellectual victory that had to have been won in order to arrive at that
seemingly rather unpromising course. For if in a sense all activist campaigns
are attempts to make a political intervention, this one is unusually clear
about its status as an intervention *at the level of collective political sensibility.*
Indeed, the slogan is precisely an insistence on the idea that sensibility is
political, and vice versa. It is as if one of the fundamental emphases of affect
theory—on sensibility as political, on the political as a matter of sensibility—is being carried through into an actual, if gestural, attempt to
encourage the development of a different range of political sensibilities in
the wider collective. It is, moreover, an attempt to encourage the development of precisely that range of political sensibilities which would allow the
collective to acknowledge what, under neoliberalism, it could not acknowledge: the viability of the underlying category of political sensibility itself—
the category within which phrases like "political depression" and "Public
Feelings" ought to work and mean. The work notionally being done here is
not literary, but it is—speaking quite precisely—aesthetic, and it tries to lay
a foundation for further aesthetic work. Within its obvious limits, it strikes
me as a genuine act of criticism, and one intended precisely as an attempt to
open up space for a criticism still to come.

One then wonders what a practice would look like that combined this
particular activist emphasis on intervention at the level of collective political
sensibility, with Miller's more evidently literary rediscovery of the critical—
affective, personal, also representative—roots of close reading, guided by

Sedgwick's nod toward something like a "reparative" or—if you like—
therapeutic motive. I think it would be something other than scholarly. I
think it would be worth having, too.

Part Three: Expansions

But by itself it would not be enough. As we have seen, one of the basic distinctions that structured the scholar/critic dispute throughout the middle
decades of the twentieth century was that between specialists and generalists:
archetypally, the "scholars" were the specialists and the "critics" were the
generalists. This basic distinction is of course complicated by many factors:
one can make it problematic simply by recalling Auerbach's *Mimesis,* which
demonstrates how widely, in exceptional cases, the often highly specialized
philological tradition was capable of opening out toward more generalist
concerns. Nor is it true that the critical tradition was *merely* generalist in any
simple sense: on the contrary, the modern critical paradigm initially distinguished itself from the more impressionistic belletrisms of the *fin de siècle,*
and thereby won for itself a place in the modern research university, precisely
by demonstrating that the work of the general could be carried out in a specialist way. In this sense, one might observe that the characteristic techniques of modern "scientific" criticism were specialist techniques by which
to approach matters of the highest generality—thus Leavis, making a case
for criticism: "[modern society is] irretrievably committed to specialization,
and no man can master all the specialisms. The problem is that of educating
a central kind of mind, one that will give the different specialisms a humane
centre, and civilization a centre of consciousness" (166).[25] Criticism, no less
than scholarship, necessarily had to find a way to put the claims of *both* specialization and generalization in some productive relationship with one
another—when thinking at any depth, one cannot simply choose a side.
And yet after registering the force of all these observations, one finds that the
accepted distinction still holds in a broad way, and that the usual claim that
the scholars were specialists and the critics were generalists really does
describe a characteristic difference in emphasis. Recall the mid-century
questions imagined by Jameson: "is Faulkner greater than Halldór Laxness,
or vice versa? Is either greater than Tolstoy? Which is more universal, *I
Promessi Sposi* or *Red Chamber Dream?*" For all its many faults, the

universalist account of aesthetic value that underpinned much mid-century criticism allowed critics to perform their intellectual work over a very broad historical, and sometimes also cultural, range. If the critical paradigm always in fact laid claim to a certain kind of specialist expertise—skating over many complexities, one might call it a specialist expertise in speaking to and on behalf of the general—it also acted as a check on the constant drive to specialization that the scientistic character of the modern university encouraged in all disciplines, and of which the scholarly paradigm was, in its unexceptional forms, the local representative.

It is therefore unsurprising to find that the scholarly turn, which removed that check, brought with it a very clear trend toward intellectual specialization. In rejecting aesthetic universalisms of a mid-century kind and insisting instead on the embeddedness of texts in specific contexts, the historicist/contextualist paradigm sharpened the focus of the discipline only at the cost of narrowing its field of view. This was evident in the nature of the work performed, of course, but also—and perhaps even more tellingly—in the harder institutional structures of hiring, publication, and promotion. Chiefly, the historicist/contextualist period saw a new institutional emphasis on field specialization, accompanied by a shift in a sense of what did, and did not, constitute a "field." Some of the more obvious features of this included a marked hardening of divisions between "fields"; the development of a range of new field-specific specialist organs (journals, professional associations, conferences, and so on), with existing field-specific organs acquiring a more central role; the creation and ever more marked presence within individual graduate programs of a field-specific professionalizing apparatus, designed to prepare graduate students for the rigors of the "job market" by ensuring their work was carried out with a clear awareness of their relationship to a well-defined preexisting field; the invention of the phrase "hiring field," with all that it implies, which went hand-in-hand with the newly created rhetoric of the "job market" itself—and so on.[26] We should note that in each case, the majority of the "fields" in question were being defined by place and period, which is to say, in the terms most immediately amenable to mainstream historicist/contextualist approaches. There were of course exceptions: at various points throughout the period, positions might become available in, say, "gender studies," "theory," "postcolonial studies," "critical race studies," or "queer theory"—just to list some obvious examples—but "fields" defined in this more thematic or methodological way tended to prove vulnerable over the medium term in a way that the core fields, defined by place and period, were not. Indeed, in many cases fields defined by principles other than place and period found that their tenure lines had a tendency to evaporate with any turn in the weather. Given the oppositional character of many of these more marginalized specialisms, it is worth observing in passing that the discipline tends to manage dissent by incorporation and evaporation, creating new fields, only to discard them later.[27] In any case, field specialism was becoming more and more central to the work of the discipline, and the bulk of those fields were being defined by place and period.

With this development being so marked at so many important levels, it was only to be expected that many would feel it as an ever-narrowing straightjacket, and therefore long to break free. No-one who has observed trends in the discipline over the last two decades can have failed to notice the repeated excitements generated by the prospect of carrying out the project of contextualization over a much, much broader range of contexts. The specific terms around which this kind of interest has clustered have of course varied greatly: any list would have to include at least "transnational," "globalization," "world literature," and most recently "Anthropocene," each of which has been the object of a great deal of collective attention at one time or another; and a longer list would find many more to choose from: "transatlantic," "Atlantic" itself, "deep time," "Pacific," "energy systems," "silk road," "Mediterranean". . . . Each of these terms has called for an expanded framing of a different kind, and each has therefore opened up a different line of questioning. To broach, in passing, just a few of the grounding questions: Does the move to a "transnational" frame make the traditional national frames less important, or more? Does "globalization" usefully describe a real phenomenon, and if so, over what timescale? Is "world literature" really just literature that circulates widely, and if so, does a "world literature" framing prevent us from attending to the specificities of local idioms? Does the "Anthropocene" overturn our existing distinctions between the natural and the cultural, thereby bringing into being a radically new subject of history—or not at all? And so on. Each of these questions is of course only a point of entry to a much larger debate, to which I merely gesture; I am not going to try to wade into all these debates simultaneously here.

My point is a more general one. Though in each case the appearance of *this* particular term, rather than another one, has been overdetermined, all the terms have functioned as means by which to organize what I take to be the same kind of excitement: the discipline's ongoing excitement at the prospect of expanding the frame. This ought to be obvious enough, but it is important to recognize. Each of the various proposals for expanded contexts has of course had its own reasons for being, many indeed having had their genesis outside the discipline (most conspicuously "globalization" and "Anthropocene"), yet in each case much of their appeal to those within the discipline has evidently derived from their ability to speak to the same anxiety: an anxiety about of the narrowness of our existing modes of contextualization. Taken together, these repeated proposals for expansions attest to a fairly widespread feeling that our strong existing commitment to specific and bounded contexts has become something of a trap, and to a fairly longstanding desire to break free. When we view this as part of the longer history of the discipline, the salient point is that in the second half of the historicist/contextualist period, a significant proportion of the discipline began to form something like an incipient consensus around the idea that breaking out into wider contexts was a worthwhile goal, though the collective, taken as a whole, has not yet been able to settle upon a means.

Before moving to justify this last clause—after all, one might wonder, why would the collective even *want* a single means? Is it not better to have many?—it is perhaps worth pausing a moment in order to attend directly to the underlying excitement that marks and even motivates these clusters of work. I am tempted to give it a name—"expansion excitement," perhaps—simply to emphasize its coherence as a single object: a coherence it retains across a range of discussions which, on the surface at least, might seem quite distinct from one another. Three quotes will suffice as a means by which to familiarize ourselves with the texture here. Let us begin with David Damrosch in 2003, explaining the excitements of a "World Literature" framing:

> The following chapters will treat materials written as far back as four thousand years ago and as recently as the late 1990s, and will include discussions of the current reshaping of our understanding of Hellenistic Egypt, thirteenth-century Europe, and seventeenth-century Mexico. One of the most exciting features of contemporary literary studies is the fact that all periods as well as all places are up for fresh examination and open to new configurations. (17)[28]

For any scholar feeling a trapped by the discipline's strong existing method-ological commitment to specialized knowledge of specific contexts, it is indeed exciting suddenly to be addressed in this expansive way. As Damrosch is aware, many also find it worrying—which is to say that the second sen-tence here is not quite true. For surely it would be more accurate to say that much of the excitement of the first sentence, with its sweep across continents and millennia, derives precisely from the fact that "contemporary literary studies" is *not* completely "open" to this kind of work—or not *yet* open to it, if you prefer? We will return to this point in a moment.

As a second example, let us take Wai Chee Dimock in 2006, showing us the excitements of a "Deep Time" framing:

> [In this chapter] the Buddhist-inflected ecology of Gary Snyder will open into a backward loop through a Sanskrit epic, the *Ramayana,* whose simian pro-tagonist Hanuman, would in turn take us to China, to the sixteenth-century novel *Hsi-yu-Chi* (Journey to the West). Meanwhile, the crisscrossing paths of Native American and Asian-American authors—Leslie Silko, Simon Ortiz, Gerald Vizenor, Maxine Hong Kingston—will weave in and out of this loop, turning it into a more sinuous fiber. (166)[29]

Though Dimock is proposing a model of literary investigation quite dif-ferent to Damrosch's, and is therefore offering us a very different set of terms, the motivating excitement seems to be quite similar, if not indeed the same. That excitement is quite vivid here, in both style and content. The aerobatics display that transforms into a loom; Snyder's near-transformation into a simian; the way that the Native American and Asian-American contexts, which one had been trained to distinguish between, here become "criss-crossed" together as parts of the same broader weave: all these, tumbling into one another, give the reader the same dizzying sensation that the list of dis-parate times and places is meant to provide—the heady scholarly thrill of bringing wildly divergent contexts into unexpected relations. It is perhaps only to point to the obvious to observe that much of the real excitement here—even, it strikes me, the central motivating excitement—lies in Dimock's refusal to be tied down to a single context as normally defined.

Before drawing out the point, let us turn to just one more example: Patricia Yaeger in 2011, showing us the excitements of an "energy systems" framing.

Instead of divvying up literary works into hundred-year intervals (or elastic variants like the long eighteenth or twentieth century) or categories harnessing the history of ideas (Romanticism, Enlightenment), what happens if we sort texts according to the energy sources that made them possible? . . . We might juxtapose Charles Dickens's tallow-burning characters with Shakespeare's, or connect the dots between the fuels used for cooking and warmth in *The Odyssey* and in Gabriel Garcia Márquez's *Cien años de soledad.* (305–306)[30]

When one sees this happening again and again, in methodological arguments that otherwise seem to point in very different directions, one wants to start the conversation again at a more general level. World Literature, Deep Time, Energy Systems: the differences between these proposed frames seem quite great, and yet one begins to wonder in what way, precisely, those differences matter, if indeed it is true that the motivating excitement is the same. Of course, it is open to us to feel that the kind of excitement I am pointing to here is marginal, or at any rate not central, to these projects, and then we are back where we started. But it seems to me at least as plausible to say that, when one steps back to try to place these things in the longer history, the scene as a whole—the whole long series of thrilling proposals for expanded frames: transatlantic, transnational, global, world literature, deep time, energy systems, Anthropocene . . .—begins to seem less invested in the specific arguments being offered than each argument, taken merely on its own, quite naturally claims. In fact, it begins to seem as if what the collective is really most excited about is simply the prospect of a convincingly rigorous way to break with the narrowness of our existing contextualisms—a break toward the general, if you like, secured as a genuine step forward rather than as a regression into universalizing mid-century modes. At the risk of doing a disservice to some rich and thought-provoking arguments, I will suggest that it would not entirely be wrong to think here about the structure of a prisoner's fantasies: for the collective, taken as a whole, the real investment has been in the breakout itself, rather than in any specific proposal about what we would do once we were free. This is a new development, and one that seems quite important in the longer view. Our period's repeated "expansion excitements" seem important to the extent that they are occasioned by the prospect of a break, not simply with the specific

boundaries of particular fields, but with field specialization per se. Drawing
the point, it seems that once again what we are seeing is an implicit collective
protest against one of the central features of the historicist/contextualist paradigm, albeit a protest that has not yet been articulated as such.

To some, it may seem that in drawing attention to this kind of excitement, I am simply offering a disproof of my first observation: that our period
has been committed to specialization above all. How can it be true to say
that the dominant tendency in the historicist/contextualist period has been
toward specialization, if it is also true that many of the more celebrated proposals of the last few decades have been for expansions outwards toward
something approximating "generalist" concerns? The answer is that it is precisely the persistence of the longing to expand that shows how completely
the historicist/contextualist emphasis on field specialization now determines
the ordinary state of things. For when we look at all these clusters of work
together, something like a pattern emerges: we have a sequence of overlap-
ping discourses, each using its own terminology as a means by which to
propose an expansion of our spatial or temporal frame of reference, with a
new central term coming to prominence, say, every five years or so, and
lasting for about a decade, before beginning to fade and being replaced by
others. The need for repetition—the repeated need for a new term that
promises once again what the last term promised—is a sign of the persistence
of the underlying concerns. Again and again, we see the same collective
excitement at the prospect of a break outwards, but the proposed expansion
never quite takes hold of the center of discipline, and the break that would
really break never quite occurs.

The picture we are left with is of a discipline still fundamentally structured by place/period fields narrowly defined, with a long-standing desire,
never quite satisfied, to broaden out. One way to see the truth of this is to
consider the principles by which the discipline governs its own reproduc-
tion. At almost any point in the second half of the historicist/contextualist
period, one could have overheard professors giving their PhD students good
advice of the following kind: by all means, perform a broader comparison;
by all means, do something that breaks out into a much wider context—
something transatlantic, transnational, global, world, Anthropocene, etc.—
that's exciting; people like that. But *of course* you should never, ever do this
at the cost of giving up your claim to be specialist in one of the existing

"hiring fields": that is simply nonnegotiable if you want to have a career in the discipline today. Both the assumed importance of a grounding in an existing field, and the excitement at breaking out of it a little, are symptomatic: it is precisely because the discipline has been so committed to the importance of deep, rather than wide, contextualization that it has seemed by turns so necessary, so exciting, and—eventually, in each case—so impossible to succeed in expanding the default frame.

What would such an expansion look like, if it ever really succeeded in transforming the core of the discipline? It is tempting to say that the question ought not to be answered, since it sets the bar too high: here one might observe that many of those proposing turns to the transnational, the global, the world and so on have not really proposed that *everyone* should use their expanded frame, only that *some* should, and that, in this view, the core of the discipline will of course always need to continue to work in the existing fields as currently defined. But in fact the argument is usually more demanding than this, amounting to the claim that the new large-scale phenomena being observed require a newly expanded periodization even at the discipline's center, if not indeed a basic revision of what it means to study literature at all. Many, unwilling to commit to a single framing but still committed to expansion in a pluralist spirit, have even called for a more complete transformation involving multiple expanded periodizations all at once. For this more demanding version of the argument, it seems that the institutional sign of a success would be a rearrangement of the temporal and spatial boundaries of the core "hiring fields." Clearly none of the tendencies toward expansion has yet met that bar, and if one is committed to an expansion of our usual contextual framing, and trying to bring it about, one then perhaps wonders why. Is it that those listening have been too obtuse to recognize good proposals for expansion when they see them? Are the institutional structures of the discipline are simply too inert to be moved by argument? Or is it that the argument has not been strong enough?

What one misses here is a sense that the problem might be deeper than simply an existing preference for specific and narrow contexts; a sense that the problem might be the underlying contextualism itself. For what these arguments are really encountering are the limits of the historicist/contextualist paradigm; a paradigm that, as we have seen, is dominant for more than simply intellectual reasons—one thinks here of the way its institutional

profile fits hand in glove with the model of specialized knowledge production that the thoroughly scientized neoliberal university assumes as the
default. As we have seen, the narrowness of our existing framing is a consequence of the turn to scholarship, and must be fought as such.

A Hidden Trajectory?

We have thus taken a glance at three recent tendencies, observing the ways
in which each has quietly registered the lack of a paradigm for disciplinary
criticism. It would of course be possible to add others. One obvious candidate here would be the various "turns to ethics" about which one sometimes
hears things said—taken together, the many clusters of work that have proceeded under that title recall the "Pendulums" with which we began, in that
those identifying with them have tried to propose a return to something like
a mid-century emphasis on literature as a site for ethical and aesthetic education. Naturally, some of these arguments have been merely nostalgic,
whereas others have been offered in a more progressive spirit. As a sign of the
distance between work of this kind and the current paradigm, it is worth
noting in passing that the central figures here have been drawn from outside
literary studies—most conspicuously from philosophy, Judith Butler and
Martha Nussbaum being the perhaps the key examples. Another candidate
for a tendency symptomatic of the "critical unconscious" in our sense would
be the various new discourses on "literature as therapy" that have sprung up
recently on the margins of literary study, often in the gap between our discipline and more directly therapeutic ones: the field of "narrative medicine,"
for instance, or various efforts to use works of literature in psychological
treatment, all of which take the old idea that criticism has a therapeutic
function in a very literal sense, without necessarily having had the benefit of
a rich engagement with the deeper thinking about aesthetics, language, and
culture that underpinned the critical paradigm in its classic forms.

Last but by no means least, there is the crucial question of the discipline's
various ongoing attempts to refigure its relationship to the "public," the
"social," or the "common." The importance of these attempts perhaps justifies our dwelling on them just a little longer than on those just mentioned.
As we have seen, where "literary scholarship" was once the discipline's primary organ of specialist knowledge-production, "literary criticism" was once

its primary organ of public engagement. One would therefore expect the demise of criticism to be associated with a collapse of the discipline's public role—and of course, this is precisely what occurred. Of course anxieties about irrelevance, over-specialization, or disconnection from the world of real affairs are very long-standing within the humanities—so much so that some have even claimed that they are *constitutive* of the humanities—and yet one misses the real character of the historical moment if one fails to see that the neoliberal restructuring of the university has given them a special urgency. In this connection there is a great deal to be said, but in the interests of conciseness I will make the point very bluntly indeed simply by observing that in the neoliberal period, unlike in the Keynesian period that preceded it, it was no longer possible for literary critics to get CIA funding for their "little magazines," to use Trilling's old phrase.

Naturally this development, too, has had its dissenters, many having chafed against what, in the introduction, we saw Eagleton describe as literary studies' willingness to convert itself into "a species of technological expertise, thereby establishing its professional legitimacy at the cost of renouncing any wider social relevance." Here again it is worth taking care to distinguish the residual formations from the emergent ones. Among the residual phenomena, one thinks first of the various well-patronized debates about the "decline of the public intellectual" that seemed to effloresce particularly during the 1990s and 2000s—debates that find their historical grounding in the decline of the Keynesian "public sphere" (so-called). The emergent phenomena have been more interesting: to my mind, the most striking development here has been the cultivation of a new and fairly vibrant literary scene of "little magazines." A brief, heterogeneous list will suffice as a gesture to the kind of publication I have in mind here: *N+1, Lana Turner, Public Books, Nonsite, The Point, The Valve. . . .* Naturally the line here continues to be anchored by the older flagships of literary journalism—preeminently the *London Review of Books,* but also the *New York Review of Books, Times Literary Supplement,* and so on—but the presence of the new smaller players is an interesting development, and one that can only partly be explained by the birth of the internet.

It would be interesting to try to develop a rigorous general account of this phenomenon. I will instead offer just two observations regarding this new wave of publications—one intellectual, the other institutional. My first observation is as follows. Recall that disciplinary criticism was once precisely the discourse that mediated between specialist scholarship and the more generalist, belletristic, and unsystematic work of literary journalism, evaluative reviewing, and so on. The absence of disciplinary criticism thus leaves a distinctive gap in these publications—a gap for which they cannot bear the blame. Though naturally the emphases vary greatly from publication to publication, my sense is that the newer publications tend to adopt a "mix" composed primarily of perhaps four main kinds of work: reviews and surveys of existing academic works of cultural analysis, written for a general rather than specialist audience; original cultural analysis of a more or less recognizably disciplinary kind, performed in public view; reviews of contemporary artistic and literary works; and perhaps a forum for response, debate, or discussion. This is merely a rough catalogue, but already one can see that, though the magazine as a whole aspires to be a site of engagement between the discipline and the public, it is not quite clear what "engagement" here really means. On the one hand, the parts of the magazine most marked by recognizably disciplinary forms of intellectual rigor often seem to understand "engaging with the public" as if it were simply a matter of exposing the public to existing disciplinary work. On the other hand, the parts of the magazine that seem to recognize the need for some other practice to supplement this—a practice that is more belletristic, evaluative, aesthetic, or similar—are left meeting that need simply by providing journalistic reviewing of contemporary artistic works—which is to say, by leaving disciplinarity behind. There is then a large gap between the emphasis on cultural analysis, which bears the mark of recognizably disciplinary forms of intellectual rigor, and the reviewing, which often feels like an activity quite different to any trained by or carried out within the discipline in its current mode. Many of the new publications have been trying (often rather heroically, in my view) to find something to put in that gap, with a range of genuinely fascinating results— yet in the absence of a rigorous and institutionally supported paradigm for criticism, their task has been very difficult indeed.

This then leads to my second observation, which relates to the project of "engaging with the public" itself. In the interests of conciseness, I will be blunt—blunter, perhaps, than many of these publications deserve. My sense is that publications of this order have been most at risk of becoming limp where their aspiration has been to connect with the "public" generally conceived. Aiming so high, they inevitably fall short, and one instead ends up in a fairly intimate academic coterie. I do not intend this as a critique of coterie publications—far from it: everyone from Leavis to Trilling has believed strongly in their importance, as do I—rather, I am simply noting the mismatch between the aspirations and the realities. For it strikes me that, when publications of this kind are conceived as more focused endeavors from the outset, they are (somewhat paradoxically) better able to generate results beyond the coterie at key moments. For somewhere between the tightness of the "coterie" and the looseness of the "public" there lies the "social movement," and it is at this median level that coterie publications are able to do their best work, when conditions allow.[31]

In summary, then, we have at least six new tendencies that seem to testify to a "critical unconscious": the "Pendulums," "Intimations" and "Expansions" we have examined, and the "turns to ethics, "turns to therapy" and "turns to the public" at which we have merely glanced. Each has had its own reasons for being; I hope by now it is clear that each can also be read as a symptom of the demise of disciplinary criticism, and an attempt to make up for the lack. No doubt further examples could be added—a whole new book of them, perhaps. Yet I think that those we have traced are sufficient at least to suggest a general pattern. To some, this pattern may seem oddly drawn, not least in that it paints some of the more notable new tendencies of the last few decades as cries from the margins—cries that call our attention both to the absence of literary criticism per se and to the poverty of literary scholarship without it. One may object to this. Many of these figures and tendencies have received a great deal of attention—surely they have been central? In emphasizing their repeated collapse back into historicist/contextualist scholarship as usual, am I not going out of my way to paint as failures movements that have evidently met with much success?

I do not think so. Certainly most of the tendencies we have examined here have been widely discussed, and there is also of course an important sense in which the only "success" that really counts lies simply in writing worthwhile and interesting work under present conditions. Yet when one is trying to bring about a fundamental shift in the orientation of the discipline, as I think at least the first three of these tendencies have implicitly sought to do, then one is setting the bar for "success" very high indeed. If it is obvious that much of the work done under the sign of these various new tendencies has been quite brilliant, significantly expanding the normative boundaries of existing research, it is also obvious that none so far has managed to become paradigmatic, nor have any yet broken with the existing paradigm in such a way as to catalyze a broader movement toward a truly alternative model of literary studies. Indeed, without wanting to underrate their real achievements, it is not unfair to observe that in the context of the longer history of the discipline relatively few of the "turns" or "movements" of the last two decades have really merited either descriptor, if one feels that those terms imply significant shifts in the center of gravity of the discipline as a whole: shifts of gravity such as may lead to a true change of direction. At a practical level, many of the "turns" we have looked at here have really been a matter of a relatively small group of academics meeting at a series of conferences and then, in due course, publishing a series of readers, edited volumes, special issues of journals, or similar. I risk being impolite here, though I hope not to be: understanding the history of the discipline demands that one face squarely this question of scale, and set it against the scale of the forces against which these efforts were ranged. It is not to underrate any of these new tendencies to emphasize the deep entrenchment of the paradigm that their most inventive proposals implicitly sought to move.

The bar for success here having been set so high—some may say impossibly high, though disciplinary paradigms do in fact change at times, as we have seen—the story I have told in this chapter might be read as the story of a series of failures: failures really to "move" and "turn." Clearly I do not think this is the right way to read it, but were one to do so, one would have to agree at least to see these failures in historical rather than in merely personal terms. It is a truism of the history of disciplines that, while a dominant paradigm remains dominant, doubts are condemned either to remain on the fringes or to be regathered into the mainstream, no matter how well-thought and powerfully articulated they may be. It is only when a change in underlying conditions brings the dominant paradigm into crisis that the various isolated instances of discontent can coalesce into a new paradigm. Viewed in this light, the fact that none of these new tendencies has yet managed to effect a decisive break with the existing paradigm is neither surprising nor even necessarily a sign that they ought to have done things differently: the external conditions for a crisis within the discipline were simply not yet in place. For if, as I have suggested, the dual "critical" and "scholarly" paradigms of the mid-century are best seen as the discipline's complex response to the demands of the Keynesian period, and if, similarly, the present historicist/contextualist paradigm is best seen as the discipline's way of riding out our own neoliberal period, then it is only to be expected that the discipline would have to await the crisis of neoliberalism before the real character of the historicist/contextualist paradigm could come into view. Seen in this light, the chapter is not the story of a series of failures, but of a series of partial successes: a richly preparadigmatic scene of local innovations that, taken together, might be seen as opening up the possibility of a genuinely critical paradigm to come.

What would all these partial successes amount to, if taken together? If we proceed as I have tried to—which is to say, if we proceed by assuming that all the more influential alternative methodological arguments of recent decades are in some sense to be honored and believed—then what is the problem with the discipline as it now stands? Withdrawing for a moment my own views, and instead limiting the discussion merely to those critiques that are already on the table, it seems that the problem with the discipline as it stands is that it is too quick to dismiss the aesthetic and/or the formal (Pendulums); too much inclined to "symptomatic,", analytical, aggressive, Jamesonian, or merely cognitivist reading (Intimations); and too tightly bound within the narrow confines of particular places and periods (Expansions). To these, let us add also the further charges that the discipline is too quick to dismiss the ethical or therapeutic claims of the literary as merely or only ideological (the turns to ethics, the turns to therapy); and that its habitual mode is now so specialized and professionalized that it no longer has a programmatic commitment to what ought to be its more directly public role (the turns to the public). Let us then try to assume that everyone is right. How are we to accept all these diagnoses at the same time? What is this hybrid thing that no single "turn" or "movement" seems to condemn on its own, but that all the dissenting descriptions seem to amount to when taken together? The enemy is anti-aesthetic; anti-formalist; takes as its prime task cultural analysis in what might be called a Jamesonian mode; is deeply committed to cultural and historical specificity, field by field; suspects the ethical and therapeutic claims of the literary as merely ideological; and is both highly professionalized and highly specialized, tending to eschew any more direct or generalized public role. I hope by this stage in the book, it is clear that what we have just described is, quite precisely, the scholarly paradigm in its current historicist/contextualist form.

On the other side of the coin, what is this hybrid thing that no single "turn" or "movement" seems to call for by itself, but that all the dissenting movements would be calling for, in effect, if one took them all together? Again, none of the following terms is quite my own—nor, indeed are *all* of them *anyone's*, since they come from such disparate places—but let them stand together here for a moment as rough approximations of a potential collective will. Merely aggregating the various proposals one already hears, it seems that the method being called for would be deeply concerned with the aesthetic and the formal; sensitive to feeling and affect both as forms of cognition and in their own right as crucial determinants of individual, collective, and historical changes; able to move broadly, in something like a generalist fashion, across times, places, and cultures; willing to use the literary as a means of ethical (or political?) education; have its emphasis on therapeutic rather than merely diagnostic uses of the literary; and would be committed in a deep and rigorous but still fairly direct way to a public role. What we want, in a word, is criticism, for this is precisely a list of the signature strengths of the lost critical paradigm in its best form. Yet in order to understand what that desire means we need to recognize firstly that the discipline lacks a true paradigm for disciplinary criticism at present; secondly that the meaning of the term "criticism" has shifted in such a way as to disguise that lack; and thirdly how long the road really is that would lead the discipline from what it is now doing toward a criticism that would truly meet the demands of our moment.

The task of creating new and rigorous intellectual forms with which to unify the best of the dissenting insights is a large one; the task of creating robust *institutional* forms in which to carry out a project of this kind is perhaps even larger. Yet something like the basic elements of such a criticism are already present in the collective, even as it stands; what we want is the collective will to bring them together. Whether or not we will muster that remains to be seen.

Conclusion

The Future of Criticism

It is famously impossible to predict the future, and so it is understandable when historians end their books by refusing to try. At the risk of seeming to want to invite absurd comparisons, I will recall here that Eric Hobsbawm ends his monumental history of the twentieth century by telling us that "it would be foolish to end this book with predictions," because history, in the end, "is no help to prophecy." "We do not know where we are going. We only know that history has brought us to this point and—if readers share the argument of this book—why."[1] This refusal to prophesy is probably wise, and certainly canny, yet reading it on p. 585 of the final book in a four-book series, I must admit to having some ungrateful feelings. Surely, I want to object, at least part of the point of spending so much time working out what happened, and why it happened, is that doing so promises to help us work out what might happen next? Is it really "foolish" to end a book by making predictions? The odd (but also everyday) task of talking responsibly about the future poses special challenges, of course, and all predictions turn out to be wrong in one way or another—but it is not as if we can therefore do without them.

In any case, I am going to close this very little book by hazarding some predictions, come what may. No doubt in a few years' time, much of what I offer here will look quaint at best, as all predictions do in hindsight, but it still seems worth the attempt—I am not trying to write history in advance, which would indeed be foolish, but simply trying to sketch a guide for present action. For we have now come to the point in our story at which the question of the future of criticism begins to seem quite pressing. The scholarly historicist/contextualist paradigm dominates the field, and for the most part, the critical paradigm that once provided a counterpart and alternative to literary scholarship is either forgotten or misremembered. Camouflaged against that background, we see an array of incipient counter-tendencies variously dissatisfied with one or another element of the dominant paradigm, many of which seem to be sensing the absence of criticism in a partial way, though none yet understands itself as a critique of the existing paradigm as such. Being partial, so far none of these critiques has managed to effect a decisive break. Having reached this point, one wants to know first how long the reign of the historicist/contextualist paradigm is likely to last, and second, whether the various counter-tendencies we have been discussing, together no doubt with others still to come, will continue simply to make proposals for local revisions of one or other element of the existing consensus, or whether, on the contrary, some catalyst will bring them to coalesce into a truly alternative critical paradigm.

How to answer this important question? Let me begin by observing that any attempt to formulate an answer here leads us rather quickly to further questions that are very broad in scope—much broader, I want to say, than is usually assumed in discussions of this kind. For I hope by this stage it is clear enough that, although the specific texture of the discipline's history has been determined in part by individual idiosyncrasy, local difference, and chance, on a larger scale the discipline has stepped out its fundamental movement from paradigm to paradigm in close synchronization with the broader advance of the social order itself from phase to phase. This has always of course been the historical materialist line in theory, but to my mind it has not often been taken seriously enough on the ground. Assuming for a moment that the three-period analysis I offer here is plausible, at least in its broad outlines, we ought to understand the early critical paradigm, in all its political ambivalence, as one expression among others of a moment in the history of capital when the balance of forces was unusually tense and uncertain; we ought to understand the peculiar coexistence of two paradigms through the bulk of the mid-century as an articulation of, and sometimes a resistance to, the demands of capital in the Keynesian period; and we ought to understand the historicist/contextualist paradigm in an equally complex relation to the rather different demands of our own neoliberal period. It is then merely to state the obvious to observe that the discipline's future shape will depend most of all on the character of whatever new period of capital emergences in the wake of the current crisis.

Our question about the various possible futures of the discipline then quite quickly becomes a very large one: nothing less, in fact, than the question of the character of the coming social order. To call this a "million dollar question" is to sell it cheaply—it is the question on which all money now depends. Are we presently living through the birth of a new period in the history of capitalism? If so, what can we say already about its likely contours—and about the demands, such as they are, that capitalism in this new period might make of literary studies? But if not, then what does a continuation and extension of the neoliberal period entail, now that the conditions that allowed for its initial development have been so radically transformed? Obviously I am not going to attempt to offer definitive answers to questions of this order, but I do not think they can wholly be avoided: they are questions about the basic conditions under which, and by which, future forms of literary study will be built. It therefore seems essential at least to glance up at this wider horizon before returning to our more local concerns.

Before taking that glance, though, I perhaps ought to say that I am not unaware of the fact that many readers will be alienated by my asking the question of the future of criticism in this manner. Indeed in the past, when I have posed questions of this kind, I have noticed that people who have never had much reason to ponder the very important array of problems known to cultural analysts under the name "mediation" sometimes seem to think I am imagining a scenario in which the head of derivatives at Goldman Sachs puts in a call to the Chair of English at Harvard, saying something to the effect of "Look, conditions have changed; here's what we need you to do. . . ." Obviously not. But to assume that *that* kind of scenario is necessary to the question is to fail to consider the long series of causal connections, metonymic shifts, and feedback loops by which what goes on in one segment of the social order regularly and quite uncontroversially comes to determine what goes on in another. One thinks of the continuous and often dramatic material restructuring of universities in response to market forces; the direct influence of senior university management, trained in the same

schools and belonging to the same class fraction as managers of for-profit
corporations, with whom they are increasingly interchangeable; the ongoing
transformation of the wider cultural situation in which those involved in
literary studies operate, a transformation that in crucial respects is determined by the underlying transformations of capital; the significant demo-
graphic overlap between elite academic formations and elite financial ones in
terms of family connections, friendships, attendance at the same educational
institutions, all of the sociological factors that go toward constituting something like a common outlook—all these have real effects on the intellectual
and political character of the work eventually produced. One can acknowledge the importance—even the determinative importance—of these kinds
of connections without even straying too far from normal language, let alone
positing a direct or one-to-one ("vulgar") causal connection between base
and superstructure, simplistically conceived. In fact, I will go so far as to say
that once one begins to consider connections of this kind, one begins to feel
that the phone call does come, after its fashion. We are then returned to the
question of the nature of the coming social order, and thus, in time, to the
question of the likely nature of capital's demands. What is the new period of
capital likely to demand of literary study? And of course, the next question
instantly presents itself: what opportunities might there be for literary
studies to work at something at odds with what capital demands?

Here I will have to risk moving very quickly through some immense and
varied territory—territory that really ought to be attended to in a more sustained way. Moving quickly then, I take it that there are three main kinds of
scenario that sensibly can be imagined. First, one might suspect that what
we are seeing around us is not a genuinely epochal change in capitalist
dynamics, but merely a prolongation and intensification of the existing neoliberal order. For it is of course quite striking that our existing political elites
have been very far from retreating from, still less breaking with, the neoliberal orthodoxy that was at the root of the crisis that closed the century's first
decade; rather, after a very brief moment of doubt in the immediate aftermath of the crisis, they have taken every opportunity to re-impose it in ever-
more-intense forms. At this level, the crash of 2008 has proved less a watershed than an excuse for "doubling down" on the policies that were its cause.
In structural terms, it is now evident that the elite interests responsible for
the crisis were able to use it as an opportunity to consolidate their position,

while imposing its costs on the bulk of the population, which may suggest to some that, considered merely in their particular capacity as corporations, capitalists, and elite class fractions, they have every objective short-term reason to oppose stabilizing reforms, whatever the resulting instability—the most glaring current examples being Trump, Brexit—may mean for their long-term collective survival as a class (whatever we now mean by "class").

In any case, there are at least three reasons to be doubtful about the prospects of any imminent change in the governing order: first, despite the seeming breakdown of a neoliberalism as usual, the hold that oligarchic interests have secured over politics as normal appears in many respects even more secure than it was before the crash; second, the process of de-democratization—a defining political dynamic of the most powerful nations since the end of the Keynesian compromise—is clearly at present being carried further rather than reversed; and third, no powerful countervailing forces have yet arisen that might be able to save capitalism from itself by forcing it to take on a less crisis-prone form. Having survived as the ideology of virtually the whole spectrum of our political and financial elites, despite having been thoroughly discredited in the most dramatic fashion, neoliberalism now begins to look oddly invulnerable, practical economics having declared, in effect, that it recognizes no standards of falsifiability. All this leaves us with a highly unstable economic situation that nevertheless works well for the purposes of direct extraction, at least for the time being. Clearly, our existing political elites recently have been dealt some rather stunning rebukes—rebukes that might be thought to indicate that the era of neoliberal globalization is now at a close. But at the time of writing, it is not yet clear that the newly reconfigured political elite will be willing to bring itself into any significant conflict with the existing financial elite. It may therefore seem as if the only reasonable conclusion is that the neoliberal period is still very much with us, and will be with us for a long time still.[2]

This all seems plausible enough, but then one begins to have one's doubts. For to focus in this way merely on the ideologies of existing elites, rather than on underlying dynamics, risks making it seem as if history functions by fiat, those in power simply declaring what will occur next. But since the crash we all ought to be in a position to see that this, at least, is false: neoliberal policies very evidently produce crises that their proponents do not intend and cannot predict. Moreover, the question is not simply one of elite desires, but of objective historical processes: neoliberalism is not a state that one can inhabit, nor be forced by diktat from above to *continue* to inhabit—rather, it is a continuing dynamic by which all levels of the social order are subjected to sweeping change. It is therefore bound continually to become something other than it is, if only because it needs to respond in new ways to the new situations it has made. This is to say that the clock cannot be dialed back, and all that was transformed by the neoliberal offensive in its first phase cannot be changed in that same way again. Therefore, even if we want to speak, not about the birth of a whole new period in the history of capitalism, but merely about a prolongation and intensification of our existing neoliberal period, it seems we must at least be willing to speak about a movement towards a neoliberalism of a different kind. The question then is as to what kind, exactly, and as to when precisely we want to say that the line has been crossed, all these quantitative changes having accumulated to such an extent that they amount to a qualitatively different phase of capital.

We may therefore find ourselves moved by shades toward imagining a second kind of scenario, in which those who try repeatedly to reimpose the doctrines of the past end up doing their part in bringing about a period of quite a different character. This would place us, not in the midst of a long neoliberal period, but in an interregnum on the way to some new phase. Looking at things from this angle, one sees our financial elites attempting to double down on the same raft of policy prescriptions that caused the crisis, while our political elites flail, and reads it not as a sign that we are heading toward a prolongation and intensification of neoliberalism, but precisely as a symptom of the increasing obsolescence of neoliberalism as a set of guiding doctrines, even for the grim purposes of capital. On this view, the relevant "crisis" is not simply the monetary crisis of 2008 and surrounds, but a broader crisis of neoliberalism per se—by which one really means a cascading series of smaller crises, each dealt with temporarily merely by shifting it to another sector, each of which does its part in laying down the sediment for a new, more stable order of some kind, the foundations of which we would already be able to see around us, if only we knew the signs for which to look. We are then returned to the question of the character of the new period, though in other terms, the task of the analyst now being to find the child by distinguishing their features from those of the parent, without being confused by resemblances.

At this stage, many signs seem to indicate we should fear the child. If it is another new form of liberalism that we see forming around us, then it evidently involves austerity for the majority and welfare for the very wealthy few, and if it is a true crisis of liberalism, then the dramatic rise of neofascist and extreme nationalist parties gives one good reason to fear a turn to the right rather than to the left. And yet there are also more hopeful signs, chief among them the new resistance movements of recent years, of which a brief list will have to suffice: the broad radicalization of democracy in Latin America; the radical energies of the early moments of the Arab Spring; Occupy; the Movement of Squares; the Indignados; 15-M, Podemos; Syriza before the collapse; Black Lives Matter; Nuit Debout; and no doubt others just around the corner. It is of course only right to observe that none of these, even at its highest moment, managed truly to break the grip of politics as usual in its sphere of action, and yet the fact that each, differently, has succeeded in forcing the principle of economic equality into view, in a way that seemed impossible during the decades prior, may perhaps be read as a sign of a shift in the wind. At the time of writing, both Britain and the United States seem to be witnessing the breakup of the neoliberal center, at least at a party-political level—to the right, we have Brexit and the rise of Trump; to the left, the Corbyn and Sanders formations. The perils of such a situation are very evident; at the same time, it is not impossible to read this breakup in an optimistic way, as a sign that for the first time in a generation, there may be opportunities to make advances on the genuine left. (As I write, Trumpism in particular is generating new forms of opposition, though much of it is evidently of a kind that evaporates with the next center-left victory; we shall see.) Note that I leave to one side the whole question of the value of electoral politics in a system such as ours, which is for another time.

So there we have two plausible scenarios: the first, a continuation and intensification of neoliberalism; the second, a movement into a qualitatively new phase. But there is of course a third scenario—one that has some plausibility, and certainly a great deal of interest, though its grand scale makes its actual probability difficult if not impossible to assess. In this third scenario, what we are seeing around us are signs of the terminal crisis, not just of the neoliberal phase of capital, but of capitalism itself. Of course, as soon as one has raised this as a serious possibility, one wants to go back and hedge one's bets. As Wolfgang Streek has recently put it:

I am willing to make exactly this claim, although I am aware of how many times capitalism has been declared dead in the past. In fact, all of the main theorists of capitalism have predicted its impending expiry, ever since the concept came into use in the mid 1800s. This includes not just radical critics like Marx or Polanyi, but also bourgeois theorists such as Weber, Schumpeter, Sombart and Keynes. (46)[3]

He continues in a footnote: "So, if history proves me wrong, I will at least be in good company." Yet, as Streek goes on to argue, there are reasons to entertain the view in earnest, especially when we understand that those proposing it at a high level are not suggesting that the whole mode of production is going to come crashing down into chaos within the next decade or two, but are rather claiming that we are at the start of a relatively long period of instability in which the mainstays of the capitalist mode of production are likely gradually to fray at the edges, obsolesce, and decay. Streek's account gives us a collapse of capital under its own weight, but refuses to make any predictions about what may come in its place; here one might contrast one of Wallerstein's scenarios, which detects around us the earliest foundations of a fairly dark neo-feudalism—though of course he proposes more positive possibilities, too.[4] I am not going to dwell on this third scenario here; I merely note it.

These, at any rate, are three visions of the future of the social order—or three classes of visions, really, since there is of course a great deal of variation within them, different observers painting their pictures differently. In a sense, they are three distinct visions of the present, too, since the first places us in the middle of a long neoliberal period; the second places us in an interregnum between the clearly neoliberal period of the late 1970s through to 2008 and whatever new period of capital will follow after; and the third places on the long tail-end of the capitalist mode of production itself. How much credence we ought really to place in them, I cannot say—certainly I am not going to attempt to arbitrate between them here. But in our effort to find a vantage point from which to take the range of the possible futures of literary studies, it seems wisest to proceed as if looking out from the middle of the three positions, which is something like a median case. Our awareness of the other two vantage points on either side gives us some ability at least to imagine other plausible angles of view, thus making clear the doubtfulness of our chosen position.

From that doubtful vantage point, what do we see? Is the new period of capital likely to have any use for criticism? Here we can begin to survey some possible futures for literary studies, starting with what I take to be the most negative. As we have seen, the critical paradigm in its mid-century form was a creature of Keynesianism and New Deal-ism at an institutional level, if not always at an intellectual one. Yet in our rapid search for a future form of criticism, one thing at least has become clear: in none of the scenarios just outlined does the Keynesian welfare state make a comeback on any grand scale. This ought to be obvious enough, but it is worth stating firmly, since at times a return to the mid-century welfare state seems the limit of what the liberal left is capable of hoping for. In the absence of a real possibility of a new welfarist regime, calls to revive the role of the "public intellectual" as a means by which to engage the humanities more fully in the "public sphere" or similar seem quite beside the point, since the conditions for the re-emergence of these things do not exist, and are not going to spring into existence in the foreseeable future. As many have shown, the Keynesian regimes propped up the humanities in part as a way to promote a kind of social cohesion in response to the ideological pressures of the cold war.[5] But today, and still more in the future, the demands on literary studies, and on the humanities generally, are likely to be of a somewhat different kind. As Göran Therborn has observed:

> [S]ocial cohesion is much less vital for the ruling elites of today. . . . [P]revail-ing economic wisdom holds that the sentiment of international investors counts for more in delivering growth than developmental unity. For Northern elites cohesion implies, if anything, pressure upon immigrants to assimilate better, in the name of 'integration'. . . . Clearly, national cohesion is no longer considered the key to imperial power—as it was in the nineteenth and twen-tieth centuries . . . .(13)[6]

This seems quite right to me, though our focus here means that it is helpful to specify the periods somewhat differently. The humanities of the mid-century university were of course largely a project of "social cohesion," in the sense that they justified themselves to their funders on the basis of their potential utility in the securing of a national cultural life—"bildung," and so on. But with the decline of the Keynesian and New Deal regimes and the global turn to neoliberalism, elites reordered their priorities. Calls for cultural unity remain part of the rhetorical arsenal, of course, and the new right seems determined to shout them loudly. Yet at an economic level, they are no longer taken seriously. The humanities, thankfully fairly resistant to the idea of taking up an official role as an assimilator of immigrants, then no longer have a place to stand: this is part of the "crisis" often spoken of. Looking forward to a future without a renewal of the welfare state, it seems very likely that the humanities will continue to find themselves without an important role to play in the maintenance of capital. The future of criticism then seems dire. If the humanities as a whole will lack a significant function, what significant function could possibly be found for the much more specific practice of literary criticism?

One possible future direction for literary studies seems clear enough: one can easily imagine a scenario in which the current paradigm, already dominant, simply entrenches itself more deeply. With even the last, vestigial organs of criticism long since having withered, and no new project of a critical kind being proposed, we would see a continuation of the current trajectory: the interventionist wing of the discipline would be hollowed out even more completely, if possible, and we would see a further scientization and sociologization of what remains. Though names like "literary criticism" and "humanities" might be retained, the critical project of forming new subjectivities and collectivities by way of the systematic cultivation of capacities for value would have been abandoned as merely ideological; left in its place would be new sciences and social sciences, producing new facts, theorizations, histories, and analyses. The fact that some of these analyses would be of a radical or resistant cast notwithstanding, a continued transformation of this kind would suit well those who seek a continuation and intensification of neoliberalism, for which all questions of value are to be given up for arbitration by the market. As the previous chapter suggested, the tendencies already moving in this direction are strong, and a scenario of this kind may therefore seem quite plausible to some.

Yet to tell the truth I do not think such a scenario is very likely, if only because it relies on nothing occurring to change the discipline's trajectory—and it seems a safe bet that *something* surely will, for good or ill. No paradigm lasts forever, and disciplines do change radically from time to time; moreover, many within literary studies seem to be searching for a way to make a change, as we have seen. Let us then imagine a second, perhaps slightly more positive scenario for literary studies, in which the new tendencies and others like them manage to come to relate to one another on something like their existing terms, and thereby acquire a kind of centrality within the discipline, modifying the existing paradigm while leaving intact its basic orientation toward cultural history, cultural theory, and cultural analysis. What would a new consensus of this kind look like? It would be historicist/contextualist in its basic orientation, but it would modify the existing paradigm by the addition of new emphases on (for example) form, on affect, on relating positively to the pleasures of the text, and on methods of analysis that are broadly transhistorical and transcultural, rather than necessarily bound to single, specific places and periods—probably achieving this last, in part, by focusing not just on contexts of production, but on contexts of reception. It would perhaps be capable of a positive "presentism," in the sense that it would make an effort to dwell, not on the past "for its own sake," but on historical and cultural matters that bear on questions of key importance today. It would be highly specialized and professionalized—of course!—but it would also make a strong effort to break out of the associated trap of irrelevance by committing to performing its cultural analyses in public view. And so on. All these changes taken together might be enough to qualify it as a qualitatively new paradigm—or else, if you prefer, as a new phase of development in the longer history of the scholarly paradigm. This is more or less what we hear being called for all around us; let us then say these calls are heard, and take their effect. What would the success then be?

There would certainly be reasons to welcome this development, just as there would be reasons to welcome, say, the transformation of a significant proportion of the existing discipline into an institutional home for quantitative literary studies. The discipline would have changed with the times, which is something; to what extent the change would have been made *against* the times is quite another question. For—merely to note the obvious—what we have just described is a modernization rather than a mobilization of the discipline, and considered merely in that capacity does not carry any necessary political significance, right or left, beyond the usual coding of modernization as the forward march of liberalism. This is despite the fact that many thinkers are currently arguing passionately for elements of the scenario just outlined, often in political terms. One can see this in a familiar way by noting that, just to take one example, a vast expansion of our habitual frame of reference out to something like the "global," "world litera-ture," or similar, could have any number of political valences: in some hands, such a methodological expansion would simply be merely a highly mediated symptom of the expansion of capital into new territories; in other hands, it could be a way of arriving at better diagnoses of a general condition.

But this way of asking the question of the politics of literary studies is a very familiar one, and part of the point of reading a book of this kind is to put our-selves in position from which to ask that question in a different way. For regard-less of the banner under which these new analyses would be pursued, and regardless also of the implied political valence of the diagnostic innovations that would be proposed, a transformation of the kind just outlined would represent a recommitment to the existing idea of the discipline as a discipline of cultural analysis and cultural theory alone, and would in that sense prevent any true mobilization at all. The scenario envisions us developing a range of sophisti-cated methodologies for the analysis of affect, for instance, but it fails to envi-sion any paradigmatic means by which cultivate new ranges of affect. Perhaps we would rely on our analysis to do that for us by implication; no doubt some bolder souls would grasp the nettle by asserting confidently with some of the Freudians and Lacanians that "analysis" simply *is the same thing* as treatment, and leave it at that. Or perhaps, somewhat better, the discipline would at least recognize the whole array of crucial questions that lie in the gap between cul-tural analysis and social change, but refer those to others outside the discipline: to the activists, perhaps, or to the politicians, or to the public at large, newly informed by our newly publicized diagnoses of cultural ills. In any case, the discipline would be left without a systematic means by which to act on its anal-yses. Ultimately, then, it seems to me that the second scenario we are envi-sioning is really another version of the first: what we are looking at is a deeper entrenchment of the scholarly model of literary studies, and an ever more com-plete collapse of the humanities into the social sciences, albeit the social sciences pursued in a less quantitative and more interpretive mode. This is precisely the analytic posture to which the discipline was forced to retreat throughout the neoliberal period; for all its value as a defensive position, it is of limited use to those who now seek to make advances on the left.

Is there an alternative scenario—a scenario in which something like criticism is reborn? Scenarios such as those we have just outlined may seem to take off the table any prospect of a return of the critical paradigm, no matter how centrist its political orientation—and yet one can easily find exceptions here. For if we believe, as many analysts do, that capitalism can only function in the long term if its excesses are tempered by a loyal opposition of some kind, and we imagine that one of the roles of that loyal opposition is promoting at least the illusion of social cohesion, the formation of ideological communities, and so on, then the fact that the Keynesian period will not return ought not to mean the complete demise of the humanities in their broader sense, nor even of criticism in something like its mid-century humanist, "liberal education" sense. One then wants to know what the sites of this loyal opposition will be. In answer to this question, it seems worth observing first that there will still be *local* sites of something like mid-century Keynesianism, particularly on the advancing frontiers of capital ("emerging markets," and similar), and here the humanities, and even something like criticism in the mid-century liberal humanist sense, might be called upon to play a role. I am thinking here particularly of the call for a Western-style humanities education that one sometimes hears coming from those who seek to educate the executive and managerial classes of some of the more strongly statist nations in Asia and the Middle East. These may seem local eddies, but in fact they connect up fairly directly with work being done at the heart of the empire. Thus Martha Nussbaum, always cited prominently in discussions of a so-called "ethical turn" in literary studies, writing in *Not For Profit: Why Democracy Needs the Humanities* (2010):

> It has been fascinating for me to learn more about current developments in Singapore and China, so often touted as successes because of their emphasis on technological education. In fact, however, both of these nations have recently conducted massive educational reforms in order to give a larger place, in both schools and universities, to both critical thinking and the arts. The reason is hardly a desire to cultivate democracy. It is, instead, the demands of a healthy business culture in a mobile world economy. Both nations have

recognized that critical thinking is a very important part of a healthy business
culture . . . . (150–151)[7]

This, it seems, is inspiring, and is intended to remind us that "one of the
distinctive features of American economic strength is the fact that we have
relied on a liberal arts education and, in the sciences, on basic scientific education and research, rather than focusing more narrowly on applied skills."
And business, in its wisdom, knows this: "many firms prefer liberal arts grad-
uates to those with a narrow training" (53). As you can see, in liberalisms of
this kind, the terms can be shifted around quite readily: a title such as *Not
for Democracy: Why Profit Needs the Humanities* would work just as well.
Nussbaum's real argument for the humanities is premised on the idea that
there is no significant tension between democracy and profit—this in 2010,
when it seemed that the rest of the world, almost regardless of political orientation, was just waking up again to precisely that contradiction. The
promise that a humanities education will provide a loyal opposition could
hardly be made more clearly, or with a stronger emphasis on the modifier.
My point is that it if we believe Nussbaum—or even simply if enough others
do—then even at the heart of the empire there will be new opportunities for
the humanities, literary studies within them, to "re-brand" as appropriately
generalist training for "corporate leaders in a rapidly changing world," as the
jargon goes.

New sites of localized Keynesianism are one thing, but perhaps even more
significant are the various new, nonstatist forms on which today's capitalism
is increasingly coming to rely as a means by which to shore up its noncapi-
talist foundations. One thinks here of the new popularity of "the commons,"
a category that is attracting the enthusiasms of both corporations and activists, though in different ways. Narrowly conceived, the idea of the commons
is a way of securing collective property rights; taken more broadly, it is a way
of thinking through, and perhaps taking advantage of, the necessary collectivity of the social. To say that capital is placing new emphases on commons
is in one sense merely to note that we are in the middle of a new round of
enclosures, but there seem also to be significant efforts to *establish* commons,
naturally under the control of the corporations, that can then be used as
permanent gardens of collective effort, ripening for corporate exploitation
on an ongoing basis, the exploitation carried out in a manner akin to tax

farming or even, if you like—returning to Wallerstein's fears of a neofeudal order—to a kind of cultural manorialism. The example always used here is that of the "social media" commons—sites of vast collective cultural production harnessed and guided by the profit imperative of large corporations, though the harnessing and guiding is (sometimes) made to feel loose and voluntary—but there are certainly others. In any case, it seems as if it may be to sites of this kind that we need to look when we search for the counter-processes that capitalism will use to stabilize itself in the new period—and it may therefore be at sites of this kind that the humanities, and perhaps something like criticism in its mid-century sense, might be able to find new ways to serve the masters.

Considerations of this kind allow us to envision a third scenario for literary studies, in which something like a paradigm for criticism proper manages to gain a foothold in the institutions, alongside and to a certain extent in competition with literary scholarship. I take it that this would have to involve something like a synthesis of the key emphases of the existing counter-tendencies, as well as of others no doubt still to come. At the very least, it would need to demonstrate its effectiveness as a method by which to address the questions that many in the discipline are now asking: questions about the role of form and of affect; about the political potential of a more positive relation to the text; about our capacity to break with the existing fields as narrowly defined in order to work transculturally and transhistorically; about the positive rather than merely diagnostic role of the literary in ethical or political education; about the discipline's broader public role, and so on—which is to say, questions about how usefully to address those things that seem to lie beyond the particular limits of historicist/contextualist scholarship as usual. But it would also need to go further by opening up a range of questions that have not been addressed within the discipline in any widespread way since the mid-century: all the many questions that lie in the gap between diagnosis and treatment; all the questions that are raised as soon as one undertakes systematically to cultivate new subjectivities and collectivities, in the service of wider cultural, political, or more deeply social change.

Let us then imagine that this third scenario comes to pass, and the existing countercurrents, and others like them, not only manage to develop a new paradigm for active cultural intervention, but also manage to win a place for criticism proper within the literary institutions. Would this be a welcome development? The answer greatly depends. It would certainly constitute a mobilization of the discipline: an attempt to find intellectually rigorous and institutionally coherent ways of putting our cultural analyses to practical use. And yet it is obvious enough that institutions can mobilize for quite different ends. In principle—which is to say, suspending for a moment one's sense of the shape of the ongoing historical transformation that would ultimately prove determinative—one can envision a centrist or even a right-wing version of this project: one that would forget the lessons of the scholarly turn and instead seek simply to reanimate something like a mid-century apparatus for the production of liberal subjectivity. Few within literary studies seriously seem to want that sort of thing nowadays, but the old, good arguments against liberal forms of aesthetic education have now been leeched down into the soil of grounding assumptions, and as such, have evidently become somewhat less available for conscious use. It may be that the discipline could simply ignore them, trying to move back in the name of moving on. The more regressive parts of the "Pendulums" tendency stand as warnings here, as do the more obviously liberal versions of the "ethical" and "public" turns.

But how much weight ought we to give those warnings today? As we have seen, for some decades now the ghost of mid-century criticism has been used to scare; surely now the white sheet is looking a little gray? For all that one has one's provisos, the broader truth is that the Keynesian regimes are long dead, and their ideological spirits will not return. Capital has passed through a whole period since then, and it is now passing forward into yet another. After decade after decade of almost unmitigated defeat, the left is at a very low point—yet it seems at least possible that we may be heading into a period in which it will have slightly more room for maneuver than it has had since the global turn to neoliberalism in the late 1970s and early 1980s. This room for maneuver will not be great, but it could be made to count greatly if used well. Moreover literary studies remains one of the relatively few places in the English-speaking world today where the left proper has something like an institutional foothold. This is true even if, as the center never tires of reminding us, the vast majority of academic radicalism is evidently merely rhetorical; and even if, as I have argued here, the left's most celebrated local victory of the last few decades—the victory of the historicist/contextualist paradigm over the critical paradigm in its mid-century form—has in many ways been a pyrrhic one, for the most part unexceptional to the general rule by which neoliberal forces have swept the field elsewhere. In this new context, there may be opportunities for a genuinely radical form of the critical paradigm to find a foothold. If such a thing were to happen in a widespread way, it would be a significant thing, even when weighed on a historical scale.

Here I think the task of those on the left of the discipline is clear. We will of course continue to need trenchant historicist/contextualist analyses of culture through a radical lens, such as are now provided by those on the left of the discipline, as well as by those situated outside the discipline to its left. But to make advances in this new period, we will also need to mobilize those analyses, setting them to work as the diagnostic element in a broader project of systematic cultural intervention. Within the discipline, achieving this would pose significant challenges, both intellectual and institutional. Intellectually, it would necessitate the creation of a new paradigm for radical criticism proper. Such a paradigm would need a clear and coherent research program together with a rigorous new pedagogy, both of which, I think, would need to be founded on an intellectual synthesis that addressed the various concerns of the major countercurrents in a systematic and unitary way. Institutionally, it would require the creation, or redirection, of a range of disciplinary sites and resources—a fraught endeavor. This would mean finding a way to outmaneuver the institution's default strategy for defusing dissent: first to ignore, second to incorporate by creating a new "field," and lastly, once the fuss has died down, quietly to let the new field go. The broader aim would be to secure a viable site within the social order from which to work at criticism in the genuinely oppositional sense. This would necessitate making broader alliances with the left outside the discipline, for it is on the broader success or failure of a more general forward movement that a movement for criticism within literary studies would ultimately depend.

That final point deserves some elaboration. Historicist/contextualist work often makes claims about its political value, and sometimes those claims are true. But one gets a different sense of what does and does not count as "political" when one tries to imagine the response that a genuinely radical, rather than liberal, project of subject formation would call down upon itself, were it to become established in any widespread way—still more a project that had real success in cultivating new collectivities that were bent on pursuing modes of life deeper than any that the existing order is willing to allow. If the left of the discipline is to make advances, it will need to do so by exposing conflict where previously one had seen merely the blank features of a dead peace, and one makes few friends in that fashion. The humanities being in as weak a position as they are, literary studies' ability to succeed at any genuinely resistant task will be dependent, most of all, on the strength and suppleness of its articulation with the larger forward movement—if indeed there is to be one. The challenge is to do our part in ensuring that there is.

Appendix

The Critical Paradigm and T. S. Eliot

I OUGHT TO ADMIT that I take some pleasure in consigning T. S. Eliot to an Appendix; it was initially a footnote, but then I repented. My purpose here is to glance briefly at a few thoughts that might lead one to want to unseat him a little from his usual position as general-in-chief of the critical paradigm—which is to say, my intentions are essentially hostile. Yet my broader aim is to rescue something that he valued from the particular manner in which he valued it, and in that sense, at least, we are in sympathy; the real argument is against those who would condemn *all* criticism as necessarily conservative on the strength of the assumption that Eliot can be treated as a synecdoche for the whole. My reason for addressing Eliot in an Appendix, rather than treating him in the body of the text itself, is that his case raises specialist considerations that are both complex and of somewhat limited relevance to the main story, at least when one is telling it in as ruthless a way as I have tried to do—ruthlessly *focused,* I mean, of course. Eliot comes first in any chronological list of the major early critics, which makes it very convenient, from the standpoint of anyone trying to write a history, to claim him as the originator and architect of the critical paradigm. Yet the real story is a bit more complicated than that. I was at one stage tempted to begin the first chapter of the book with Eliot, showing first his continuity with the belletrisms of the *fin de siecle* and then, second, drawing attention to his innovations, only to point out, third, the ways in which many of those innovations really constituted a false start; then beginning the story once again with

Richards, only to return to Eliot later in a discussion of the process by which the whole scene turned to the right. This would have been chronologically accurate, but as this summary indicates, it would have involved paying a price in both conciseness and readability. For better or worse, I have opted instead to start the book where the critical paradigm really begins, with Richards, and instead glance briefly at the exceptional case of Eliot here.

Nowadays Eliot is almost always considered the key figure in the critical revolution. This seems natural enough, given that Richards, Leavis, and the New Critics each claimed him as their figurehead at one time or another—which is to say, all the major thinkers associated with the new paradigm, barring Empson. But when one looks a little deeper, noticing that these thinkers and movements in fact claimed him in the name of quite different and sometimes even quite opposing principles, one begins to harbor certain doubts. If, as Louis Menand tells us, "the genius of Eliot's literary strategy might be characterized as the genius of a weak pragmatism," meaning in part that his characteristic ambivalence was a deliberate strategy that allowed him, for a time, to seem to be all things to all people, might the same not be true of his criticism?[1] It is not to underrate Eliot's real achievements to observe of him also that he had the happy knack of delivering gnomic pronouncements in an authoritative tone of voice, and that he often did so opportunistically in order to take full advantage of the various possibilities the situation offered. My point is the gnomic-ness of the utterances, the ambiguity of which allowed him to function as a figurehead for a range of quite disparate movements. His mystique was of such a kind as to conceal the real contours of his position, which allowed his name to be used to authorize the pursuit of quite opposite ends. Here it is perhaps telling that when he finally came to declare a position (the famous "classicist in literature, royalist in politics, and anglo-catholic in religion" of the preface to *For Lancelot Andrewes*), his celebrity was still on the rise, but his substantive influence on other thinkers was beginning its decline.[2]

In this connection, it is perhaps worth recalling the letter of the same year in which Virginia Woolf informs her sister of Eliot's conversion:

> Then I have had a most shameful and distressing interview with poor dear Tom Eliot, who may be called dead to us all from this day forward. He has become an Anglo-Catholic, believes in God and immortality, and goes to

church. I was really shocked. A corpse would seem to me more credible than he is. I mean, there's something obscene in a living person sitting by the fire and believing in God.[3]

These lines have been much discussed as an index to Woolf's views, and as a place at which to debate the secular or religious character of high modernism generally. But they are also remarkable for something quite different. How can Eliot's Christianity come as such a "shock" to her? Knowing what we now do about Eliot's later views, it is hard to recover Woolf's surprise. Surely the traces of Eliot's religious brand of conservatism were obvious enough, even in his earliest writings? They certainly seem so today. Yet here we have Woolf, surely one of the most perceptive observers of her time—and an observer, moreover, who was very close indeed to Eliot; an observer with the most serious interest in divining the implications of his views—and still, when Eliot reveals his position, it leaves her "shocked" and "distressed." She is performing for Vanessa here, of course, but the underlying surprise seems real. Reflecting on this gives one a strong sense of how ambivalent Eliot's position had seemed before this point.

One then begins to wonder what Eliot's influence in the early period was, precisely, beyond the obvious rhetorical weight of his perceived authority. How much control was he really exercising over the critical paradigm as it formed? What *kind* of control? To clarify the precise nature of Eliot's relationship to the whole early scene, it is necessary to see that he exercised at least three kinds of influence, each of which needs to be distinguished from the others and then assessed accordingly. I will be brief. First, there is his influence on modernist poetry, and thence on the poetry of subsequent generations. This is of course very considerable indeed. Yet for the purposes of assessing the influence of his critical thought, it is obviously of only indirect relevance—certainly the fact that he was *both* a deep and provocative thinker in criticism *and* a sophisticated poet of a startlingly new kind made him tremendously convenient as a figurehead for the critical revolution, but, at least in principle, this is quite distinct from the question of his substantive influence on particular critical doctrines, still more from the question of his influence on the birth of the modern critical paradigm itself.

Second, there is his influence on the specific doctrines of key critical movements from the 1920s through to the mid-century. This influence was of

course also very considerable—even a cursory survey would show that Eliot
was responsible for at least four ideas, or sets of ideas, that became central to
the many of the most important critical movements of the early-to-mid century: first, his subtle and deeply-thought conception of "tradition"; second, his
historical thesis of the "dissociation of sensibility" and his consequent revalua-
tion of the English poetic canon; third, his doctrine of "impersonality"; and
fourth, his suggestive remarks on the "objective correlative." Each of these was
received as a key intervention at the time Eliot pronounced it, and it was then
incorporated as a central element in some of the most important critical positions of the 1920s, 1930s, and 1940s. Indeed, it is not too much to say that,
taken together, these four related passages of thought did more than any other
to determine the specific political, aesthetic, and historical content of literary
criticism in those decades. The politics of this are also clear enough: with the
benefit of hindsight, it is not difficult to see that of these four key terms,
two—"tradition" and the "dissociation of sensibility"—were being framed by
Eliot in such a way that they would prove significantly easier to use for conservative purposes than for liberal or radical ones.

At this point, the discussion of Eliot's influence usually stops, and we are
left with the conclusion that he was the central figure in the critical revolution, which then proves itself an essentially conservative endeavor after all.
Yet there remains a third level of influence, one quite distinct from the
others, and specifying it here allows me not merely to make observations
about Eliot's role in the early history of criticism, but also to reemphasize
some of the central methodological stakes of the book as a whole. For when
one is stepping back to discern, over the century of the discipline's development, the traces of its present lines of force, one must consider not merely
how a thinker was received by their contemporaries, nor their influence on
the specific doctrines of subsequent movements, but their influence, over
the whole period, on the basic structure of the discipline itself. What *was*
Eliot's influence on the critical paradigm itself, as distinct from his influence
on the particular doctrines held at one time or another by the movements
that sought, in their various ways, to put that paradigm into practice? This
is where one's doubts about the extent of Eliot's influence come to a head,
because here in truth his contribution seems surprisingly slight. To many in
the 1930s and 1940s, Eliot's key terms seemed central to the revolution in
criticism, yet by the 1950s and 1960s they were starting to be left behind

even by those who were still strongly committed to the practice of criticism itself. One then wants to ask what the underlying paradigm was, such that later thinkers could understand themselves as literary critics, as distinct from literary scholars, without feeling any need to commit themselves to Eliot's specific doctrines. Putting it differently, one might say that the boundaries of the paradigm established by the critical revolution were evidently significantly broader than those drawn by Eliot. Who then established those broader boundaries?

If the need for conciseness requires that you focus on a single figure, then the short answer to this is Richards, and it is only a surprising answer if we forget the problem the belletrists faced—the problem that the critical revolution proved able to solve. How does one pursue the tenuous task of cultivating an appreciation for the aesthetic without lapsing into mere impressionism? How does one pursue this task with a rigor sufficient to qualify one's work as disciplinary in the scientistic terms recognized by the modern university? We are returned to the centrality of the new methods of "close reading" and "practical criticism," and here I think it starts to feel uncomfortable to emphasize the centrality of these methodological innovations and at the same time take as the central figure T. S. Eliot, who contributed little to either.[4] In this circumstance it seems better to say that, while Eliot served as a convenient figurehead for the critical revolution, this was for complex and in many ways quite contradictory reasons, and while many of his particular emphases were determinative for particular schools and movements in the 1930s and 1940s, the crucial break that enabled the birth of the critical paradigm itself derives most centrally from the work of Richards and Empson.[5] This was quite well understood by many all the way through the mid-century: thus Stanley Edgar Hyman in 1947: "No treatment of modern criticism is possible without discussing Richards, since in the most literal sense Richards created it. What we have been calling modern criticism began in 1924, with the publication of *Principles of Literary Criticism*" (278).[6] Later on, much of the discipline was to forget this: by the 1970s it was becoming increasingly normal to assume Eliot's centrality, and by the 1980s one heard little else. Today, though, it ought to be possible to return to the better view, rejecting the widespread assumption that the critical paradigm was born as Eliot's creature, as well as the sense of the necessary conservatism of the critical paradigm that this assumption has been taken to authorize.

Notes

Introduction

1. In the United States, the "scholars" versus "critics" distinction was brought to the attention of many by Gerald Graff's *Professing Literature* in 1987, but it is not simply a historian's terminology: throughout much of the century, many thinkers in the field explicitly referred to the conflict in substantially the same terms.

2. John Guillory with Jeffrey J. Williams, "Towards a Sociology of Literature: An Interview with John Guillory," *Minnesota Review* 61 (2004): 95–109.

3. For sensitive reflections on the "heroic age" of criticism, see Stefan Collini, *Common Reading: Critics, Historians, Publics* (New York: Oxford University Press, 2008).

4. I address these new tendencies, together with others, in the final chapter—but some of the central reference points are as follows. For new formalism, see for example Marjorie Levenson, "What is New Formalism," *PMLA*, vol.122, no. 2 March 2007, pp. 557–569; and Caroline Levine, "Strategic Formalism: Towards a New Method in Cultural Studies," *Victorian Studies* 48 (Summer 2006): 625–657. For surface reading, see Stephen Best and Sharon Marcus, "Surface Reading: An Introduction," *Representations* Vol. 108, No. 1 (Fall 2009): 1–21. For distant reading, see the papers collected in Franco Moretti, *Distant Reading* (London: Verso, 2013).

5. Fredric Jameson, *The Political Unconscious: Narrative as a Socially Symbolic Act* (Durham: Duke University Press, 1981).

6. Later published as Perry Anderson, *In the Tracks of Historical Materialism* (London: Verso, 1983).

7. Terry Eagleton, *Literary Theory: An Introduction* (Minneapolis: University of Minnesota Press, 1983) 185–186.

8. Terry Eagleton, *The Function of Criticism* (London: Verso, 1984), 56–57.

9. To see what I mean here, one only has to look at the many graphs of, say, income inequality that circulated during, and then in the wake of, the movements of 2011. See, for instance, Thomas Piketty's *Capital in the Twenty-First Century* (Cambridge: Harvard University Press, 2014).

10. Perry Anderson, "Renewals," *New Left Review* 1 (January–February 2000), 5–24.

11. Susan Watkins, "Shifting Sands," *New Left Review* 61 (January–February 2010), 5–27.

1. The Critical Revolution Turns Right

1. Chris Baldick, *Criticism and Literary Theory 1890 to the Present* (London: Longman, 1996), 20.

2. Gerald Graff, *Professing Literature: An Institutional History* (Chicago: Chicago University Press, 1987), 55.

3. John Guillory, "Literary Study and the Modern System of the Disciplines" in Amanda Anderson and Joseph Valente, eds. *Disciplinarity at the Fin de Siecle* (Princeton: Princeton University Press, 2002). Guillory's essay focuses on these two main tendencies, presumably because he finds them central, but it is perhaps worth noting that in regard to the 1890s scene, he zooms in, as it were, to a lower level of generality and detects "four different disciplinary practices (philology, literary history, belles lettres, composition)" (35). This seems right. Once the critical revolution of the 1920s remakes *belles lettres* as a forcefully defined and combative "criticism," both the language-based studies that resemble the old philology and the continuing practices of literary history will increasingly be understood as within the broad tent of "scholarship," leaving composition, as so often, out in the cold.

4. Gerald Graff, *Professing Literature: An Institutional History* (Chicago: Chicago University Press, 1987), 14.

5. John Guillory, "Literary Study and the Modern System of the Disciplines" in Amanda Anderson and Joseph Valente, eds. *Disciplinarity at the Fin de Siecle* (Princeton: Princeton University Press, 2002), 24. In passing, it is worth noting here that Guillory believes that the philologists, for their part, *also* failed to achieve disciplinary status, though for the opposite reason: they "overextended their claim to scientificity" (36).

6. Stanley Edgar Hyman, *The Armed Vision: A Study in the Methods of Modern Literary Criticism* (New York: Vintage, 1947).

7. Christopher Hilliard's wonderfully rich *English as a Vocation: The Scrutiny Movement* (Oxford: Oxford University Press, 2012) is the source of many of my examples here. On the connection between the critical paradigm in its Leavisite form and adult education movements in Britain, see also John McIlroy and Sallie Westwood, eds. *Border Country: Raymond Williams in Adult Education* (Leicester: National

Institute of Adult Continuing Education, 1993). On the connection to the birth of cultural studies, see Tom Steele, *The Emergence of Cultural Studies 1945–1965: Cultural Politics, Adult Education and the English Question* (London: Lawrence and Wishart, 1997). The *Doctor Who* is from Hilliard, page 99.

8. Chris Baldick, *Criticism and Literary Theory 1890 to the Present* (London: Longman, 1996), 13. The fuller context of this line of some relevance here:

> The heroic phase of modern Anglo-American criticism, from the 1920s to the 1960s, was marked by the subordination of literary-historical and literary-biographical study to the ascendant discourses of critical analysis and evaluation. In terms of method, this entailed a new practice of 'close reading', attending to the specific formal features of texts rather than to the general world-views of their authors. Nothing distinguishes twentieth-century literary criticism more sharply from that of previous ages than this close attention to textual detail. (13)

This emphasis on the centrality of close reading strikes me as quite correct. Francis Mulhern, focusing on the British scene, draws the same emphasis: "Richards's theories were the main formative influence on Cambridge English. His 'practical criticism' soon became independent of the liberal theory of communication on which it rested, and passed into currency as the key instrument of literary analysis in general." Francis Mulhern, *The Moment of 'Scrutiny'* (London: New Left Books, 1979) 27. This is right on.

9. For examples of the first kind of account, which treat "close reading" mainly as a New Critical innovation, see Frank Lentricchia and Andrew DuBois eds., *Close Reading: The Reader* (Durham: Duke University Press, 2003), especially DuBois' introduction; Franco Moretti's "Conjectures on World Literature" *New Left Review* 1 (2000) 54–68; and Jane Gallop's "The Historicization of Literary Study and the Fate of Close Reading," *Profession* (2007), 181–185, as well as her "Close Reading in 2009" *ADE Bulletin* 149 (2010), 15–19. For examples of the second kind of account, in which "close reading" is seen as originating with Richards and Empson, but Richards and Empson are then seen as "proto-New Critics," see John Guillory's very interesting "Close Reading: Prologue and Epilogue" *ADE Bulletin* 149 (2010), 8–14 (Richards is the "prologue" here); and Jonathan Culler's very fine piece "The Closeness of Close reading" *ADE Bulletin* 149 (2010) 20–25, which makes the same move via the formulation "Anglo-American New Criticism."

10. Richards on another occasion: "I can't add anything about my 'followers' not having known who they could be or easily acknowledging any who seemed to regard themselves so." These statements are Richards' way of divorcing himself entirely from New Criticism as a critical tendency, and should not of course be taken literally: as Richards' biographer John Paul Russo notes, Richards in fact knew a great deal about the New Critics, being personally acquainted with many of them. John Paul Russo, *I. A. Richards: His Life and Work* (Baltimore: Johns Hopkins UP, 1989) 524. Empson's charges ("dogma" and "absurd") were levelled specifically at the view, associated with the New Criticism and with Neo-Christian criticism more generally, "that the reader

of poetry only has the words on the page, and the author didn't mean him to have anything else so he mustn't *know* anything [else]." See William Empson, "The Argument about Shakespeare's Characters," *Critical Quarterly* 7:3 (Autumn 1965), reprinted in John Haffenden, *Selected Letters of William Empson* (Oxford, Oxford University Press, 2006) 389.

11. CK Ogden, I. A. Richards, and James Wood, *The Foundations of Aesthetics* (London: Allen & Unwin, 1922); C. K. Ogden and I. A. Richards, *The Meaning of Meaning: A Study of the Influence of Language Upon Thought and of the Science of Symbolism* (London: K. Paul, Trench, Trubner & Co, 1923). References to *Principles* are to I. A. Richards, *Principles of Literary Criticism* (London: Routledge, 2001[1924]). References to *Practical Criticism* are to I. A. Richards, *Practical Criticism: A Study of Literary Judgment* (London: Harcourt Brace Jovanovich, 1956 [1929]).

12. A word here on the reception of *Practical Criticism*. Richards' central finding in this work was that, by and large, the students tested found even fairly simple poems very difficult to make sense of, and moderately complex ones completely unintelligible. One initial conclusion he drew was that we had overestimated most people's ability to construe language: a more direct and focused form of education in simple comprehension was required—this is one of the convictions that leads him to develop "close reading." Yet much of the subsequent reception of *Practical Criticism* has offered a rather different account of what the experiment revealed: an account that emphasizes that the students were unable to distinguish poems by authors generally considered geniuses from those by authors generally considered dunces—that is, that the students had made a failure, not of "construing" in its most basic sense, but of "taste," of aesthetic judgment. In many cases readings of this kind are symptomatic of the history I outline here. As we shall see, as the century proceeds Richards' distinctive emphasis on training basic cognitive and affective capacities rapidly gets buried beneath the Leavisite and New Critical emphasis on coming to the "correct" aesthetic judgments about specific works. It is only when we read *Practical Criticism* back through the lens of those later texts that it starts to appear, first as an exposé about the failures of literary studies as aesthetic education, and then, as the century proceeds, as a kind of unwitting critique of the aesthetic *per se*.

13. There is a great deal to be said at this point about Richards' student William Empson. For our purposes, it is enough to note that, like Richards' *Practical Criticism*, Empson's *Seven Types of Ambiguity* (Norfolk: New Directions Press, 1947 [1930]) is often read back through the history of its influence in America: its focus on "ambiguity" and its very close attention to fine linguistic detail in poetry allow it to be read as an early work of New Criticism. Yet Empson's work in *Seven Types* is less a model of close attention to "the poem itself," and more a detailed investigation into reader responses: a tracking of, and speculation about, the sorts of associations an ordinarily competent language user makes when encountering poetic language. As with Richards' *Practical Criticism*, the primary effort is not to sever the text from its context, but to investigate the nature of the relationship between the text and its context of reception.

14. A good example here would be Terry Eagleton, who overlooks this diagnostic aspect of the project when he tells us that:

> To my mind . . . much the most interesting aspect of [*Practical Criticism*], and one apparently quite invisible to Richards himself, is just how tight a consensus of unconscious valuations underlies [the students'] particular differences of opinion. Reading Richards' undergraduates' accounts of literary works, one is struck by habits of perception and interpretation which they spontaneously share. . . . [Richards] as a young, white, upper middle-class male Cambridge don was unable to objectify a context of interests in which he himself largely shared, and was thus unable to recognize fully that local, 'subjective' differences of evaluation work within a particular, socially structured way of perceiving the world. (*Literary Theory: An Introduction.* London: Verso, 1996:13–14)

This is of course one of the left's classic critiques of liberalism—that liberals like Richards fail to see how individual cases are determined by larger social forces. In so many places, this is a necessary and principled critique. Yet it seems odd to apply it to the Richards of *Practical Criticism,* for here he cannot really be accused of failing to perceive larger structures: his project in the second half of the work is precisely to observe and analyze the ways in which the various students' different errors of reading fall into broader, socially determined patterns of perception and response. The left critique should rather be that Richards analyses these structures at what we might now call a "cognitive" level, without then going on seriously to interrogate the political, economic, and ideological structures which would help to explain the production and distribution of the cognitive ones. Yet for the left the analysis of cognitive patterns remains of considerable value as long as we are prepared to see it in light of a broader account of determining forces. For a much more nuanced reading of this diagnostic part of Richards' project, we can turn to Eagleton's teacher, Raymond Williams, who tells us that *Practical Criticism* demonstrated:

> [T]hat the cultural consensus around certain earlier notions of cultivation or taste could be quite brutally refuted by presenting people with texts without any cultural signals like the author's name, or any other cues to 'the right response.' If you asked people about the authors who had written these pieces, they knew what to say within the terms of the consensus. When they actually had to read and describe their writings, the result was radically different—in some cases nearly the reverse. So the effect of Richards' practical criticism was anti-ideological in a very crucial sense: it exposed the disparity between the cultural pretensions of a class and its actual capacities. (Raymond Williams, *Culture.* London: Fontana, 1981:192–193)

As a way of recuperating Richards' project for leftist purposes, Williams' reading of *Practical Criticism* as an insistence on the gap between the "cultural pretensions of a class and its actual capacities" seems rather useful. Yet, by reading the results of Richards' experiment as evidence of a failure in "taste," a failure of aesthetic education,

Williams here threatens to elide what is really the more fundamental point revealed by the experiment: that the institutions of literary study, as well as the broader social order, had failed to provide the students with the ability to construe basic meanings in simple poems—that is, simply that they were unable to read, even in the ordinary sense of the term.

15. For reasons I note when I come to address Williams' work directly, it is not clear to me that the first task is inherently more politically viable than the second. See chapter two, footnote 9.

16. *Principles,* page x.

17. Twelve Southerners, *I'll take My Stand: The South and the Agrarian Tradition* (Baton Rouge: Louisiana State University Press, 1977 [1930]).

18. The key study here would be Mark Jancovich's *The Cultural Politics of New Criticism* (Cambridge: Cambridge University Press, 1993).

19. It is worth noting that Brooks insists on this distinction again and again: he likes the practical Richards of *Practical Criticism,* and he rejects the theoretical Richards of *Principles of Literary Criticism.* "The *practical* effect of Richards' discussion [in *Practical Criticism*] of his thirteen selected poems was almost overwhelming, and was to make its fortune in the world of letters. The *theoretical* aspect of the work, however, was another matter . . . (587; my italics); "[The] 'precepts' and 'admonitions' urged in *Practical Criticism. . . .* impressed me so much that they made up in part for what I found difficult or distasteful, particularly in *Principles*" (589); "I wrote long letters to John Ransom and Allen Tate in which I argued that, *in spite of his philosophy and his terminology,* Richards was a perceptive critic of great power who, *at least in his application,* arrived at judgments that were almost wholly compatible with mine" (589; my italics); "His practical criticism tends to correct his inadequate theory" (592); and so on. Cleanth Brooks, "I. A. Richards and *Practical Criticism,*" *The Sewanee Review* Vol. 89, No. 4 (1981): 586–595.

20. See William K. Wimsatt, *The Verbal Icon: Studies in the Meaning of Poetry* (Lexington: University of Kentucky Press, 1954).

21. John Crowe Ransom, *The New Criticism* (Norfolk: New Directions Press, 1941).

22. See John Crowe Ransom, "Criticism, Inc." *Virginia Quarterly Review* 13 (Autumn 1937) pp. 586–602. Ransom was of course responding directly to R. S. Crane's "History Versus Criticism in the Study of Literature," a traditional landmark for anyone looking to track the development of the critic/scholar distinction. See R. S. Crane, "History Versus Criticism in the Study of Literature," English Journal 24.8 [1935] pp. 645–667.

23. *Practical Criticism,* 327.

24. John Paul Russo, *I. A. Richards: His Life and Work* (Baltimore: Johns Hopkins University Press, 1989) 542.

25. Empson, with his keen interest in, among other things, historical contexts, literary biography, and even authorial intention, is the exception here.

26. On the Anglophone left, the classic reference points for understanding Leavis and Leavis-ism more generally are Perry Anderson, "Components of the National Culture," *New Left Review* 1, no. 50 (July–August 1968): 3–57, which is excellent, though it is worth noting that the section addressing Leavis is much shorter than the long shadow the piece casts in subsequent debates might lead one to suppose; and Francis Mulhern's brilliant, and much more extensive, *The Moment of 'Scrutiny'* (London: New Left Books, 1979). For a careful defense of Leavis—very, very thin on the ground nowadays—one can do little better than Michael Bell, *F. R. Leavis* (London: Routledge, 1988). (I remain grateful to Stefan Collini for having referred me to Bell's book). Anderson and Mulhern's accounts of the role that Leavis-ism played in tipping to the right a cultural moment that was otherwise rather delicately balanced are, I think, exceptionally perceptive, and as a result the picture they offer has largely been taken for granted in the left's subsequent reception of Leavis. At one level, this is as it should be—yet Bell's claim that neither really does justice to the depth of Leavis' view of language is, I think, worth taking on board. The question then is as to how much really rests on this. I have tried to conduct something like a preliminary scouting of that question in the main text.

27. See Philip Smallwood and Philip Trew, "British Theory and Criticism: 5. 1900 and After," in *Johns Hopkins Guide to Literary Theory and Criticism,* 2nd ed. (Baltimore: Johns Hopkins University Press, 2005).

28. I quote this as Leavis reproduces it in "Mass Civilisation and Minority Culture." See F. R. Leavis, *Education and the University* (Cambridge: Cambridge University Press, 1979), pp. 143–171. The original passage, in its full form, can be found in I. A. Richards, *Principles of Literary Criticism* (London: Routledge, 2001), pp. 54–55.

29. I quote from F. R. Leavis, *The Living Principle: English as a Discipline of Thought* (Chicago: Ivan R. Dee, Inc., 1975).

30. One can of course also note the ways in which these broad similarities in the larger positions play out in the smaller details. One example: a few pages after his parsing of the phrase "criticism of life," Leavis moves to defend Arnold on grounds that could be taken straight from the pages of *Practical Criticism:* "It is only by bringing our experience to bear on it that we can judge the new thing, yet the expectations that we bring, more or less unconsciously, may get in the way" (61). This is quite precisely Richards on "stock responses"; the fact that Leavis feels no need to cite him here is evidence of how thoroughly internalised these sorts of considerations had by then become.

31. It may help those more familiar with philosophy than with criticism if I note here that it is a view of language somewhat reminiscent of the kind later associated with the Wittgenstein of the *Philosophical Investigations* (1953), who was of course at Cambridge while the critical revolution was in full swing.

32. I am thinking here particularly of Richards' characteristic rejection of aestheticist views of the artist as, *qua* artist, a special or an especially idiosyncratic person, essentially different in kind from the rest of us, and his contrary insistence on the necessary

"normality" of the artist, by which he means, in effect, the potential representativeness of the artist's experience. See "The Normality of the Artist," the twenty-fourth chapter of *Principles of Literary Criticism*. In passing, as a gloss for future readers, let me draw attention to the casual racism with which the chapter opens, the very odd and intriguing theory of artistic form to which it proceeds, and the more humane note on which it ends.

33. I am grateful to Francis Mulhern for clarifying this for me. "Leavis himself never called for a return to the 'organic community,' which he expressly ruled out. The 'finest use of language' was in his view the surviving trace of such a community and the practical point in the present was the defense and development of that in the hands of 'the critical minority': elitism was the programmatic obverse of his retrospective populism. The motif of the organic community receded in *Scrutiny* with the departure of Denys Thompson in 1939." Francis Mulhern, personal communication.

34. Later in "Mass Civilization and Minority Culture," Leavis repeats almost precisely the same move. He quotes a number of those with whom he disagrees, and then states, characteristically, that "such pronouncements could be made only in an age in which there were no standards, no living tradition of poetry spread abroad, and no discriminating public. It is the plight of culture generally that is exemplified here" (157). He then offers, as one of his few footnotes, the following long quote from Richards' *Practical Criticism:*

> For there is no such gulf between poetry and life as over-literary persons sometimes suppose. There is no gap between our everyday emotional life and the material of poetry. The verbal expression of this life, at its finest, is forced to use the technique of poetry; that is the only essential difference. We cannot avoid the material of poetry. If we do not live in consonance with good poetry, we must live in consonance with bad poetry. And, in fact, the idle hours of most lives are filled with reveries that are simply bad private poetry. On the whole evidence, I do not see how we can avoid the conclusion that a general insensitivity to poetry does witness a low level of general imaginative life.

Once again, Leavis selects a passage in which Richards is at his most judgmental, and once again, even in the passage selected, Richards' central aim is really to insist on the continuity of artistic experience with ordinary experience, in contrast to Leavis who wants instead to emphasise the collapse of "standards" and the "plight of culture generally."

35. This strange fixation on staging and restaging the scene of judgment is replayed at the level of Leavis' treatment of critics, too. Thus his final endorsement of Arnold as a critic is made in the following terms:

> [Arnold's] actual achievement in producible criticism may not seem a very impressive one. But we had better inquire where a more impressive is to be found. As soon as we start to apply any serious standard of what good criticism should be, we are led towards the conclusion that there is very little. If Arnold is not one of the great critics, who are they? Which do we approach with a greater expectation of profit? Mr Eliot himself—yes; and not only because his preoccupations are of our time; his

best critical writing has a higher critical intensity that any of Arnold's. Coleridge's pre-eminence we all recognize. Johnson?—that Johnson is a living writer no one will dispute, and his greatness is certainly apparent in his criticism. Yet that he imposes himself there as a more considerable power than Arnold isn't plain to me, and strictly as a critic—a critic offering critical value—he seems to me to matter a good deal less to us. As for Dryden, important as he is historically, I have always thought the intrinsic interest of his criticism much overrated . . . (63–64)

And so on. The testy shuffle around precedence, and the essay as a whole, finally ends with: "I can think of no other critic who asks to be considered here, so I will say finally that, whatever his limitations, Arnold seems to me decidedly more of a critic than the Sainte-Beuve to whom he so deferred" (64). Unless we have a particular interest in the re-ordering of tables of precedence, this is a pretty flat note on which to end.

I make this somewhat abstruse point at such length not merely to emphasize the distance between Leavis and Richards, but also to note that this sort of thing has had such an influence, not only on mid-century criticisms, but on our own. In this regard, it is perhaps worth recording here my sense that a surprising proportion of the best British writing in the world of letters—in the exceptionally fine *London Review of Books,* for instance—defaults to something like this mode even today, when the arguments and conditions that were once thought to underpin and justify it can no longer seriously be defended. Readers of Stefan Collin, for example—a writer whose work I greatly admire—are importantly, I think, being treated to the spectacle of a fair and measured judgment, as if the critic were really a kind of judge whose task, finally, is to come to a fair-minded and lasting assessment of the achievements of various figures, the better to know who is and who is not truly "first-rate." This is despite the fact that Collini himself would no doubt repudiate the kind of canon-policing that characterizes the mode in its earlier incarnations. Of all his work to date, this is perhaps seen most clearly in *Common Reading: Critics, Historians, Publics* (New York: Oxford University Press, 2008). It should perhaps be added that Collini's more recent work appears to be moving in a slightly different direction—I am judging from a distance, so it is possible that my eye is off, but it seems to me that in recent years his work has become increasingly open to partisan commitments. If so, then it is a development for which one can only cheer. I say this with a sense that something more is at stake than the work of a single person; I am hardly alone in thinking of Collini as one of the strongest contemporary representatives of a certain tradition of cultural criticism in Britain. This may be the moment to refer readers to the extended debate between Collini and Mulhern that appeared in the pages of *New Left Review* in the early 2000s—a debate that bears quite directly on what one might call the "Leavis question." See Francis Mulhern, *Culture/Metaculture* (London: Routledge, 2000); Stefan Collini, "Culture Talk." *New Left Review* 7 (Jan.–Feb. 2001): 43–53; Mulhern, "Beyond Metaculture." *NLR* 16 (July–Aug. 2002): 86–104; Collini, "Defending Cultural Criticism." *NLR* 18 (Nov.–Dec. 2002): 73–97; Mulhern, "What is Cultural

Criticism?" *NLR* 23 (Sept.–Oct. 2003): 35–49; Collini, "On Variousness; and on Persuasion." *NLR* 27 (May–June 2004): 65–97.

36. Though there were a few exceptions to this general rule. See for instance *The Living Principle: English as a Discipline of Thought* (Chicago: Ivan R. Dee, Inc., 1975) 19–69, where Leavis engages with, and selectively endorses, an idiosyncratic grouping of philosophers.

2. The Scholarly Turn

1. For the view from the fulminating right wing of the United States, see Roger Kimball's media favorite *Tenured Radicals: How Politics has Corrupted our Higher Education* (New York: Harper Collins, 1990) usually paired with Allan Bloom's *The Closing of the American Mind: How Higher Education Has Failed Democracy and Impoverished the Souls of Today's Students* (New York: Simon and Schuster, 1987). The subtle titles come with the territory. For a more serious account from the left, see Perry Anderson, "A Culture in Contraflow," *New Left Review* 182: 85–137.

2. A good starting point here is Nancy Fraser, *Fortunes of Feminism: From State-Managed Capitalism to Neoliberal Crisis* (London: Verso, 2013).

3. Here Jodi Melamed's question is a good one: in the United States in particular, to what extent did the new race critiques contest the United States' role as the guarantor of capital at the international level, and to what extent did they instead allow the United States to redescribe itself as an "internalized model of global diversity," thereby disguising its expansionism as merely that of "a universal nation fulfilling its destiny"? See Jodi Melamed, *Represent and Destroy: Rationalizing Violence in the New Racial Capitalism* (Minneapolis: University of Minnesota Press, 2011), 35.

4. See for instance Benita Parry, *Postcolonial Studies: A Materialist Critique* (London: Routledge, 2004) and Vivek Chibber, *Postcolonial Theory and the Specter of Capital* (London: Verso, 2013).

5. A good place to start here is Holly Lewis, *The Politics of Everybody: Feminism, Queer Theory, and Marxism at the Intersection* (London: Zed Books, 2016).

6. See for instance Daniel Zamora and Michael C. Behrent, eds. *Foucault and Neoliberalism* (Cambridge: Polity, 2016)

7. It is possible to take this argument a step further, albeit into some quite speculative territory, by examining some of the patterns that structured this confusion. As Marc Redfield, among others, has observed, the "Theory" debate was notable, not merely for its confusion, but also for the especially central role played by personifications, with the names of key theorists coming to stand for arguments, positions, qualities, affects, insults in complicatedly mediatized ways. Once one has appreciated the force of this observation, it begins to seem worthy of note that the two names that became perhaps most iconic of "theory," Foucault and Derrida, would, if classified according to the older dichotomy, fall on both sides of the traditional "scholars versus critics" debate: Foucault roughly in the former camp, Derrida very roughly in the latter.

I note this merely in order to observe that, if the new battle lines within Anglo-American literary studies were vague, they nevertheless formed themselves in just such a way as to muddy the older distinctions. It is then open to one to suspect that one of the most important effects of the shift into these vague terms, straddling the traditional dichotomy, was to mask what was, in the longer historical view, the truly momentous change going on within the discipline in just this period: the collapse of the distinction that had been the central axis of dispute in the discipline since the 1920s, and the eventual victory of the "scholar" over the "critic" model. Of course, this was far from being anything like the result that any of the main practitioners intended.

Our rough classification bears this out, for if one were to insist on imagining, perversely, the subsequent history of the discipline as, in part, a competition between Foucauldian "scholars" and Derridean "critics," one would find first that the history resists being split in this way, since the various attempts that were made to paint the two as opposing never really took on, but second, and perhaps just as important, that the Foucauldians win. For if the most obviously "critical" forms of deconstruction—de Manian and "Yale School"—were rather quickly to acquire a period flavor, Foucauldian "scholarship" was to make its way to the top of the field and remain there, in a wide array of differing forms, from the new historicism through to queer theory. Of course, as I just noted, this is a perverse way to read the history, since one forces these continental philosophers into Anglo-American literary-critical categories only at considerable cost. The analogy is very rough indeed. And yet, to continue the thought experiment, the particular texture of that roughness is perhaps itself an indicator of the turn toward scholarship, and away from criticism: Foucauldian reading, while radically new in its day, was still recognizably "scholarly" in that it took the form of archive-based cultural analysis. Yet deconstruction, for its part, was "critical" only in a very specialized sense: though Derrida, de Man, and the "Yale School" of deconstruction each resembled the older "critics" in their commitment to something like "close reading" and their associated determination to make use of the text as, in Richards' terms, "a machine to think with," rather than as a source of historical knowledge, they nevertheless represented a break from criticism towards a distinctly scholar-like specialization and professionalization, in that their aim was to use literary texts as a means by which to (un)think high-level philosophy, rather than as a means by which to cultivate the sensibilities of general or "common" readers. The key difference here lay in the fact that deconstruction was understood as having hollowed out the aesthetic—precisely the category that, in its various forms, had done most to provide the *raison d'etre* for criticism in its paradigmatic form. With apologies to Gayatri Spivak, who has at times made a valiant attempt to turn this deconstructive tradition in the direction of something like the more critical task of "aesthetic education," it is necessary to say that the training that the theory of the "double bind" offers is, I think, primarily cognitive—which is not to say that the double bind is not often also emotionally fraught. See Gayatri Chakravorty Spivak, *An Aesthetic Education in the Era of Globalization* (Cambridge: Harvard University Press, 2012).

8. Perry Anderson, "Renewals," *New Left Review* 1 (January–February 2000).

9. For Williams' demurrals about the applicability of the term "Left-Leavisism" see Raymond Williams, *Politics and Letters* (London: Verso, 1981), 195. The whole section from 190–195 is of considerable interest with respect to Williams' sense of the relationship between his own early methods and those of Leavis, and before him, Richards. But see also 65 where he makes the link in the most explicit terms, noting of the editorial board of the Journal "Politics and Letters," of which he was one of the three founding members: "Our intention was to produce a review that would, approximately, unite radical left politics with Leavisite literary criticism."

In this connection, it is perhaps helpful to reflect on Christopher Hilliard's claim that "'Left-Leavisism' was not a synthesis of *Scrutiny* and Labour or Marxist politics: it was a process of working with or working through the assumptions and analytical practices established by [Leavis'] *Culture and Environment* and arriving at a point where that book's governing principles no longer held" (170). Hilliard generally sees the scene with great clarity, and this is a fine line. I wonder, though, whether it is really true. It certainly points to something real: he is speaking not just of Williams but of a whole adult education scene, the other prominent name being Richard Hoggart, and often in work of that kind, it seems as if it was precisely the depth of the commitment to the given (broadly Leavisite) task that led to the position being developed in quite new ways. Pointing this out has the virtue of showing the power of Leavis' (or if you like, Richards') initial premises, which, taken forward, outstrip the limitations he placed on them—which is precisely my larger point. Yet if we take Hilliard's line at face value, then the claim is also that "Labour or Marxist politics" were ultimately irrelevant to left-Leavism: that the critique was entirely an immanent one, and that Williams, Hoggart, and company either could have arrived, or did in fact arrive, at their anti-Leavisite positions in the absence of any external influence from forces of that kind. *That* claim would be quite wrong: to say that Williams' development out of the Leavis tradition took nothing significant from Marxism is very much to overplay Leavis' hand.

10. Raymond Williams, *Politics and Letters* (London: Verso, 1981).

11. Raymond Williams, *Drama from Ibsen to Eliot* (London: Chatto and Windus, 1952)

12. In this respect, it is of some interest to observe that for Williams here "English literary sociology" itself begins with the practical criticism of the *Scrutiny* group:

> English literary sociology began, in effect, from this need of a radical critical group to locate and justify its own activity and identity: the practical distinction of good literature from the mediocre and the bad extending to studies of the cultural conditions underlying these differences of value . . . (18)

Apart from noting here once again that practical criticism began, not with Leavis' and the *Scrutiny* group's project of distinguishing "good literature from the mediocre and the bad" but with Richards' project of using both good literature and bad "as a means of ordering our minds," it is worth thinking back to what we earlier called the diagnostic part of Richards' project—his proposal for literary studies as, in part, "fieldwork in comparative ideology." Would it not be more accurate to say that "English literary sociology" within the university really begin there, with Richards, at the start of the discipline? See Raymond Williams, *Culture and Materialism: Selected Essays* (London: Verso, 2005).

13. In this regard, it is worth noting in passing that in accepting this emphasis, thinkers in the discipline whose primary intention was to reject the influence of Leavis were in fact implicitly accepting his retrospective construction of a tradition of criticism-as-judgment that ran behind him all the way back to Arnold. There is much to be said here about the history of the idea of "criticism" before its entry into the university as part of the discipline of English Literature; naturally I cannot say it here.

14. The two territories of the United States and United Kingdom can hardly be considered separately in this regard: Williams himself notes that his opposition to literary criticism as a project built on the assumption that it was possible to make impersonal judgments of works of literature "was really much more [an opposition] to later developments in New Criticism than to Leavis" (*Politics and Letters* 335). At this level of analysis, it is important to insist that the Anglo-American intellectual tradition moves as a unit, propelled in part by imbalances in the relative power and sophistication of the various national formations within it.

15. Raymond Williams, *Marxism and Literature* (New York: Oxford University Press, 1977).

16. Here it is of interest to observe that in mopping up, as it were, Williams goes on to argue that the term "beauty" cannot, as the tradition often claims, be used to secure a further specialization of the concept to *positive* sensory experiences, since the positive sensory experiences cannot finally be distinguished, in principle, from the negative ones—precisely the second move in Richards' argument.

17. The reader may perhaps excuse a long note here, for without wanting to digress too far from the main line of our history, there is also much to be said about Williams' sense that criticism is at fault for focusing too closely on the *context of reception* ("effect") and that it therefore needs to be supplemented (or really, replaced) by scholarly methods that can focus more effectively on the *context of production* ("intention and performance"). When we think of the particular forms of criticism he is trying to do battle with, we must, I think, agree that he is largely right: there was, in both Leavis and the New Criticism, a programmatic refusal to come seriously to grips with real problems of "intention and performance" in this sense. We could even go further to agree also that the "scholar" model of literary study—literary study as the production of knowledge about culture—has tended to favor approaches like Williams' that treat the text, finally, as an index to its context of production, whereas in contrast "criticisms" of various kinds, conceiving of literary study as a matter of developing and disseminating certain cultural capabilities through training readers, creating an educated public, and similar, have naturally enough tended to focus their attentions on the context of reception, often with very problematic results.

But we need to make some finer distinctions here, too, for as we have seen, there are "criticisms" and "criticisms." Can we really say that the Leavisite and New Critical obfuscation of the conditions of textual production was the consequence of their placing too great an emphasis on "effect"—on the context of reception, per se? I think the answer is no: the real error here has mostly been to deny "context" altogether in the name of a spiritualized and autotelic concept of "the text itself." After all, the New Critics were at pains to excoriate *both* the "Intentional Fallacy" *and* the "Affective Fallacy"—to exile both the writer *and* the reader, as it were. Leavis is less explicitly idealist here, but as we have seen, still represents a shift of emphasis, not *onto* questions of "effect," as Williams seems to think, but away from them, and instead onto the process by which the critic judged the text "itself"—a shift of emphasis that was to become decisive. Noticing this allows us to observe, once again, one of the key differences between criticisms of what I am calling the first and the second periods: what was initially, in Richards and Empson, a deliberate focus on the context of reception becomes, in Leavis and then even more evidently in the New Critics, a rejection of context altogether.

If Williams misses this here, it is because of his tendency to feel that the context of production is the only thing that really counts as a context for leftist purposes. In this, he is again very much of our period: "context" is now reflexively used in this way, in reference to the context of production alone. Yet surely this is overly restrictive: the various contexts of reception are at least as important, and there are good reasons to want to distinguish between past contexts of reception and present contexts of reception, too. Williams focuses his analysis on the context of production because for him such an analysis can entail—and indeed, for a Marxist, must entail—an analysis of the conditions of material production more generally. His proximity to Leavis makes him very aware that there were, in criticisms of the second period, ways of focusing on "effect" that amounted to an evasion of this more political, because more material, analysis: that amounted, really, to an ideological obfuscation of the conditions of material production by way of a redirection of our attention onto consumption. It is this, I think, that sometimes leads him to make too quick an equation between the specific context of textual production and the conditions of material production more broadly.

From our present vantage point, it is perhaps easier for us that it was for Williams to observe that there is no necessary identity between the two. In Williams' writings, an analysis of the specific context of textual production (the "structure of feeling") amounted to an analysis of the conditions of material production more broadly, but this is by no means always the case, as is attested by the countless pages of politically inert literary history that the discipline has produced both before and since Williams. Moreover, one might ask, could not an analysis of a text's relationships to its contexts of *reception* reveal just as much about the conditions of material production in the society at large? We might even say that, to the extent that for an activist such as Williams, useful cultural analysis must finally be a matter of describing the conditions of material production as they stand in the present, rather than as they stood in the past, it seems more promising to try to focus our attention on the present context of reception, rather than on past contexts of production. Yet this would of course still be to think in the mode of the cultural analyst. If we want to move forward into criticism proper, then we have to begin to see that analyses of contexts of production, and past contexts of reception, can be made to engage with the real, present conditions of material production only insofar as they can be brought to bear on the present context of reception: real, living readers—what I would perhaps term the "context of use." Praxis is only ever in the present, though it is of course essential to bring the past to bear on it as sophisticatedly as we can.

But this takes us into deeper methodological waters than a historical book of this kind is built to weather. For present purposes, the historical point is simply that we need to be able to appreciate the ways in which Williams' careful insistence on the importance of "intention and performance" offered a valuable corrective to criticisms of the second period, while also acknowledging that he misdiagnosed the real problems with that criticism in such a way as to dismiss also criticisms of the first period—criticisms to which William's argument ought not, in all rigor, have been applied. As the remainder of this chapter begins to show, the generalization of Williams' argument against Leavis and the New Critics into an argument against criticism *per se* did much to pave the way for a wholesale replacement of the "critic" by the "scholar" model, and so inadvertently did much to direct the discipline, as well as his particular branch of thinking on the left, into the respective impasses they have reached today, when our various highly developed practices of cultural analysis fail to bite in the absence of any equally developed practice of cultural intervention.

18. Of course, none of this is to say that Williams was not deeply committed to "practice" in other fields of endeavor; I merely mean to observe that he understood his disciplinary work in scholarly terms, as cultural analysis, cultural history, and cultural theory, rather than understanding it in critical terms as the systematic cultivation of sensibility. Naturally, the two are not finally distinguishable, and any powerful work of scholarship moves readers to try on different ranges of sensibility, etc., etc. But the "practice" of scholarship, conceived of as cultural analysis, is necessarily neither direct nor systematic in this respect. I ought to add that Williams' work as a novelist (to which I am personally very partial, for whatever that may be worth) is itself a significant form of "practice" in just this respect, the novels naturally seeking to engage readers' sensibilities directly, rather than indirectly via the medium of scholarly analysis—though even here I feel myself bound to add, reluctantly, that one of Williams' weaker points as a novelist is his tendency to lapse into sociological description, relying on the force of the underlying analysis to achieve effects that would be better wrought more directly on the reader's tastes, incipient responses, habits of evaluation, and so on. A longer account here might attempt to situate the aesthetic work performed by Williams' novels in its precise relation to his rejection of just that kind of work in his scholarship. I am grateful to Francis Mulhern for pressing me on this.

19. One of the members of the editorial board of the *New Left Review* put this succinctly during the interview with Williams: "What Morris really represents is the

first time that this whole tradition [that is, the tradition that Williams outlined in *Culture and Society*] centrally connects with the organised working class and the cause of socialism" (*Politics and Letters* 128). This seems right. Of the many passages by Morris that confirm his status as the point of confluence between the Romantic revolt and the revolt of the working class, let me just quote one:

> [T]here is a revolt on foot against the utilitarianism which threatens to destroy the arts. . . . For myself I do not indeed believe that this revolt can effect much, so long as the present state of society lasts; but as I am sure that great changes which will bring about a new state of society are rapidly advancing upon us, I think it a matter of much importance that these two revolts should join hands, or at least should learn to understand one another. (*Useful Work Versus Useless Toil*. London: Penguin, 2008, 31)

I cannot resist directing readers toward the obvious point of reference here: E. P. Thomson's extraordinary biography of Morris. See E. P Thomson, *William Morris: Romantic to Revolutionary* (London: The Merlin Press, 1955).

20. Raymond Williams, *Culture and Society 1780–1950* (New York: Columbia University Press, 1958).

21. "How I became a Socialist" 93, in *Useful Work Versus Useless Toil*. (London: Penguin, 2008), 88–94.

22. William Morris, 'The Lesser Arts' 83, in *Useful Work versus Useless Toil* (London, Penguin, 2008), 56–87.

23. "Why I am a Communist," *Labour Monthly* (December 1954): 565–568. Originally published in *The Why I Ams* (London: Liberty Press, 1894). The italics are mine.

24. Showing how this move comes through the various moments in the history of U.S. pragmatism would be a larger project. For now, it will have to suffice if I simply remind the reader of one of the clearest examples, from John Dewey:

> Wherever conditions are such as to prevent the act of production from being an experience in which the whole creature is alive and in which he possesses his living through enjoyment, the product will lack something of being esthetic. No matter how useful it is for special and limited ends, it will not be useful in the ultimate degree—that of contributing directly and liberally to an expanding and enriched life. The story of the severance and final sharp opposition of the useful and the fine is the history of that industrial development through which so much of production has become a form of postponed living and so much of consumption a superimposed enjoyment of the fruits of the labor of others. (*Art as Experience*. New York: Penguin, 2005, 27)

As so often in Dewey, the language here might well be called vague, but the strength of the thought comes through. Did he learn this from Morris? He doesn't cite him. But then

Dewey cites no one. In this connection it is perhaps worth noting that in *Art as Experience* (1934), Dewey, who cites no one, does cite Richards—disparagingly, of course.

3. The Historicist/Contextualist Paradigm

1. Terry Eagleton, *Literary Theory: An Introduction* (Minneapolis: University of Minnesota Press, 1983).

2. As we also noted in the Introduction, this appearance of success is somewhat deceptive, since one might fairly have doubts about the extent to which these kinds of arguments actually effected the changes they called for. What has been underestimated here is the extent to which the movement from "critical" to "scholarly" models of literary study—a movement called for and seemingly brought about by the left—was substantially the result of much broader political, economic, and cultural forces of a fundamentally conservative nature, viz., the crisis of Keynesianism and the turn to neoliberalism.

3. Terry Eagleton, *Literary Theory: An Introduction* (Minneapolis: University of Minnesota Press, 1983); *The Function of Criticism* (London: Verso, 1984).

4. *The Function of Criticism* (London: Verso, 1984), 38.

5. Terry Eagleton, *The Ideology of the Aesthetic* (London: Blackwell, 1990).

6. The best account here would still, I think, be Jameson's classic analysis of the plebeianization of culture under late capitalism. See Fredric Jameson, *Postmodernism, or The Cultural Logic of Late Capitalism* (Durham: Duke University Press, 1991).

7. Since we are talking here about national formations, this may the moment to note my sense that French conservatism, too, is sometimes still able—residually, I think, but not therefore negligibly—to shelter to a certain degree behind aesthetic distinctions. This bears on the question of why the other main lines of anti-aesthetic critique arrived specifically from France—though obviously there are also other factors. The emblematic figure here would be Bourdieu. A brief survey of this line of thought, which runs in parallel to the line developed by Williams, would move from Pierre Bourdieu, *Distinction: A Social Critique of the Judgment of Taste* (Cambridge: Harvard University Press, 1984) through John Guillory, *Cultural Capital: The Problem of Literary Canon Formation* (Chicago: University of Chicago Press, 1993), to, most recently, Pascale Casanova, *The World Republic of Letters* (Cambridge: Harvard University Press, 2007). This has proven to be a very significant line of thought during the period of the dominance of the "scholar" in literary studies, and indeed Bourdieu's work, as it was received within the discipline, played a key role in justifying the "scholarly turn." Of it, let me simply ask: even if we assume that this critique was aimed at a live target in France in the 1980s, can the same be said of it when it is made in the US-dominated Anglosphere today?

8. Catherine Gallagher and Stephen Greenblatt, *Practicing New Historicism* (Chicago: Chicago University Press, 2000).

9. This line is from *Culture and Materialism* (1980) 20. The best example of the New Historicist critique of materialism is probably Chapter 4 of *Practicing New Historicism,* "The Potato in the Materialist Imagination"; the explicit critique of Williams is at 112–113; the associated critique of E. P. Thomson is at 122–126. Those interested might see also the more extended discussion of Williams on 60–66 of the same work. Without attempting to adjudicate this issue in any thorough way here, I will simply record my sense that the New Historicists have a point to the extent that Williams, particularly when trying to engage with others who accept a very simplistically hierarchical account of base and superstructure, does sometimes have a tendency to accept formulations that involve the positing of "primary needs" that precede any process of culture, representation, or signification. To this extent, the New Historicist insistence on the omnipresence of representation is a welcome and valuable correction. Yet the central thrust of Williams' critique moves us in the opposite direction, toward an insistence that most or all of what has been considered superstructure must, in various moments of analysis, be considered part of the base. Much of the time, his moves to posit primary needs are in fact provisional ones, made at a certain stage in the argument specifically in order to explain his rather drastic revision of the base and superstructure model to Marxists who, he feels with some justification, may otherwise have difficulty coming to accept it. It is in this sense that one can say that the New Historicist move is merely a repetition of Williams'. For Williams' own critique of base and superstructure, see his essay "Base and Superstructure in Marxist Cultural Theory," *Culture and Materialism* (1980) 31–39, as well as *Marxism and Literature* 75–82. For an interrogation of Williams' position on base and superstructure that is wonderful and illuminating, even in its moments of comedy, see *Politics and Letters,* 140–147, 350–358.

10. For a very fine discussion of the whole issue, see Williams *Politics and Letters* (1979), pp. 78–83, and *Politics of Modernism* (1989), pp. 151–162.

11. Frank Lentricchia, *After the New Criticism* (Chicago: University of Chicago Press, 1980).

12. Readers may well want to check whether these phrases have any richer meanings in their original contexts, which I here provide:

[S]everal of us particularly wanted to hold on to our aesthetic pleasures . . . (4)

[We invited in] texts that have been regarded as altogether non-literary, that is, as lacking the aesthetic polish, the self-conscious use of rhetorical figures, the aura of distance from the everyday world, the marked status as fiction that characterize belles lettres . . . (9)

The conjunction [between literary and non-literary texts] can produce almost surrealist wonder at the revelation of an unanticipated aesthetic dimension in objects without pretensions to the aesthetic. (10)

But the new historicist project is not about "demoting" art or discrediting aesthetic pleasure . . . (12)

[O]ur effort is not to aestheticize an entire culture, but to locate inventive energies more deeply interfused within it. To do so is hardly to endorse as aesthetically gratifying every miserable, oppressive structure and every violent action of the past. (12)

To wall off for aesthetic appreciation only a tiny portion of the expressive range of a culture is to diminish its individuality and to limit one's understanding even of that tiny portion . . . (13)

13. From "World Literature," a lecture given as an acceptance speech for the Holberg International Memorial Prize, University of Bergen, Norway, November 25, 2008. For comments to the same effect in his written work, see, for example, *Archaeologies of the Future* (New York: Verso, 2005), p. 18, note 11, where "traditional aesthetics" is said to be "obsolete" on the grounds, really, that its "standard aim" is simply to "identify the specifics of the aesthetics as such."

14. For those who are interested in following this up, Jameson makes this fairly clear in his response to two questions from Leonard Green in an interview for *Diacritics* in 1982. See Leonard Green, Jonathan Culler, and Richard Klein, "Interview: Fredric Jameson," *Diacritics* 12:3 (1982): 72–91; reprinted in Ian Buchanan, ed., *Jameson on Jameson: Conversations on Cultural Marxism* (Durham: Duke University Press, 2007), 11–43. I have in mind Jameson's answers to Green's first two questions.

15. For relatively recent instantiations of the debate, see for instance the papers collected in Frank Lentricchia and Andrew DuBois, *Close Reading: The Reader* (Durham: Duke UP, 2003), as well as the three papers by Jonathan Culler, Jane Gallop, and John Guillory in the *ADE Bulletin* 149, 2010. As I observe above, Culler's paper seems particularly helpful in its attempt to get us thinking about the many things that "closeness" here might mean. He concludes by calling for us to "reflect on the varieties of close reading and even to propose explicit models." He explains:

> We would be better equipped to value and to promote close reading if we had a more finely differentiated sense of its modes and a more vivid account of all the types of nonclose reading with which it contrasts and that give it salience, making it more than something desirable that is taken for granted. (24)

Culler's quick, suggestive catalogue of various typologies of reading practices seems a good place to start this kind of project. Generally, his call for us to try to specify different modes of reading within the general category "close reading" seems to me very helpful—and even more his suggestion that this may involve the proposing of "explicit models."

16. "The Historicization of Literary Study and the Fate of Close Reading," *Profession* 2007:181–185, and reiterated in "Close Reading in 2009" *ADE Bulletin* 149 (2010).

17. Moretti subsequently developed this methodological argument in a series of further papers, which now have been conveniently collected in a single volume entitled *Distant Reading* (London: Verso, 2013). I will cite from this edition.

18. Jonathan Culler, "The Closeness of Close Reading" *ADE Bulletin* 149 (2010): 20–25.

19. Not to belabor the point, but it is also worth asking what happens to this kind of argument once one has recognized that close reading was in fact invented by secular—in Empson's case, radically atheist—left-liberals, precisely as a critique of "theological" idealisms of a New Critical kind.

20. Franco Moretti, *Graphs, Maps, Trees* (London: Verso, 2005).

4. The Critical Unconscious

1. Rei Terada, "The New Aestheticism," *Diacritics* vol. 23, no. 4, (1993): 42–61. This may also be an appropriate moment to thank Francis Mulhern for suggesting "The Critical Unconscious" as a title for this chapter.

2. One's sense of this is reinforced when one notes that some of the specific figures within the broader tendency were operating with an unusually accurate account of precisely how all this had come to pass. Winfried Fluck, for instance, saw the history of the anti-aesthetic turn with exemplary clarity. Thus:

> It has become one of the starting moves of recent revisionist scholarship in literary and cultural studies to emphasize the historical relativity of all aesthetic judgments and to stress their function not only as cultural but also as political acts. This argument can be traced back to one of the founding texts, if not the founding text, of cultural studies, Raymond Williams's *Culture and Society* [which] describes the emergence of the term aesthetic as a response to an alienating division of labor between artist and artisan. In *Marxism and Literature,* he takes one step further and characterizes aesthetic theory as a form of evasion, that is, as an instrument of obfuscations. (79)

> I want to claim that the new revisionism has systematically misunderstood and misrepresented the issue of aesthetics because it has conflated the New Critical version of aesthetic value with the issue of aesthetics in general. (84)

Observing the widespread turn against the aesthetic, Fluck saw clearly that it had one of its central roots in Williams, and he saw also that in accepting the argument in its broadest form the discipline was, in effect, allowing an argument against New Critical aesthetics to serve as an argument against aesthetics per se. Few saw the situation as sharply as that. Obviously such clear sight was not typical of the tendency as a whole, and nor, perhaps, would we expect it to be. Still, it can fairly be said that the new aestheticist position was founded on a perceptive analysis of the state of the discipline. See Winfried Fluck, "Aesthetics and Cultural Studies" in Elliot, Caton, and Rhyne, eds. *Aesthetics in a Multicultural Age* (Oxford, Oxford University Press, 2002).

3. John J. Joughin and Simon Malpas, "The New Aestheticism: An Introduction," in John J. Joughin and Simon Malpas, eds. *The New Aestheticism* (Manchester: Manchester University Press, 2003), 1–19.

4. This was despite the fact that Fluck's own position in aesthetics did tend toward breaching the traditional Kantian boundaries by way of a turn to pragmatism, and thus bears comparison, in certain respects, with the more radical work of Isobel Armstrong, to whom we will turn in a moment. See Winfried Fluck, "Aesthetics and Cultural Studies" in Elliot, Caton, and Rhyne, eds., *Aesthetics in a Multicultural Age* (Oxford: Oxford University Press, 2002), 79–103. He makes this particular argument about the "aestheticization of politics" at great length in "Radical Aesthetics." *REAL. Yearbook of Research in English and American Literature.* Vol. 15, *Pragmatism and Literary Studies.* Ed. Winfried Fluck. (Tubingen: Narr, 1999): 227–242. Fluck's analysis can be very incisive, but it must be noted that the central themes here are very staid ones, at least to my mind: academic radicals are all poseurs, their very existence is a testament to the generosity of the dominant liberalism, etc., etc. On the central points, Heinz Ickstad agreed: see "Towards a Pluralist Aesthetics" in *Aesthetics in a Multicultural Age* (Oxford, Oxford University Press, 2002) 263–278.

5. As Peter de Bolla notes, the debate is as interesting for its confusions as for what it illuminated. Peter de Bolla, "Toward the Materiality of Aesthetic Experience" *Diacritics,* Vol. 32, No. 1, Rethinking Beauty (Spring, 2001): 19–37.

6. George Levine, "Reclaiming the Aesthetic," in *Aesthetics and Ideology* (New Brunswick: Rutgers University Press, 1994).

7. Timothy Peltason, "The Way We Read and Write Now: The Rhetoric of Experience in Victorian Literature and Contemporary Criticism," p. 1010. *ELH*, Vol. 66, No. 4, (Winter, 1999): 985–1014; Paul J. Alpers, "Renaissance Lyrics and Their Situations," p. 309. *New Literary History,* Volume 38, Number 2 (Spring 2007): 309–333; Stephen Cohen, *Shakespeare and Historical Formalism* (Padstow: Ashgate, 2007), 14. Cohen opens the book by observing: "Without overmuch simplification, the institutional history of literary studies over the last hundred or so years can be characterized as a series of agonistic oscillations between the discipline's two mighty opposites, form and history" (1). This is a popular view, but it does not seem right.

8. Rachel Sagner Buurma and Laura Heffernan, "Interpretation, 1980 and 1880," p. 616; *Victorian Studies,* 55, No. 4, Special Issue: The Ends of History (Summer 2013): 615–628. It is worth noting that Buurma and Heffernan actually go on to take the argument in a different direction.

9. Another way to see my point here is to ask what is being elided when "materialist critique" in a Jamesonian mode is conflated with "activism." I think both are necessary, but we gain nothing by pretending that the former counts as the latter. Working within the discipline, I see this trick practiced every day, but it ought to belong to the right.

10. In a sense, Levinson is even unusually clear-sighted about the significance of the latter, in that she sees that the paradigm to which the better "new formalists" are seeking recommit themselves has its roots in the Marxist tradition. Thus she talks of

returning us to the "original" mode of "historical reading" and refers us back, in effect, to Marx (as the list of figures just quoted suggests, her campsite is really just the Marxist line, plus Freud). Yet I think perhaps the implied reference to a whole Marxist tradition is an exaggeration, and the phenomenon to which she is really responding is one that must be measured on a much smaller timescale. As she notes elsewhere, "Jameson is relentlessly held up as the good example"—the gesture, repeated again and again, is really towards the much more local history of the historicist/contextualist paradigm itself.

11. Levinson: "one cannot help noticing the striking agreement to exempt by name the founding figures of historicist critique from the charge of reductiveness, while maintaining the anonymity of those hapless "followers" and mere practitioners (Levine 2), those "less careful and subtle critics" (Clarke 9), who *are* held accountable for the sorry state of our criticism." (560). The references here are to the George Levine piece we have just been looking at, and to Michael Clark's *Revenge of the Aesthetic: The Place of Literature in Theory Today* (Berkeley: University of California Press, 2000).

12. Levinson is appropriately dismissive of "new formalist" reductionism here: "In many of these essays, *new historicism* serves as a catch-all term for cultural studies, contextual critique; ideology critique; Foucauldian analysis; political, intersectional, and special-interest criticism; suspicion hermeneutics; and theory. This is regrettable" (559).

13. Isobel Armstrong, *The Radical Aesthetic* (Oxford: Blackwell, 2000).

14. Dave Beech and John Roberts, "Spectres of the Aesthetic" in Beech and Roberts, eds. *The Philistine Controversy* (London: Verso, 2002), 13–47. This was a common reading, on both sides of the left/liberal divide. Emory Elliott read the book in the same way in his introduction to *Aesthetics in a Multicultural Age*: "*The Ideology of the Aesthetic* makes a good beginning in the attempt to mediate between those who argue that aesthetics is somehow independent from political ideologies and those who hold the view that aesthetics is merely a component of a bourgeois ideology to be purged from the discipline of the arts and humanities" (17).

15. These are scattered throughout her work, but a fair concentration of them can be found in her essay "Textual Harassment," which attempts to lay the groundwork for a new paradigm of reading, beyond "close reading" as normally understood. One example: "Empson saw his own revolutionary thinking co-opted by the conservative neo-formalism of Cleanth Brooks and W. K. Wimsatt after the Second World War" (90). In the first chapter, we saw the truth of this, and in the third, we saw how completely it is usually overlooked; again, Armstrong is unusually clear-sighted about many of the things that matter.

16. The phrase is Paul Ricoeur's, but it has since been taken up and used by many others. See e.g. Paul Ricoeur, *Freud and Philosophy: An Essay on Interpretation* (New Haven: Yale University Press, 1970).

17. Best and Marcus's much-discussed proposal for "surface reading"—or, elsewhere, "just reading"—is a good example here: it strikes me as perceptive in its

identification of "symptomatic reading" as a hallmark of the dominant paradigm, and its choice of Jameson as a synecdoche for that reading practice is of course quite right. Yet, to my mind, the real contours of the history are obscured when one critiques the turn to "symptomatic reading" as if it were merely a turn to the analysis of deep or occluded structures: as we have seen, it is really most significant as part of the scholarly turn to cultural analysis *per se.* In that sense, the proposed alternative, "surface reading," simply continues the existing project by another name. Note that I do not here mean to offer any assessment of the merits of "surface reading" as a method for cultural analysis; that would be quite a different project. See Stephen Best and Sharon Marcus, "Surface Reading: An Introduction," *Representations* 108.1 (2009): 1–21.

18. *Novel Gazing: Queer Readings in Fiction* (Durham, NC: Duke University Press, 1997). The essay was later reprinted with some minor modifications, under a slightly different title in *Touching Feeling* (Durham, Duke University Press, 2003). I will quote from the earlier, slightly more extensive version.

19. Michael Warner, "Uncritical Reading," pp. 17–18 in *Polemic: Critical or Uncritical,* ed. Jane Gallop (New York: Routledge, 2004): 13–38.

20. D. A. Miller, *The Novel and the Police* (Berkeley: University of California Press, 1988).

21. In passing, I would like to offer a thought here on the status of the "lyric" in Miller's argument. The category seems crucial to the argument, though he never seems to want to talk about it. Look again at these lines from the first page of the book:

> Here was a truly out-of-body voice, so stirringly free of what it abhorred as "particularity" or "singularity" that it seemed to come from no enunciator at all. It scanted person even in the linguistic sense, rarely acknowledging, by saying I, its originations in an authorising self, or, by saying you, its reception by any other. We rapt, admiring readers might feel we were only eavesdropping on delightful productions intended for nobody in particular.

"Voice"; "I, you"; "eavesdropping": it strikes me that what is really at stake here, as at so many crucial points throughout the book, is the possibility of lyric speech and of lyric reading. This is interesting for many reasons, but for our purposes I simply want to recall that both "close reading" and the critical paradigm itself have historically been quite closely associated with the genre (or mode, if you prefer) of lyric—certainly more closely than with any other genre. Having recalled this, it is intriguing to see lyric returning here as one of the central stakes of a reading that does not acknowledge it—a reading that, as I am trying to show, seems in many ways to be an attempt to win a way back, through "close reading," to something like criticism in the older sense. There is much more to be said here, but it will need to await another occasion.

22. See for instance Sianne Ngai, *Our Aesthetic Categories: Zany, Cute, Interesting* (Cambridge: Harvard University Press, 2012).

23. The first and last quotes from Richards here are from *Principles of Literary Criticism* (London: Routledge, 2001[1924]), p.103 and p.102, respectively. The second

and third quotes are from *Practical Criticism: A Study of Literary Judgment* (London: Harcourt Brace Jovanovich, 1956 [1929]) p6.

24. Lauren Berlant, "Critical Inquiry, Affirmative Culture" *Critical Inquiry,* Vol. 30, No. 2 (Winter 2004): 445–451.

25. F. R. Leavis, "The 'Great Books' and Liberal Education" in G. Singh, ed., *The Critic as Anti-Philosopher: Essays and Papers by F. R. Leavis* (Chicago: Elephant Paperbacks, 1998), 156–170.

26. On the invention of the phrase "job market," and on its ideological character, see Marc Bousquet, *How the University Works: Higher Education and the Low-Wage Nation* (New York: New York University Press, 2008).

27. Graff gives a good account of the first part of this process when he observes that, when challenged by contrary views, a discipline organized by "field-coverage" can simply add an additional field, thereby assimilating the contrary view without actually engaging with it. Writing in 1987, with memories of the Keynesian expansion of the universities still quite fresh, and the neoliberal offensive still in a relatively early phase, Graff is perhaps not as aware as we are today of the second part of the process: he focuses on the addition of new fields, but says less about possibility of those newly created fields later being stripped away. See Gerald Graff, *Professing Literature* (Chicago: University of Chicago Press, 1987). Speaking more broadly for a moment, this process of managing dissent by expanding to incorporate it is characteristic of many Keynesian institutions, certainly including the mid-century university. In contrast, speaking broadly, in their neoliberal phase those same institutions have often opted instead to starve dissent, presenting this as a collective tightening of belts in response to a general condition of scarcity, while actually shifting resources to the top. Within universities, the classic example of the latter is the claim that the market demands austerity from everyone, meaning students, staff, and faculty (humanities faculty in particular), while in fact resources are being shifted to upper university management. I note without surprise that this analysis keeps being rejected in some circles without much serious evidence being offered to refute it, when in fact the general picture has been made quite clear by a range of persuasive, detailed, and responsible studies. For the British context, see, among others, Stefan Collini, *What Are Universities For?* (London: Penguin, 2012) and Andrew McGettigan, *The Great University Gamble: Money, Markets, and the Future of Higher Education* (London: Pluto, 2013). For the U.S. context, see for instance Sheila Slaughter and Gary Rhoades, *Academic Capitalism and the New Economy: Markets, State, and Higher Education* (Baltimore: Johns Hopkins University Press, 2004); Christopher Newfield *Unmaking the Public University: The Forty-Year Assault on the Middle Class* (Cambridge: Harvard University Press, 2008); and Marc Bousquet, *How the University Works: Higher Education and the Low-Wage Nation* (New York: New York University Press, 2008).

28. David Damrosch, What is World Literature? (Princeton: Princeton University Press, 2003).

29. Wai Chee Dimock, *Through Other Continents: American Literature Across Deep Time* (Princeton: Princeton University Press, 2006).

30. Patricia Yaeger, "Editor's Column: Literature in the Ages of Wood, Tallow, Coal, Whale Oil, Gasoline, Atomic Power, and Other Energy Sources," *PMLA* 126, no. 2 (March 2011): 305–326.

31. The best available case study here is Francis Mulhern's survey of *N+1*, particularly where it bears on Occupy Wall Street. See Francis Mulhern, "A Party of Latecomers." *New Left Review* 93 (May–June 2015): 69–96.

Conclusion

1. Eric Hobsbawm, *The Age of Extremes: A History of the World, 1914–1991* (New York: Vintage, 1996) 584, 485.

2. For a more carefully elaborated version of something very like this scenario, see Colin Crouch, *The Strange Non-death of Neoliberalism* (Cambridge: Polity, 2011). Of interest here is Jamie Peck's "Explaining (with) Neoliberalism," in *Territory, Politics, Governance* 1, no. 2 (2013): 132–157.

3. Wolfgang Streeck, "How Will Capitalism End?" *New Left Review* 87 (May–June 2014): 35–64.

4. Here I am thinking particularly of the old collection *Historical Capitalism with Capitalist Civilization* (London: Verso, 1995 [1983]), but see also *After Liberalism* (New York: New Press, 1995).

5. This has been noted by many. For two rich accounts that bear directly on our concerns here, see Greg Barnhisel's *Cold War Modernists* (New York: Columbia University Press, 2015) and Evan Kindley's *Critics and Connoisseurs: Poet-Critics and the Administration of Modernism* (forthcoming with Harvard University Press). Both of these are recommended reading for anyone interested in tracing the connections between mid-century criticism and the cold war, the old question of CIA funding, and so on. For the more general picture, see for example Noam Chomsky et al., *The Cold War and the University: Toward an Intellectual History of the Postwar Years* (New York: The New Press, 1997).

6. Göran Therborn, "New Masses?" *New Left Review* 85 (January–February 2014): 7–16.

7. Martha Nussbaum, *Not For Profit: Why Democracy Needs the Humanities* (Princeton, NJ: Princeton University Press, 2010).

Appendix

1. Louis Menand, Discovering Modernism: T. S. Eliot and His Context (Oxford: Oxford University Press, 1987), 4.

2. T. S. Eliot, *For Lancelot Andrewes: Essays on Style and Order* (London: Faber and Gwyer, 1928), ix.

3. Nigel Nicholson and Joanne Trautmann, eds. *The Letters of Virginia Woolf Volume III: 1923–1928* (New York: Harcourt Brace Javonovich, 1977) 457–458.

4. Again here, Chris Baldick is the most sophisticated representative of what I take to be the informed consensus view. His account of the "modernist revolution" in criticism puts Eliot in the guiding role, and the development of close reading is then consigned to a second phase, a move which involves conflating Richards and Empson with the New Critics (the title of the relevant section makes the point succinctly: "Close Reading and The Rise of the New Criticism"). In my view, this emphasis on the centrality of Eliot sits problematically next to his emphasis on the centrality of close reading (see Chapter 1, note 8). Baldick resolves this problem by tracing the development of close reading itself back to Eliot's early essays, in which Eliot "takes care to produce particular exhibits of verse exemplifying [the] poetic qualities of complex response to experience" in a way that anticipates Richards (78). Certainly Eliot's sense that "poetry gives us more than just a versified 'idea' or feeling, but an intense fusion of associations within the complex concentration of its images" strikes a distinctively modernist note, but *does* Eliot's practice of quoting itself here really constitute an early form of close reading? It strikes me as quite consistent with earlier Edwardian, *fin de siècle* or even late Victorian practices of quoting, Eliot's obvious modernism in other respects notwithstanding. If *this* is really the innovation that "sharply distinguishes twentieth century criticism . . . from that of previous ages," then it is a bit difficult to see what the fuss is about. One might note also that, when Richards comes to discuss Eliot in *Principles of Literary Criticism* (1924), he discusses him as a poet, rather than as the originator of a newly rigorous practice of reading.

I should perhaps add that Baldick's account is wonderfully rich, and strikes me as the best available. One way to reconcile my account with his might be to say that he is focusing on what I take to be the second level of Eliot's influence, at which level we agree; what I am most interested in here is the third. See Chris Baldick, *Criticism and Literary Theory 1890 to the Present* (London: Longman, 1996) 64–115.

5. Menand, not a believer in the importance of "close reading," strikes what I take to be the right balance here while assessing Eliot's influence on the basic form of the critical revolution itself:

> It cannot really be said . . . that the critical vocabulary that came to be so strongly associated with Eliot was his own invention, but it might be said that Eliot did invent, for a common set of terms and judgments, a manner—judgmental, hierarchical, but "scientific"—perfectly suited to the needs of the modern academic critic.

I think this is quite right, though I would put it slightly differently. If we are trying to trace Eliot's influence at this third level of analysis, his specific doctrines do not seem the place to look; rather, we might suspect that his central contribution to the effort to turn the old belletrism into the new, more rigorous critical paradigm was the development of a style and tone suited to the occasion. His manner was of course much copied. See Louis Menand, *Discovering Modernism: T. S. Eliot and His Context* (Oxford: Oxford UP, 1987), 155.

6. Stanley Edgar Hyman, *The Armed Vision: A Study in the Methods of Modern Literary Criticism* (New York: Vintage, 1947).

Acknowledgments

Some of these thanks perhaps ought to be accompanied by apologies; in this book I have tried to avoid dwelling on the work of people with whom I am personally acquainted, so if your name appears in these acknowledgments, it is a good sign that your thinking does not get treated in depth in the book itself. Whether you consider this a curse or a blessing is up to you.

I very much want to thank Sarah Cole, Nicholas Dames, and Erik Gray, who were extraordinarily generous both to me and to this work over a long period. From the same period, warm thanks also to Deborah Aschkenes, Jennifer Davis, Anne Diebel, Jessica Fenn, Matthew Hart, Darragh Martin, Sarah Minsloff, Sherally Munshi, Bruce Robbins, Lytton Smith, Gayatri Spivak, Kate Stanley, and Marion Thain.

I owe particular thanks to Langdon Hammer, Amy Hungerford, and Michael Warner—and indeed to the whole English Department at Yale, for taking a risk on work that was not easy to agree with, and that was in any case not being conducted within an established "hiring field." For various moments of intellectual engagement around this project, I would also like to thank Jessica Brantley, David Bromwich, Ardis Butterfield, Wai-Chee Dimock, Marta Figlerowicz, Paul Fry, Ben Glaser, David Kastan, Jonathan Kramnick, Anthony Reed, Jill Richards, Caleb Smith, Katie Trumpener, R. John Williams, Sunny Xiang, and Ruth Bernard Yeazell. From the same period, thanks also to Andrew McKendry, Heather McKendry, and Tim Kreiner, for keeping things sane.

Jonathan Culler, John Guillory, and Francis Mulhern were all kind enough not only to read the manuscript at various stages, but also to offer extensive commentary, criticism, and support. Rarely have I seen truly deep expertise brought to bear in such a generous way.

At the Press, I would like to thank Lindsay Waters for his continuing enthusiasm about the project, as well as Joy Deng, who guided it to completion. I am also grateful to Amanda Peery, who was kind enough to offer extra feedback when she had no formal responsibility for doing so.

Warm personal thanks to Janice, Samuel, Blainey, and Samuel Ingemar; Beck, Daniel, Matthew, Oscar, and Richard; Gaurav, of course.

For Deborah Friedell, a paragraph of her very own.

Special thanks to Adam Alexander, Jason Alexander, David Backer, Chris Casuccio, Aleksandra Perisic, and Jason Wozniak—after such an intense period of thinking together, my thoughts are no longer quite separable from theirs.

Lastly, thanks most of all to Katja Lindskog, for so many things—not least for her brilliant and incisive thoughts about this project, at every stage of its development, over the better part of a decade. For whatever it may or may not be worth, this book is dedicated to her.

My article "What's 'New Critical' about 'Close Reading'? I. A. Richards and His New Critical Reception" (copyright © 2013 New Literary History, University of Virginia), which first appeared in *New Literary History* 44, no. 1 (Winter 2013), pages 141–157, is incorporated into sections of Chapter 1: "First Period: Criticism Established," "I. A. Richards, Close Reading, and Practical Criticism," and "The New Criticism: Close Reading for Kant." Thanks to *New Literary History* for the permission to make use of that work here.

Index